DREAMS WITHIN A DREAM

DREAMS WITHIN A DREAM

THE FILMS OF PETER WEIR

Michael Bliss

Southern Illinois University Press | Carbondale and Edwardsville

03 02 01 00 4 3 2 1

Library of Congress Cataloging-in-Publication Data
Bliss, Michael, 1947–
Dreams within a dream : the films of Peter Weir / Michael Bliss.
    p.   cm.
Filmography: p.
Includes bibliographical references and index.
1. Weir, Peter, 1944– —Criticism and interpretation.
I. Title.
PN1998.3.W44B58 1999
791.43′0233′092—DC21   99-27241
ISBN 0-8093-2284-6 (alk. paper)   CIP

For My Brothers: Richard Bliss, Randy Neir, and Ronald Bliss

CONTENTS

ILLUSTRATIONS

DREAMS WITHIN A DREAM

INTRODUCTION

The infinite attraction of unresolved, antithetical forces is one of the prime bases for the popularity of the films of Peter Weir. Coming as he does from an Australian film tradition replete with films involving clashes between civilization and savagery, Weir has managed to establish for himself a distinctive place in international filmmaking by insisting that dreams and the unconscious, and clashes between civilization and so-called savagery, far from being mundane notions, are in fact still undervalued and overlooked in contemporary culture. And while the director, well spoken on many topics, sometimes seems reluctant to comment on the structural and philosophic sources of his films, we can nonetheless ascribe them to certain trends in fiction, psychology, and philosophy.

To appreciate Weir's work, it is helpful to understand the national heritage to which he is heir. Australian cinema has a long, well-established tradition. In 1906, Australian director Charles Tait produced what may very well be the world's first feature-length motion picture, *The Story of the Kelly Gang,* a film whose focus on Australians who act outside the law anticipates a theme with which contemporary Australian cinema is still concerned.[1] By 1911, four years before the release of D. W. Griffith's *The Birth of A Nation* (a film that is generally regarded as revolutionary with regard to its length and narrative sophistication), "no fewer than fifty-one Australian [feature] films were released."[2] For the next twenty-eight years, Australian cinema remained strong, developing into a truly national cinema concerned with the country's landscape, its people, and its people's problems.

Over time, though, two prominent factors contributed to the industry's decline. Competition from British and American films became more and more pronounced (not even trade quotas and the imposition of import taxes made a significant dent in the onslaught); and the Second World War, with attendant

1

"investor caution and film stock shortages," significantly slowed production (only one major Australian film was released between 1942 and 1945).[3]

Eventually, production fell off so dramatically that in 1962, only one feature film was produced.[4] By the 1970s, it became necessary to fund Australian filmmaking in a way other than through the efforts of individual producers. This goal was accomplished via government support.[5] The Australian Film Development Commission (which was created in 1970)[6] was succeeded in 1975 by the Australian Film Commission, which aided in the financing of such internationally renowned films as Fred Schepisi's *The Devil's Playground* (1976), Bruce Beresford's *The Getting of Wisdom* (1977), and Weir's *Picnic at Hanging Rock* (1976) and *The Last Wave* (1977), leading examples of a resurgence in production that came to be known as the New Australian Cinema. As critic Brian McFarlane asserts, "in 1976, virtually no film could be made without government money."[7] One of the effects of government funding, though, was a strong influence over the thematic content of the films being financed. As McFarlane notes, "The film corporations tended to favor nationalist themes and projects which bespoke 'quality' in theme and treatment (for example adaptations of classic Australian novels),"[8] an attitude appreciable in the films just cited.

From the beginning, one of the major influences on Australian filmmaking was a narrative approach that characterized (some would say crippled) British and American filmmaking as well: melodrama. McFarlane (one of the most prolific advocates of Australian cinema) and writer Geoff Mayer regard melodrama as a genre with "no interior depth to the characterization," and as "an excessive form, with extreme pressure placed on the 'surface' of the text."[9] One might ask, then, as does Kevin Brownlow in *The Parade's Gone By*, his study of silent cinema,[10] why melodrama emerged as such a basic dramatic principle in early filmmaking. I believe that the genre was popular because it appeals to the most basic instincts in human storytelling: the desire, derived from biblical tales, to see good and evil displayed in striking opposition. And though melodrama's oversimplifications have their drawbacks, they can also lend themselves to representations of sophisticated issues. The dramatization of the contradictory forces of light versus darkness, reason versus mystery, rationality versus magic in Weir films such as *Picnic at Hanging Rock* and *The Last Wave*, for example, can be seen as reflecting a melodramatic emphasis,[11] as do the polarized characterizations in such films as *Witness* (1985), *Dead Poets Society* (1989), and *The Truman Show* (1998).

As we might expect, there are recurrent attributes common to Australian films that emerge most forcefully in Weir's work. Ockerism, "the depiction of

Australian men as boorish but good humored"[12] is a quality that thankfully, except as it is parodied in *The Cars That Ate Paris* (1974), is absent in Weir's films; however, Weir does dramatize mateship, the celebration of men's communal adventures. This characteristic is endemic to many American films and traditional in Australian works as various as "the short stories of Henry Lawson, . . . the bush ballads of A.B. Paterson [who wrote the ballad on which Australian director George Miller's 1982 film *The Man from Snowy River* was based],[13] and . . . the demotic verse narratives of C. J. Dennis."[14] Mateship is clearly evident in such Weir films as *Gallipoli* (1981), *The Year of Living Dangerously* (1983), and the American production *Dead Poets Society*, films in which Weir gives mateship a new meaning by making self-knowledge dependent upon action involving one's friends.

One of Australian films' most striking characteristics is their emphasis on the starkness of the country's landscape. As Ross Gibson points out, "non-Aboriginal Australia is a young society [the country was claimed for Great Britain by Captain James Cook in 1770], under-endowed with myths of 'belonging'. The country is still sparsely populated and meagerly historicised."[15] Gibson goes on to observe:

> The idea of the intractability of Australian nature has been an essential part of the national ethos. It is a notion with its genesis in the ancient legends of the hellish antipodes; a notion promoted by First Fleet annalists who detailed the anguish of a harrowed and perverse society's struggling to understand and subsist in a seemingly bizarre habitat . . . a notion perpetuated to this day by the myriad legends of the bush, that mythic region of isolation, moral simplicity, homelessness and the terrible beauty of "nature learning how to write."[16]

Despite its significance for Australian filmmakers, though, there is no romanticizing of the landscape in most contemporary Australian films.[17] Although for Weir the outback (the uninhabited portions of the countryside) is allied with desirable forces (e.g., a sense of myth and history and a respect for nature, concepts that Weir often associates with Aborigines), its presence (literal or figurative) nonetheless represents to the white characters in his films a threat to their placid existences, a force to be reckoned with—so much so, that it seems to function as a character that affects human behavior. In films such as *The Cars That Ate Paris* and *Gallipoli*, the landscape is, respectively, either a hazard or a deadly challenge.

Yet the landscape may be favorably viewed as well. In American films by Weir such as *Witness* and *Dead Poets Society*, the natural world provides a respite from the anxieties of repressive cultures, while in the 1990 film *Green Card* (which, like *The Cars That Ate Paris, Picnic at Hanging Rock, The Last Wave,*[18] *Witness,* and *Dead Poets,* can be viewed as an urban drama of rural longing), a character attempts to literally transplant the soothing effects of the "green world" (a symbolic realm in which fertility triumphs over sterility) into the city.[19] Thus, the earlier-mentioned sense of "under-endowed . . . belonging" has yielded to the feeling that one's healthy adjustment is dependent upon an acknowledgment of nature's positive qualities. This change in attitude on Weir's part, from depicting nature as threat to nature as comforting presence, is possibly a result of the director's appropriation of ideas in American mythology. Working in the United States, Weir seems to have been influenced by notions elucidated by writers such as Frederick Jackson Turner and Leo Marx, who draw attention to Americans' romanticization of the wilderness, which is dependent upon an unconscious denial of the wilderness's hardships.[20]

Australian films' attitudes toward the depiction of women and Aborigines are polarized. As we might expect given the centrality of the mateship theme in Australian films, women—even in the films of someone who considers himself intellectually progressive, as does Peter Weir—are often tangential figures. To say that this situation represents sexual bias would be to oversimplify, though. Rather, it seems apparent that women are marginalized in Australian culture not only because Australia has traditionally been "a male-dominated society, in which the national myths and the historical situations which promoted them are essentially male-centered,"[21] but also partially because Australian men are embarrassed about dealing directly with feelings.[22] Indeed, in Weir's early films (from *The Cars That Ate Paris* through *Gallipoli*), romance is either absent or marginally situated. It is only with *The Year of Living Dangerously* that Weir begins to realize that his filmic heroes, whose redemption previously was dependent upon the embracing of distinctly intellectual concerns such as recognition of one's dark counterpart or a merging with the primal forces of nature, are incomplete outside of a productive heterosexual relationship.

Another prominent aspect of Weir's films is their use of characters of color. In this regard, an historical perspective is useful. Racism was not just the result of individual Australian citizens' attitudes; bigotry and fear of foreigners were codified by the Australian government. The rationalization for what became known as the "white Australian policy"[23] (which applied not only to the country's Aborigines but also to immigrants from countries such as Polynesia, the Philippines, China, and Japan) actually derives from an Australian Federal Parliament law, the Immigration Restriction Act of 1901, which required that in order to be admitted into the country, immigrants had to write out passages from dictation "in any European language directed by the [immigration] officer."[24] The Australian Workers Union, which asked the Arbitration Court in 1945 to restrict the employment of Aborigines, held onto the ban against them until 1969.[25] It takes very little effort to see a strong parallel between these attitudes and those of whites toward Native Americans and African-Americans in the United States;[26] and as Leslie Fiedler convincingly demonstrates in *Love and Death in the American Novel*,[27] the effect on our literature of what are essentially policies of psychological exclusion and imbalance is still in evidence, just as these attitudes are dramatized not only in Weir's films but also in the work of other major Australian filmmakers.

The Australian film industry's slow acceptance of Aborigines is striking. If Aborigines were depicted at all in Australian films before the 1960s, they were usually portrayed stereotypically. In fact, aside from their use in films as clichéd, threatening dark "others," Aborigines didn't even appear in films that depicted them individually until the late 1950s, a situation that invites comparison with the characterization in American films of Native Americans, who for the most part were represented as either a threatening presence or patronized good friend until revisionist films such as *Cheyenne Autumn* (1964) and *A Man Called Horse* (1969). Originally, Aborigines in Australia were viewed as nothing more than "a melancholy footnote to Australian history."[28] As anthropologist W. E. H. Stanner notes, Aborigines,

> were widely regarded as scarcely human, and were left to the fitful paternalism of government, the hard mercy of pastoralists, and the charity of Christian missions. There was no line of battle, as with the Maori or Redskins, no true conquest, because the truth of it is that we inched and filched a continent into our possession. . . . [N]othing in the whole affair made us deeply conscious of the Aborigines as a people or a race, but nevertheless I think that the emptiness of conscience and compassion that made the melancholy business tolerable had something to do with our racial views later.[29]

The psychological effects of this attitude, and the manner in which it exemplifies a Freudian fear of the dark "other" (an extension of a pathological sense of guilt that appears repeatedly in Weir's early films), will be dealt with in more detail later. It suffices to note here that the effects of racism, at least in terms of an approach to characterization that conceives of individuals opposed to and fearing one another, are still being felt in Weir's films.

White colonialism is a recurring, if sometimes unstated, theme in Weir's films. This situation is not unusual given the fact that Australia had colonized part of New Guinea[30] and, as Stanner points out, that the country was stolen from its Aboriginal population. It is one of colonialism's prominent aspects, racism, that is particularly important to a consideration of Peter Weir's films.

In films such as *Picnic at Hanging Rock, The Last Wave,* and *Gallipoli,* blacks—by which term I mean both people of color and individuals of African-American descent—or the idea of blacks are used, respectively, to suggest mystery, wisdom, or friendship. Even though Aborigines or people of color are not literally present in films such as *The Cars That Ate Paris, The Plumber* (1980), and *Dead Poets Society,* their presence is felt in the manner in which the films invoke themes and ideas associated with the Aboriginal realm,[31] such as the sense of threat or the unknown. In Weir's American films, this black or Aboriginal quality is present in the corrupt "underground" police of *Witness,* the nighttime rituals of *Dead Poets Society*'s students (which at one point are linked with Vachel Lindsay's poem "The Congo"), and so on. In *Playing in the Dark,* her study of American literature, Toni Morrison refers to symbolic uses such as these as "the denotative and connotative blackness that African peoples have come to signify."[32] Morrison contends that this "Africanist" quality in American literature works to define what it means to be white: "it may be possible to discover, through a close look at literary 'blackness,' the nature—even the cause—of literary whiteness."[33] And indeed, as we will see, the "other" in Weir's films works to facilitate an understanding of the identity of white characters.

Morrison's book is about American literature as a codification of national views about race, but, as I earlier stated, the similarity between American attitudes toward people of color and Australian attitudes toward Aborigines seems to be quite strong. Obviously, Weir is not compelled to use blacks in his films; but when he does so, he tends to use them as types rather than as individuals. Combine this quality with Weir's disparagement of colonialism (a theme implicit in such films as *The Last Wave, The Year of Living Dangerously,* and 1986's *The Mosquito Coast*), and we have a paradoxical approach: the director appears to use blacks as suggestive symbols for ideas about the unconscious and repression at the same time as he condemns blacks' exploitation.

Although Morrison decries the unrealistic portrayal of blacks in American literature, and criticizes the manner in which they are used as "signs" rather than as real people, she nonetheless acknowledges the almost necessarily symbolic function that they assume in the literature. (It is precisely this function that dark "others" perform in Weir's films.) Morrison writes:

> images of blackness can be evil *and* protective, rebellious *and* forgiving, fearful *and* desirable—all of the self-contradictory features of the self. Whiteness alone is

mute, meaningless, unfathomable, pointless, frozen, veiled, curtained, dreaded, senseless, implacable. Or so our writers say.[34]

Morrison refers to this manner of representing blacks (and whites) as "economy of stereotype. This allows the writer a quick and easy image without the responsibility of specificity, accuracy, or even narratively useful description."[35] The language here is obviously disdainful and, if applied to Weir's films, would have a negative critical effect. However, in Weir films from *The Cars That Ate Paris* to *Gallipoli,* this "economy" seems to be democratically applied to both whites and blacks. In these films, virtually all characters function as types, since at this point in his career the director is more interested in representing ideas than people.[36] By the time of *The Year of Living Dangerously,* the necessity of pleasing the audience seems to have compelled Weir to make his fictions more popular by emphasizing character rather than types. Yet even in the films from this period onward, symbolic dark "others" do not disappear from the films. One thinks immediately of *Year's* Billy Kwan, Kumar, Hortono, and Tiger Lily; of *Witness's* major villain, an African-American cop gone bad (a character complemented by the presence in the film of an honest African-American policeman); of the malicious headmaster in *Dead Poets Society,* who takes on a sinister tone; of *Fearless's* Carla, a Latin woman who functions as a dark rival for the affections of the white Max Klein, who is married to a Caucasian woman.

While Morrison's notion of figurative blackness is only hinted at in *Cars* (via the town's avariciousness), it is prominent in *Picnic,* whose girls disappear into an Aboriginal realm that is associated with sexual threats (snakes) and implicit self-realization of a sexual nature. Other Weir films contain characters such as *The Last Wave's* Chris and Charlie; *The Plumber's* Max; *Gallipoli's* Egyptians and Turks; the inhabitants of Mosquitia in *Mosquito Coast,* all of whom function as dark (or darkly conceived) "others" who represent repressed attitudes, fears, and desires.[37] In Weir's films, the most intense investigation of the relation between whites and blacks occurs in *The Mosquito Coast,* a film derived from Joseph Conrad's *Heart of Darkness.* Although I do not want to anticipate my remarks on the film at this point, it should be noted here that Weir does not deserve to be faulted for his method of characterization, any more than Conrad should be faulted for not fully characterizing blacks in his short novel. Critic David Denby notes that writers such as Chinua Achebe and Edward Said (who, like Morrison, find biased representations of dark "others" in literature) have "alerted readers to possible hidden assumptions in language and point of view" in many fictions.[38] Nevertheless, Denby feels that Achebe and Said go too far when they condemn Conrad (and other writers who supposedly approve implicitly of colonialism, such as Austen, Carlyle, and Thackeray) as racist simply because these authors do not directly condemn some of the things that they portray. (As Denby notes, "one has to wonder if blaming writers for what they *fail to write about* is not an extraordinarily wrongheaded way of reading them.")[39] Denby writes of Conrad in terms that implicitly refer us back to Morrison's essay: "Conrad practices a narrow economy and omits a great deal."[40] However, Denby goes on to observe that many authors of fiction who are critical of Conrad also use economy and omission as a means of quick characterization.[41] It is also important to realize that while Conrad gives us virtually no insight into Congo culture, we receive or are referred to a great deal of information about "others" in Weir's film, a fact that might to a degree temper our responses to his films.

As one might expect, Australian filmmaking has a history of reflecting (and thereby supporting) the country's racist policies. Historian H. O. McQueen's comment on literary representations of miscegenation bears particular relevance to Weir's work.

> The psychological inhibitions which underlay the unsatisfactory nature of interracial sexual relations are presented in Katherine Susannah Prichard's [novel] *Coonardoo* (1929) where Hugh Watt destroys himself because of the revulsion he experiences after his liaison with Coonardoo. The essentially furtive and harsh nature of these sexual encounters should be considered in examining the idealized conception of white women that arises in the literature of the outback and in the white males' fear that coloureds, both Aborigines and Chinese, had little in their minds other than the rape of white women.[42]

As I point out in chapter 2, one of the underlying themes in *Picnic at Hanging Rock* is the fear of sex with blacks. Weir would go on to focus on the disparity between the demonstrative sexuality of dark others and whites' repressed sexuality in films such as *The Last Wave*, *The Plumber*, and *Fearless*, in which this quality is present via the strong contrast between Carla's passionate nature and the cool veneer of Max's wife.

Given this emphasis, should we read the entirety of Weir's output as a gloss on interracial sexuality? Not necessarily. Writing about *Heart of Darkness*, David Denby refers to what he calls Conrad's "philosophical meditation on the complicity between 'civilization' and savagery."[43] We might regard Weir's insistent returns to questions of interraciality in this way as well.

How can we determine what Weir's point of view is with regard to race? One way to begin is by considering a piece of dialogue from an early scene in *Gallipoli*. Palling around with his Aboriginal friend Zack, the film's main character, Archie, is excoriated by one of his parents' ranch hands. "Prefer the company of blacks, eh Archie?" the man asks with a sneer, to which Archie replies, "Zack is my mate." We might conclude from this exchange that Weir disapproves of racism; I think that his films tend to bear out the truth of this assertion. Still, there lingers the nagging suspicion that Weir's representations of people of color are somewhat skewed.

In her review of *The Last Wave,* Pauline Kael, whose insights have relevance to our reading of all of Weir's films, criticized Weir for the manner in which he used the film's Aborigines.

> Instead of seeing the victims of expansionist drives and colonial policies . . . as people whose rights were violated and must be restored as quickly as possible, [movies such as *The Last Wave*] romanticize the victims. They are seen in terms of what whites are supposed to have repressed. A few generations ago, whites saw the victims of white civilization (as racist bigots still do) in terms of sexuality and savagery; now the victims are seen in terms of magic, dreamspeak, nobility, intuition, harmony with nature. The white bigots saw them as mentally inferior; the modern, guilt-ridden whites see them as spiritually superior. In neither case are they granted what is their plain due: simple equality. . . . The aborigine actors are by far the most vital element in "The Last Wave," yet they're kept on the margins and used as universal forces.[44]

Clearly, Kael feels that Weir is doing more than simply romanticizing the film's blacks. Her implicit comparison of the attitudes of white bigots with those of "modern, guilt-ridden whites" suggests that there is very little difference between the two responses. Her assertion about bigots viewing "victims" in terms of "sexuality" is obviously applicable to Weir's work in *Picnic at Hanging Rock* as well as *The Last Wave.* Earlier in the review, Kael asserts that *The Last Wave* embodies an attitude that she refers to as "the white man's burden of alienation."[45] Given what she subsequently says, the implication is that this attitude is not only an example of self-serving posturing but, quite possibly, a veiled form of bigotry with an overlay of progressive intellectualism.

Weir does seem to use *The Last Wave*'s Aboriginal characters as a form of racial shorthand in a manner similar to the kind to which Toni Morrison draws attention. The film's characterizations may not be racist, but they are very close to it; they may be referred to as "racialist" or akin to racist with regard to the manner in which the characterizations are used.[46] By saying that *The Last Wave*'s Aborigines are mysterious bearers of great truths and, by implication, that the lower classes (who in Weir's films seem to have the simple qualities that Weir associates with dark characters) are the only ones capable of direct sexual expression (a bias present in *Picnic, Wave,* and *The Plumber*), Weir is in effect stereotyping these groups. Indeed, one could say that examples of stereo-typing are present throughout Weir's work: in *The Year of Living Dangerously*'s "mysterious" Indonesians, *The Mosquito Coast*'s trusting natives, *Fearless*'s ultra-religious Carla.[47] Has Weir, then, unknowingly appropriated—albeit in somewhat modified form—the racism that characterizes a great deal of Australian society?

When Michael Dempsey interviewed Weir in 1978, he asked the director an interesting question about the manner in which he appears to stereotype many of his films' characters.

> *Dempsey:* Some critics in [the United States] accuse you of romanticizing primitive people—aborigines, working-class people, whoever—and caricaturing "civilized" people, intellectuals, by making them bloodless, sexless. What do you think about this?
>
> *Weir:* Well, if you make films with a strong style, and with a strong sort of hand, inevitably you will create strong reactions for and against. I would say to those sorts of criticisms, "oh, really?" I mean, I have no interest in intellectuals, bloodless or otherwise. I have no interest in primitive peoples one way or the other. I'm interested in stories. I'm interested in the details that come across.
>
> *Dempsey:* In *The Last Wave*, someone must have thought of this matter given the moment when a supporting character denounces the hero for suddenly acquiring a sentimental, patronizing interested in aborigines.
>
> *Weir:* Ah, yes. I wasn't unaware of it. I remember rewriting that scene to drop that line in, because I had already picked up some of that criticism from some people who had read the script. But I'm probably just more interested in . . . catastrophic events, like death or revolution.[48]

Yet as Weir himself observed (in a quote to which I'll return), not only does an astute viewer begin to see patterns in an artist's work, but such a viewer can also develop a good sense of the artist behind the work. Weir feels that the latter reaction is "not unreasonable."[49] Judging from his films, then, Weir's statements to Michael Dempsey, in which he veers off from addressing his potentially clichéd attitudes toward his characters, seem disingenuous.

It's not that Weir doesn't try to be liberally fair about his films' characterizations: with regard to people of color, for example, he attempts to avoid stereotyping by including in his films characters such as *Witness*'s Sergeant Carter and *Mosquito*'s Mr. Haddy. Unfortunately, these characters, and their counterparts in other films, are so minimally developed that they fail to compensate for the drawbacks of Weir's occasionally stereotypical approach to characterization.

I don't think that the appropriate response to all of these considerations is to brand Weir a racist, as Achebe or Said might, or to denigrate his cinema. It might be productive to keep in mind that like anyone, Weir has limitations; in this case, those limitations are to a great extent those of the society in which he grew up. I think it's quite clear that Weir recognizes these limitations, and that he's trying to address them. It may be unreasonable to expect Weir to completely transcend his upbringing and background. In my opinion, we do his filmmaking an injustice by accentuating this shortcoming at the expense of the rewards that his films bring us.

Moreover, the kind of revisionist, politically correct criticism that is brought to bear on Weir's work often seems to be as much of an automatic reaction (which disregards not only authorial tone but the social and historical context in which the artist works) as the automatic, presumably racist response with which the artist is faulted. Writing about criticisms of *Heart of Darkness,* David Denby said

> Poor, stupid Conrad! Trapped in his own time, he could do no more than write his books. A self-approving moral logic has become familiar on the academic left: so-and-so's view of women, people of color, and the powerless lacks our amplitude, our humanity, our insistence on the inclusion in discourse of all people.[50]

By no means am I advocating a return to the values of Conrad's time. I do feel, though, that there's a suspicious rigidity to Kael's critique and to what I perceive as the implicit threat of Said and Achebe against Weir's work. Weir may be a flawed filmmaker. Yet Weir's films repeatedly draw attention to the problems attendant with racial and cultural clashes, and Weir himself clearly believes in cultural blending. If the form that this message takes is sometimes stereotypical, that quality detracts from the films' dramatic success—but not from the integrity of Weir's repeated attempts to confront racial issues.

Many other thematic concerns of Australian cinema emanate from the nature of the nation's consciousness. Although the Australian sensibility derives from the country's origins as a British colony, the Australian national personality, probably owing to the penal background of many of the early settlers, is characterized by a spirit of rebellion. Thus, the typical Australian attitude toward Britain is a mixture of both allegiance and antagonism. In Peter Weir's films, this conflicted response emerges most strongly in *Gallipoli,* in which the film's two principals, Archie and Frank, respectively embrace and criticize Australia's helping the British during the First World War. Yet this quality of attraction to and repulsion from British culture is also present in *Picnic at Hanging Rock* and *The Year of Living Dangerously.* Commenting on the conflicted Australian reaction to British institutions, Neil Rattigan notes

> While [in Australia] there was continuity of many of the ideological state apparatuses of England—legal system, Westminster system of government, public administration, education, church, and so forth—a cultural identity developed

(which would in turn become a national identity) based upon the denial (as much as possible) of class distinction, based upon ideas of egalitarianism, collectivism, and the distinctly Australian mythos of mateship. These ideals were not universal, of course; they did not extend to the aboriginal population in any way, shape, or form, and they did not really apply to women in certain circumstances. They were, however, cultural perceptions that developed from "down below" and might have taken the form, had they ever coalesced sufficiently, of a radical political doctrine.[51]

As Rattigan implicitly demonstrates, there is an inherent contradiction in the Australian sensibility, as the "ideals" to which Rattigan refers did not extend to the groups that he mentions as exceptions. What we see here, then, is another example of the playing out of the basic contradiction in the Australian character between idea and impulse, between the notion that racism and sexism are abhorrent and the negative feelings that some Australians experience when confronted with "others," dark or otherwise, a reaction characterized by a great deal of anxiety and fear. In Weir's films, this antagonism results in the conflict between the rational and unconscious realms, the canny and the uncanny—in other words, in a profound dualism.

Where does this focus on dualism come from, and why is Weir so interested in the subject? I believe that the major source of this attitude comes from Weir's experience while attending college. In a 1983 interview, Weir was asked about his university education. "It just seems that I cannot get all of the education that I got cleaned out of my head. I've done as much as I can to eliminate the system of thinking that I was taught but I think you're never free of the analytical system. . . . I left the university in the second quarter."[52]

Weir recalls being in a poetry class during which the instructor was

putting up rhyming couplets on the blackboard or analyzing a scene or whatever and finding out what made it tick. And the very thought that you could analyze and remove the emotive response, the magic, things that were the last fragments of childhood that were being eroded! The moment that changed me totally was in a class in poetry, a seminar, at Sydney University in the early 60s. [A poem by Blake was put up on the board.] . . . I loved it and . . . I thought, there's something embarrassing about that emotion. . . . The education system . . . was training spontaneity out of me and dulling the edge of emotion, and these were things, of course, that I later came to realize that I drastically needed if I was going to make films.[53]

Weir's comment is quite interesting, especially in the way that it shows him drawing such a dramatic distinction between emotion and thought, as though the two realms are, and always must be, exclusively independent. Despite the wide range of Weir's reading, it is clear from his films (which are almost exclusively about the disparity between two very different realms—usually the intellectual and emotional or the conscious and the subconscious—and the difficulty encountered in attempting to resolve them) that he is in flight from the intellectual and (in his opinion) pejoratively academic realm, so much so that he has embraced what he views as the opposite extreme: the emotional, the mystical, the romantic. Clearly, though, the two realms are not mutually exclusive. Many academics, for example, find that intellectual pursuits sharpen their emotional responses, and that emotional responses often precede intellectual insights. Indeed, it seems that the intellectual and emotional realms are not separate but complementary; we often experience a work of art in terms of both ideas and feelings.

Moreover, we can't completely trust what Weir is saying here. Surely in his filmmaking he must blend the intellectual and emotional, must consciously make editorial and structural decisions at the same time as he is aware of one of the bases for these decisions: an emotional reaction to the film on which he's working. Yet we can't discount the significance of Weir's university story, especially since the conclusion that he drew from it has been one of the prime narrative bases for his films ever since. What we see in Weir's films, then, is what we might expect of any intriguing artist: a playing out of the artist's psychology in a way that reflects the artist's attitudes far more transparently than he or she may be aware.

Weir's films overcome their occasional deficiencies by repeatedly giving us what Sam Peckinpah (speaking about his own films) called "moments," junctures at which something extraordinary or extremely touching happens. Thus we get the affecting simplicity of Witness's barn-raising sequence; the point at the end of Dead Poets Society at which the music swells during the boys' tribute to Keating; the end of Fearless when Max, in tears, feels that he has returned from the dead; the point in Truman Show when Truman repudiates Christof. By virtue of these moments, we forgive the films their occasional incongruities, their dramatic lapses, their deficiencies in conception. At these junctures, Weir seems to have truly moved beyond art and craft into a region in which nothing else matters except the exhilaration that we feel.

To appreciate Weir's films, one must accept their wild swings between ideas and feelings, and must wait for those times when everything comes together. In this sense, don't the films reflect the way that many people experience the world? Richard Combs's comment on Weir, to which I'll later return, is quite apt: he refers to Weir as a "cool lyricist."[54] The contradiction in that description tells us a great deal of what we need to know about Weir and his films.

Although *The Cars That Ate Paris,* the first of Weir's features currently available for viewing,[55] seems to posit a rather simple set of oppositions,[56] intentionally unresolved ambiguity would characterize Weir's next two productions, *Picnic at Hanging Rock* and *The Last Wave.* The strong emphasis in *Picnic* on the beauty of the settings, the gauze-like quality of the cinematography, and the evocative nature of the music track, combine with the fluid cutting, slow-motion shots, and languorous pacing to work in opposition to the harshness of the landscape and the inexplicable disappearances that occur in the film. Additionally, what Weir manages to achieve in *Picnic* is an undercurrent not so much of sexual tension (something we might expect in a story about young women in an all-female school) but sexual threat, much of which seems to emanate from the impending onset of heterosexual relationships that will destroy the girls' sense of sorority. The significant aspect of the film, though, is its understated tone, which is in striking contrast to the intentional excesses of *Cars.* Yet excess reappears in the apocalyptic *Last Wave,* in which ambiguity and irresolution once again predominate.

Weir is adept at creating credible settings, as is evident not only from the period recreations in films such as *Picnic at Hanging Rock* and *Gallipoli,* but also in films with a contemporary setting, such as *The Year of Living Dangerously* (1982) and *Witness.* Nevertheless, the physical details in Weir's films are secondary to the ambience that the films create.

The feeling of otherworldliness in many of Weir's films is primarily a function of a dramatic approach that emphasizes the unusual awareness that results from a confrontation with an alien milieu or violent circumstances. A premium is placed on rendering psychological, as opposed to physical, action; in the director's filmic universe, consciousness often takes precedence over behavior. Watching Weir's films, we're repeatedly made aware that our normal type of perception is nothing more than the result of customary, socialized cultural attitudes.[57]

Perhaps one of the most important keys to the nature of Weir's films derives from Miranda's voiceover statement at the beginning of *Picnic at Hanging Rock:* "What we see, and what we seem, are but a dream, a dream within a dream."[58] What is being referred to in this statement is the illusory aspect of existence, the feeling of unreality regarding our sensory and emotional impressions of the world. Such an attitude derives from the notion that what we perceive with our senses is, at best, an unreliable indication of what really exists. The behest, derived from Plato's parable of the cave, is to trust to our philosophic and spiritual intuition to make sense of the world. For Weir, "reality" resides in dreams, in myths, in states of heightened consciousness resulting from exposure to stress, strongly contrary impressions, or strange objects. In each of these cases, along with the characters in the films, we experience psychic displacements that dislodge us from traditional ways of thinking. "What we see, and what we seem"—in other words, what we know through our senses, and whom we think we are—can only be correctly understood through extrasensory or intuitional experiences. Moreover, such an ultra-reality, if perceived, is for both characters and audiences doubly displaced in Weir's cinema: first, because it occurs within the dream-like life that we all (with varying degrees of awareness of this condition) lead; and second, because it occurs within a larger dream-like realm, through literal dreams—or movies, which we may regard as a ribbon of dreams. As both Weir and many writers have observed, the act of viewing films, which involves a passive perception of fleeting images received in the dark, bears a strong resemblance to dreaming.[59]

Unfortunately, Weir tends to place so much emphasis on atmosphere that his films' narratives occasionally suffer. This aspect is not a problem in films such as *Cars* or *Picnic*. The first film's narrative is virtually nonexistent, while the second film is more interested in ambience than story (indeed, the whole point of *Picnic* seems to be a repudiation of traditional narrative and the empirical world view that it implies). But in films that are supposed to tell a strong story, Weir's narrative weaknesses cripple the films. We can enjoy the atmosphere in *The Year of Living Dangerously* or *The Mosquito Coast,* and can appreciate the films' music and visuals, but sometimes events have ascribed to them a significance out of proportion to their function in the films. Billy's death in *Year* and Allie's obsessive qualities in *Mosquito* don't seem to propel actions so much as serve as intellectual reasons for what goes on emotionally. These examples show us Weir as a man strong on mood but occasionally weak on character motivation, a situation that parallel's Weir's privileging the realm of the mysterious over the material. Weir attempts to bypass these problems by taking the audience with him into the nonintellectual realm via an emphasis on discontinuity and the importance of dreams, and by avoiding traditional closure. Let's examine each of these techniques.

Historian Roger Shattuck regards Alfred Jarry as one of the precursors of surrealism. Shattuck says that artists who deal in the realm of the absurd often attempt to meld the subconscious and conscious realms, precisely the effect toward which Weir is working. "Jarry pushed systematic absurdity into the realm of hallucination, of violated consciousness. And this is the third trait of the arts of the period: the eruption of dream into waking experience. The tendency is already a commonplace for our century."[60]

Yet if this is so, the tendency has become so common as to often make its products seem pejoratively quotidian, thereby precluding the sense of outrage and surprise that the use of dream imagery is meant to create. Moreover, as philosopher of science Thomas Kuhn notes, human beings also tend to ignore things that are strikingly unusual; according to Kuhn, we often prefer to treat uncommon events as though they were normal.

> [T]he previous awareness of anomaly, the gradual and simultaneous emergence of both observational and conceptual recognition, and the consequent change of paradigm categories and procedures [is] often accompanied by resistance. There is even evidence that these same characteristics are built into the nature of the perceptual process itself. In a psychological experiment that deserves to be far better known outside the trade, Bruner and Postman asked experimental subjects to identify on short and controlled exposure a series of playing cards. Many of the cards were normal, but some were made anomalous, e.g. a red six of spades and a black four of hearts. . . . Even on the shortest exposures many subjects identified most of the cards [correctly], but the anomalous cards were almost always identified, without apparent hesitation or puzzlement, as normal. . . . Without any awareness of trouble [on the part of research subjects, these cards were] immediately fitted to one of the conceptual categories prepared by prior experience.[61]

The psychological reaction toward which Kuhn draws attention is one that artists like Weir must work hard to waylay by creating ever-new and unusual discontinuities that resist being ignored. Weir also uses surrealist technique, as when he juxtaposes elements with disparate implications (such as the lizard moving past a girl's arm in *Picnic at Hanging Rock* or the radio leaking water in *The Last Wave*).[62] However, as Kuhn notes, "in science, as in the playing card experiment, novelty emerges only with difficulty, manifested by resistance, against a background provided by expectation."[63] Weir attempts to preclude this resistance in his audience by situating his visual and verbal incongruities in the midst of stories that themselves have a dream-like aura, and in which the narrative is often concerned with unusual events or situations, thereby doubling the dream effect.

In an article on Alfred Hitchcock's *Vertigo* (1958), psychiatrist Stanley Palombo inadvertently points us toward an appreciation of the manner in which Weir uses the dream realm in his films. Palombo observes that

> Munsterberg (1916) recognized that isolated camera shots, the raw material furnished by the camera, could be assembled and organized into larger and more substantial dramatic structures only by "overcoming the forms of the outer world, namely space, time, and causality, and by adjusting the events to the forms of the inner world, namely, attention, memory, imagination, and emotion."

Munsterberg's work suggested that all film is inherently fantastic or dream-like. The *departures* brought about by the technique of film composition, even when "reality" itself is being represented, produce an *intensification* of the viewer's everyday experience.[64]

When he compares the dream experience with the art of editing as practiced by Eisenstein, who "showed that montage was not merely a device for enhancing narrative sequence, but a method for creating new meanings by combining familiar objects and ideas in unexpected juxtapositions,"[65] Palombo provides us with a compact description of a working method that Peter Weir uses in many of his films. The coincidence in Weir's work of the mundane and the fantastical, light and dark forces, waking and dreaming states encourages us to synthesize these apparently contradictory realms by dissolving their differences.

Palombo notes that "as it can be understood today, dreaming is an essential step in the processing of new experience, linking new events with related events stored in long-term memory."[66] In Weir films such as *The Last Wave* and *The Year of Living Dangerously*, though, what we see is characters realizing that dreams themselves can become the new experience, thus preparing the way for the integration of the dream consciousness (which effortlessly blends the ordinary and extraordinary) into one's conscious life. Virtually all Weir characters struggle toward a new mode of awareness. By using uniquely filmic techniques of image sequencing (e.g., empirical shots followed by dream shots, a structure effectively complicated in *The Last Wave* via an intentional confusion of realms) and stylization (e.g., altered film speeds), Weir repeatedly draws attention to the cinematic nature of the experiences undergone by many of his protagonists, who often dream within the dream realm of the films in which they appear.

In the process of dramatizing the weaving of dreams, directors often draw attention to themselves as the weaver; and the "irregular succession on the screen of objective and subjective worlds" not only "creates the montage effect described by Eisenstein,"[67] but also, in its focus on the (often irresolvable) antagonism between the objective and the subjective realms, provides us with an accurate identification of the psychological experience that many of Weir's characters undergo. One need only add that Weir places an extra spin on this structure by making it difficult for the viewer to determine precisely what the "objective . . . world" actually is.

Not only do Weir's films often refuse to identify reality; they also avoid traditional closure, refusing to resolve at their ends the troublesome issues raised by the conceptual confrontations that they depict. Admittedly, this quality is not unique to Weir; it is present as well in a great deal of European cinema, such as Michelangelo Antonioni's *L'Avventura* (1960), as well as in Australian films such as Ken Hannam's *Sunday Too Far Away* (1975), which ends on an image rife with irresolution: as the bruised protagonist prepares to throw a final punch, the image freezes.[68] However, some critics feel uncomfortable with this aspect of Weir's filmmaking. McFarlane and Mayer, for example, attempt to make the endings of many Weir films seem traditional by asserting that the films' conclusions are melodramatic and, therefore, somewhat conventional. Pointing to the reliance of many of the films on the representation of "polarities [such] as guilt and innocence, innocence and corruption, [the] ordinary and the bizarre and of imagery that reinforces these [concepts],"[69] McFarlane and Mayer go on to contend that films such as *The Cars That Ate Paris*, *Picnic at Hanging Rock*, and *The Last Wave* "all make some use of melodramatic structures"; they then refer to the endings of these films (as well as the conclusion of *Gallipoli*) as "oddly low-key," and go on to contrast them with "the emotional frissons generated by some of [Weir's] American films."[70]

Yet I should note that aside from McFarlane and Mayer's preference for traditional endings, they tend to misinterpret the films. The "low-key" finales of Weir's first three features represent Weir's refusal to answer questions such as: What is reality? What constitutes acceptable behavior? How does one deal with the apparent contradictions between the conscious and unconscious realms? As for *Gallipoli*, there is very little that is low-key about it. We're meant to feel deeply melancholic after watching the deaths of so many young men.

McFarlane and Mayer point to the "unequivocally . . . victor[ious]" John Book at *Witness's* end and "more powerfully still . . . the inspired last moments of *Dead Poets Society*, in which the students' tribute to their departing teacher ends the film on a note of affirmation of goodness."[71] They observe of these conclusions that "the enigmatic Weir of his Australian films has responded with melodramatic flourish to the melodramatic challenges of two of his American films."[72] Again, though, the two critics seem to be incorrectly describing the films. John Book is hardly triumphant at the end of *Witness*; indeed, he leaves the Amish farm in defeat, having accepted the impossibility of remaining with Rachel. As for *Dead Poets Society*, McFarlane and Mayer overlook the complexity of the film's final image, which problematically encloses the shot of one of the boys standing on his desk within the legs of another student.

The oppositions in Weir's films may be more than the result of melodramatic dictates or Weir's university experience; they also derive from insights that

Weir has achieved in response to his readings on the unconscious. One of the reasons that Weir often doesn't end his films traditionally is because to do so would be to affirm that a conventional resolution of contraries is not only possible but preferable, an attitude completely at variance with the director's ethic, which—rooted in the values of surrealism, the unconscious, and dreams—avoids the pedestrian assurances of the material realm in favor of an irresolution that, while potentially frustrating, is nonetheless for Weir a more truthful representation of what he considers reality.[73]

In 1987, Weir was with some justification referred to by one critic as "the strongest heir to 60s dreaming—someone who, wherever he calls home (the America of *Witness* or *The Mosquito Coast*, the Australia of *The Last Wave* or *Picnic at Hanging Rock*), is always looking for some alternative to it, some romantic dissolution in distant times and faraway places."[74] Nevertheless, his filmmaking has been open to negative assessment. In a challenging article, "Peter Weir and the Cinema of New Age Humanism,"[75] Gary Hentzi contends that the type of spiritualism exhibited in Weir's films is nothing more than "pop spiritualism . . . a way of making a virtue of necessity . . . a kind of tonic for the feelings of loss and anxiety and vulnerability that are inseparable from the loss of traditional communal structures . . . [a] product of the frustrated desire for a sense of communal wholeness and purpose."[76] Hentzi further contends that Weir is "unable to capture on film the subterranean powers that so fascinate him" and that Weir is guilty of one of the failings of New Age thinking: the inability to identify precisely what the forces are that are absent in contemporary life and consciousness.[77]

Hentzi's critique seems to point to potential problems with Weir's filmmaking. Hentzi contends that New Age thinking deals in absolutes without defining what it is talking about, and points to Weir's fascination at the approximate time of the production of *Picnic at Hanging Rock* and *The Last Wave* with the work of Carl Jung, Carlos Castaneda, and Immanuel Velikovsky as suggesting the kind of vague thinking that led to what Hentzi considers the failure of both films to successfully communicate an otherworldly atmosphere. However, to describe in this way the director's technique in these films is to miss the point. It's characteristically Western to insist on art grounded in factual narration and concrete imagery. Yet such an approach is clearly inappropriate if, as is true for Weir, one is attempting to demonstrate that empirical reality is nothing more than a shadow of what is real. One could contend that it's not vagueness but precision to sketch in reality via suggestion rather than assertion, ambiguity rather than emphatic statements. Once again, Roger Shattuck's study proves to be illuminating, providing us with insights that we can apply to our inquiry into Weir's work. While he recognizes that ambiguity has its dangers, Shattuck also highlights its unique strengths.

> All this embracing of ambiguity makes the arts difficult of access and occasionally irresponsible. It often renders the extraction of a single meaning infeasible. On the other hand, it permits the complexities and conflicts of mental operations to carry over into their products. This may seem an idle virtue, for clarity has long been one of the supreme artistic standards. Yet there are subjects about which one cannot be clear without fraud. Every emotion and conviction has its reverse side, and ambiguity can stand for a profound frankness, an acknowledgment of the essential ambivalence of truth and experience, of life itself. Striving to apply a rigorous and simultaneous attention to several meanings, ambiguity aims beyond vagueness at *inclusiveness,* for which the only other method is monumental size.[78]

Keeping Shattuck in mind makes Hentzi's subtext clearer: Hentzi fails to tell us that his essential argument with Weir's filmmaking is based less on a disagreement over technique than on a difference of opinion as to what constitutes reality. Moreover, despite Hentzi's annoyance with Weir's search for universal meaning, he never demonstrates that there is any reason not to be dissatisfied with the lack of a communal, spiritual dimension in the world; nor does he identify precisely what he finds wrong with writings such as Jung's. Further, in aligning Jungian psychology with the work of Velikovksy and Castaneda, Hentzi conceptually renders them equivalent, although it seems quite clear that Jung's hypotheses concerning the collective unconscious, archetypes, and the function of dreams are far more sophisticated and empirically based (many were borne out in clinical applications) than the work of these other two authors, who respectively deal with worlds in collision and the teachings of a (fictional) Yaqui master. In essence, what Hentzi does is to set up the Jung/Castaneda/Velikovksy triumvirate as an easy target in a straw man argument that is used as a link in what only seems to be a deductive chain.

Additionally, Hentzi not only faults Weir for not portraying a mysterious realm in a non-mysterious way, but goes on to overlook Weir's refinement of his early filmmaking technique. Even though Hentzi, whose article appeared in 1990, quotes Weir as stating that he has moved away from the eclectic reading of the period that gave rise to his early films, he ignores the implications of Weir's assertion, as well as the director's increasing emphasis on stronger scripts and more restrained dream effects.

When asked by Michael Dempsey in 1980 whether or not he was trying to film his own dreams, an attempt that might make Weir seem to fit into the pattern of vagueness that Hentzi later asserted, Weir replied,

Not at all, no . . . to answer the question a little more fairly, I have lost interest in certain themes. There was a period when I read a tremendous amount of Carl Jung. I was dazzled, overwhelmed. And, hell, I read very little of it now, nor do I either agree with or understand all of his theories. The film we're [currently] working on, *The Year of Living Dangerously,* has moved in another direction. It's about a very real situation, but in an extraordinarily hallucinatory setting.[79]

As we will see throughout this book, though, Weir has not abandoned Jung's ideas so much as integrated them into his own thinking.[80] Rather than using dream imagery indiscriminately, Weir eventually began to use such elements more moderately, perhaps realizing that their depiction would be more effective if they acted as periodic counterpoints rather than as recurrent elements. Moreover, we need not take Weir at his word, as Hentzi often does. By merely looking at *The Year of Living Dangerously,* for example, it is clear that in his depiction of Indonesia, Weir has retained the otherworldly aspect of his early filmmaking and complemented it by introducing factually based political elements. We need to recognize that Weir's diverse reading from the 1960s is only part of the basis of his work, which also derives from his feelings and ideas about the unknown. Weir's work posits alienation (and a resultant shift toward an emphasis on the unconscious) as prime attributes not only of his own reading but of the Australian experience. (Weir characterizes Australians as "colonial people, the dispossessed of the world";[81] the director's countrymen are obviously in sharp contrast to the Aborigines, who have a long history.) This aspect of Weir's filmmaking might account for some of what Hentzi sees as the vagueness in the director's films. Additionally, if there is a lack of traditional narrative clarity to some of Weir's early work, even this quality has its place and is functional: it represents the filmmaker working our problems that derive from a clash of the empirical and dream realms. Instead of exemplifying answers, the films emblematize a strong desire to know, even if the end point of the journey toward knowledge results in our realizing that we cannot know everything. As Richard Combs puts it in a comment on Weir's early work, "one of the pre-eminent signs of Weir's cinema has been his tendency to suggest more atmospherically than he was prepared to develop thematically."[82] Critic Jan Dawson notes, "Weir admits that he's always been more interested in atmosphere than character, and insists that he works from instinct rather than 'premeditation.'"[83] Again, we see that the films often disparage thought in favor of feelings; and whether Weir creates this effect consciously or not, the films reflect their director's concerns.

It is easy to see the point at which Weir most notably gave up his fascination with the intellectual realm: it occurred when he began to make a pitch to become an international filmmaker.[84] The beginning of this change in Weir's technique started with the production of *Gallipoli,* during which Weir began to move away from the intellectual approach that characterized the making of *Picnic* and *Last Wave* in favor of feelings, in this case, the strong feelings that the devastating Gallipoli campaign occasions in many Australians. During one point in the film's production, Weir says that along with screenwriter David Williamson he decided to "turn . . . away from . . . the analytical, intellectual, the academic [approach], the very training we'd both had, and go flat out for the feeling."[85] Despite Weir's opinion that "*Gallipoli* was the last major step in . . . allowing myself to be so emotional,"[86] one can see that although the film attempts to be highly emotional, much of it does not reflect this emphasis. With *Gallipoli* finished, Weir seems to have decided to further develop this side of his filmmaking.

While it might seem as though Weir's career could be easily divided into two periods defined by where his films were directed—one in which he directed films in Australia, one in which he directed films in the United States—it nonetheless appears that the most significant dividing line in Weir's cinema is not geographic but emotional.[87] I contend that Weir's Australian period begins with *The Cars That Ate Paris* and ends with *Gallipoli*, and that the director's "American" period begins with *The Year of Living Dangerously*. Aside from the fact that Year was completely financed by MGM, a major American studio, the film evidences a dramatic change in the director's work, away from heavily symbolic renderings of abstract concepts (the unconscious, the unknown, etc., notions that do not disappear from Weir's work but are, rather, more organically integrated into the films) in favor of emotions as the arbiter of knowledge and a prerequisite to self-realization, as well as a concomitant use of intense climaxes that, if they don't always solve the social and personal problems posited in the films, at least leave the audience emotionally satisfied. Perhaps more importantly, though, this apparent change in Weir's approach signals a recognition of the relation between love and religion in life. The "cool" aspect of early films such as *Picnic at Hanging Rock* and *The Last Wave*—in which love is, respectively, either repressed or absent—gives way to a view in which human affection mediates the conflict between conscious and unconscious urges. The dramatization of the secular love between Guy and Jill in *The Year of Living Dangerously* yields, in *Witness*, to a passionate relationship that has religious overtones. By the time of *Fearless*, love and religion are represented as equivalent.

The distinction between the earlier and later films represents a shift in emphasis from films in which the predominant stress is on ideas to films in which ideas and feelings are of equal importance. In the later films, we meet characters whose dilemmas are at least as much based on sentiments as on concepts. Perhaps as a result of his early films' obsessive inquiries, Weir came to understand that one could resolve contradictory issues, could transcend duality, by embracing a combination of thought and feeling, that indeed, to do otherwise is to risk falling short of complete self-realization.[88] In fact, it might be fair to assert that the spiritual, otherwordly aspect of the love that these characters feel has the same elevating effect on them as do the Jungian mysteries on characters in the earlier films. Love thus becomes a breakthrough, a revelation, a means of moving toward spiritual enlightenment.

Although an initial response to the early films might suggest that they were interested in ambience instead of themes, it's more likely that the heavily visual atmosphere of films such as *Picnic at Hanging Rock* and *The Last Wave* is the themes. In his later work, Weir created films that blend mood and dialogue, context and action, a combination embodying that fusion of inner and outer forces toward which the earlier films (which may most profitably be viewed as investigations in search of a solution) seem to be working. The later films do not, it should be clear, provide answers to the questions earlier posed; however, they do suggest avenues of further inquiry, all in the service of an attempt to reach a life-affirming fusion of one's body and soul, flesh and spirit, an end successfully achieved at the conclusion of Weir's most spiritually satisfying film, *Fearless*.

Weir seems to have found a basis for many of his notions about the magical and mystical in the writings of Sigmund Freud and Carl Jung. In his essay "The Uncanny," Freud inquires into the nature of our reaction to a situation in which we experience a sense of unfamiliarity with regard to an event or person, a reaction that, Freud notes, occurs quite often in relation to "death and dead bodies," "the return of the dead," and spirits or ghosts.[89] Freud posits that there is a degree of repression involved in the experiencing of such events.

> If psycho-analytic theory is correct in maintaining that every affect belonging to an emotional impulse, whatever its kind, is transformed, if it is repressed, into anxiety, then among instances of frightening things there must be one class in which the frightening element can be shown to be something repressed which *recurs*. This class of frightening things would then constitute the uncanny; and it must be a matter of indifference whether what is uncanny was itself originally frightening or whether it carried some *other* affect. In the second place, if this is indeed the secret nature of the uncanny, we can understand why linguistic usage has extended *das Heimliche* ("homely") into its opposite, das *Unheimliche*; for this uncanny is in reality nothing new or alien, but something which is familiar and

old-established in the mind and which has become alienated from it only through the process of repression.[90]

The uncanny appears in many Weir films: in the form of the threatening Max in *The Plumber,* who concretizes Jill's unrecognized apprehension about her sexuality and identity; in the person of *Dead Poets'* Keating who, unbeknownst to the school's administration, represents the embodiment of youthful rebellion, not the authoritarianism that they cherish. However, its most obvious occurrence is in the person of *The Last Wave's* central Aboriginal character, Chris, who passes out of the dreams in which David, the film's white protagonist, sees him and into David's reality, within which Chris's return presages David's psychological reorientation. In all of its appearances in Weir's films, the uncanny person or object signals, not so much a state of fear as an anxiety that functions as the first step toward self-revelation.

Freud's elucidation of a significant mechanism in our reaction to the uncanny—although it stops short of proposing the type of reciprocity between realms that will be asserted by Jung—nonetheless bears particular relevance to the manner in which the actions and images in many of Weir's films affect us:

> an uncanny effect is often and easily produced when the distinction between imagination and reality is effaced, as when something that we have hitherto regarded as imaginary appears before us in reality, or when a symbol takes over the full functions of the thing that it symbolizes, and so on. . . . [I]t may be true that the uncanny . . . is something which is secretly familiar . . . which has undergone repression and then returned from it.[91]

This explanation suggests one possible way of accounting not only for the otherworldliness of the action in such films as *The Cars That Ate Paris, Picnic at Hanging Rock, The Last Wave*, and certain sections of *The Year of Living Dangerously,* but also for the power of the imagery in most of Weir's films. Much of the impact of Weir's visuals seems to be achieved via a number of carefully wrought mechanisms: the intentional resurfacing of unusual images and domains (the seeing of visions, the entrance into a dream-like realm); the psychological dislocation that results from a confrontation with upsetting forces or the unknown (characters who find themselves in "foreign" cultures, as do John Book in *Witness,* Allie Fox in *The Mosquito Coast,* and Truman Burbank in *The Truman Show*); the alienating effects of disasters (*Fearless's* plane wreck), tidal waves or storms (*The Last Wave, The Mosquito Coast*), immigrant status (Georges in *Green Card*); the psychological trauma resulting from car crashes (Arthur's reaction in *The Cars That Ate Paris*) or intrusive, insulting, and sexually threatening workmen (Jill's anxiety in 1979's *The Plumber*)—in short, an onslaught of responses that, like the one to things uncanny, are initially repressed and then resurface.

Freud says that "the finding of an object is actually the refinding of it."[92] Palombo observes that Freud's assertion is

> as much a statement about knowledge as desire. We can't recognize what we haven't known earlier, and we can't desire what we don't recognize as desirable. It isn't possible to *experience* anything *for the first time.* In the double imagery of the dream we register the yet to be experienced, acquiring as we do the ability to respond in kind. Art reflects our desire back to us as a special kind of knowledge, always, relative to the objective world, as a double image incorporating the past as well as the present.[93]

This insight, which affirms that the "uncanny" is always the "canny" or already known, makes it clear that what Weir was working toward in the eerily familiar otherworldliness of early films such as *The Cars That Ate Paris* and *Picnic at Hanging Rock* is the necessarily ambiguous answer to the riddle that he persistently poses: what do we really know, and how do we know what we know? A possible answer is to adopt the dream wisdom that does not inquire but merely accepts. Paradoxically, the end point of Weir's inquiries in his films is to lead us to conclude that inquiry is itself unproductive, that acquiescence to the knowledge contained in the subconscious is all.

The notion of a clash between two apparently distinct realms of perception not only invites comparison with Freud's work but is also structurally related to the classic notion of the double, which may take the form of shadows or ghosts as projections of the soul or actual, apparently identical beings, as in Dostoyevsky's novel *The Double,* Poe's "William Wilson," and Stevenson's *Dr. Jekyll and Mr. Hyde.* Otto Rank asserts that

> the primitive belief in souls is originally nothing else than a kind of belief in immortality which energetically denies the power of death; and even today the essential content of the belief in the soul—as it subsists in religion, superstition, and modern cults—has not become other, nor much more, than that. The thought of death is rendered supportable by assuring oneself of a second life, after this one, as a double. As in the threat to narcissism by sexual love, so in the threat of death does the idea of death (originally averted by the double) recur in this figure who, according to general superstition, announces death or whose injury harms the individual.[94]

It should seem apparent that "the uncanny" to which Freud refers reappears in Rank's work as the double, which Rank at one point conceives of as a harbinger of ideas (in this case ideas associated with death) that one attempts to deny.

In Peter Weir's films, the "other" or double appears to the films' whites in the form of the Aborigine, immigrant, or group whose world view is foreign to that of the predominant, white social class. In its milder forms, this attitude on the part of whites manifests itself as fear and uneasiness concerning outsiders or those ideas and concepts alien to one's usual experience; but it may also appear as threats that are either racially based (the Aboriginal realm as a threat to the "purity" of white civilization, a concept implicit in *Picnic at Hanging Rock*); intellectual (the outsider as a threat to the white version of history, as in *The Last Wave*); sexual (the threats against Jill in *The Plumber*); or psychological (threats to the integrity of the self, which appear in films as varied as *Dead Poets Society, Green Card, Fearless,* and *The Truman Show*). Perhaps the greatest threat of the outsider is as the representative of a system of thought that differs so significantly from the one held by certain characters in a film that it represents an alternative view of reality. For example, in *Picnic at Hanging Rock* and *The Last Wave,* the forces at the rock (in *Picnic*) and the Aboriginal view of reality that sees nature as an integrated system meant to be respected and, if possible, lived with harmoniously (in *Wave*) are alien to the manner in which "white" characters such as Miss McCraw, Mrs. Appleyard, and David Burton—who regard nature as something extraneous to them—live. The different world view of an outsider or outside force, sometimes coupled with antagonistic actions, may also threaten the cohesion of a town or community, and can result in a radical shift in a community's perspective. We see this mechanism in action in the persons of *The Cars That Ate Paris*'s Arthur, who does not share the town's view of cars as objects from which people may profit, and *The Truman Show*'s Truman, who eventually rebels against his town's imposed reality.

There is another realm to which changes in perception or a collapsing of distinctions may draw us: the religious. Highlighting the split between Freud and Jung's conception of religion throws into relief Weir's views on the subject, as well as the attitudes of his characters, who represent different sides in the debate between materialism and spirituality.[95]

For Freud, transcendent, religious feelings are an indication of neurotic thinking. Freud traces these feelings back to "an early phase of ego-feeling," during which, Freud says, there is a need for a protective father figure.[96]

> The psychical origin of religious ideas . . . are [sic] illusions, fulfillments of the oldest, strongest and most urgent wishes of mankind. The secret of their strength lies in the strength of those wishes. As we already know, the terrifying impression of helplessness in childhood aroused the need for protection—for protection through love—which was provided by the father; and the recognition that this helplessness lasts throughout life made it necessary to cling to the existence of a

father, but this time a more powerful one. Thus, the benevolent rule of a divine Providence allays our fear of the dangers of life.[97]

Freud's view seems to correspond to that of the materially oriented characters in Weir's films (e.g., *Picnic's* Mrs. Appleyard and Miss McCraw, or the original attitude of *Last Wave's* David), for whom the realm of the mysterious and otherworldly is nothing more than an aberrant distortion of the real world. In these films, "male" figures acting as arbiters of order and control either disappear or are notably elusive (thus Mrs. Appleyard's expression of regret over the loss of Miss McCraw, whom she refers to as having a "masculine" intellect, and David's [unconscious] search for an alternative to his stepfather, which he finds in Charlie).

Although Weir doesn't seem to disparage religious feelings as does Freud, he is, like Freud, fascinated with the dream realm. For Freud, though, dreams were either a function of wish fulfillment or a dramatization of events experienced during waking hours.

> If we seek the help of analysis, we find that every dream without any possible exception goes back to an impression of the past few days or, it is more probably correct to say, of the day immediately preceding the dream, of the "dream day." . . . Dreams are never concerned with things with which we should not think it worth while to be concerned during the day, and trivialities which do not affect us during the day are unable to pursue us in our sleep.[98]

For Freud, then (whose attitude is reflected in the early portions of *The Last Wave* by David), dreams are not visionary but merely dramatic; and though dreams contain apparently mysterious images, Freud feels that these images are only "displaced" aspects of the material world.[99]

By contrast, Weir's attitude toward dreams is strongly allied with that of Carl Jung. In Jung's view, "dream analysis is the central problem of the analytical treatment, because it is the most important technical means of opening up an avenue to the unconscious."[100] For Jung, "our dreams are most peculiarly independent of our consciousness and exceedingly valuable because they cannot cheat."[101] Jung felt that "dreams are a guide just as the compass is guide,"[102] and agreed with the view that "dream material has a sort of logic of its own."[103]

Most significantly, in opposition to Freud, Jung holds that dreams have concrete significance, that they function not as neurotic mirrors but, virtually, as objects.

> I suppose you have seen that [in dreams] there are certain motifs which occur from time to time—a machine, or the mandala principle is hinted at, or the cauldron, the anima, etc. These are principles, motifs, of worldwide frequency and

great stability of meaning and interpretation. And these motifs can be grasped: here is something rather concrete, a fact, like a hard handle which one can take hold of.[104]

When Jung notes, "This is where I differ with Freud. You cannot say [as Freud does, that] the symbol in a dream is merely a facade behind which you can hide and then say what the dream is. The symbol is a fact . . . ,"[105] he might as well be speaking for Weir. Moreover, Jung felt quite strongly that to treat dreams with suspicion (in much the same manner as the otherworldly forces or characters in Weir's films—for example, the rock in *Picnic at Hanging Rock,* the Aborigines in *The Last Wave*—are regarded by empirically oriented characters as strange) is to commit a serious error of interpretation. "The dream is such a difficult and complicated thing that I do not dare to make any assumptions about its possible cunning or its tendency to deceive. The dream is a natural occurrence, and there is no earthly reason why we should assume that it is a crafty device to lead us astray."[106]

The most significant link between Jung and Weir is in their conception of the implicit connection among the unconscious realm, dreams, and religion. For Jung, the religious realm is not (as it is for Freud) an example of neurosis but the very essence of human psychology. "The *mysterium magnum* is not only an actuality but is first and foremost rooted in the human psyche."[107] In his commentary on contradictions, Jung elucidates the notion of irresolvability as it relates to religion, a notion that plays an important part in Weir's filmmaking. Jung's statement that "the paradox is one of our most valued *spiritual* possessions, while uniformity of meaning is a sign of weakness"[108] (my emphasis) helps us recognize Weir's stress on ambiguity as a mechanism that not only allows integration of uncanny elements into one's psychology but also makes possible the reciprocal acceptance of intellectually incomprehensible, often paradoxical religious elements into one's life as well. When Jung later goes on to note that "in the psychic archetype of the self" opposites as inherently contradictory as good and evil "seem to be united,"[109] he points us toward the realm in which all contradictions seem resolved, and which he identifies as religion. "The archetypes of the unconscious can be shown empirically to be the equivalents of religious dogmas."[110] In what manifestation of the unconscious, we then may ask, does this resolution of contraries take place? Given our understanding of Weir's films, it is probably not surprising that for Weir, this resolution occurs in that part of the unconscious occupied by dreams. For Weir, there is a virtually unbroken continuity among the unconscious, dreams, and religious feelings, all of which emanate from or help us penetrate to that psychological region that is the basis and source of all profundity, secular or not.

According to Jung, "the dream compensates the conflicts of the conscious mind . . . the unconscious does not simply act *contrary* to the conscious mind but *modifies* it more in the manner of an opponent or partner."[111] This conception is present in *The Last Wave,* in which the unconscious, in the form of the film's Aborigines, is first viewed as opponent and then partner. Indeed, all of Weir's films portray conflicts between the conscious/material and unconscious/dream realms. Yet there is a solution to this dilemma. When Jung notes that "human wholeness [is] the goal to which the psychotherapeutic process ultimately leads,"[112] the applicability to Weir's films should seem plain: what the films dramatize is a process involving conflict and inquiry whose end point is psychological unity. Just as the Fall of Man in the Garden of Eden story is viewed as a *felix culpa,* a happy (and essential) fault that paved the way, after repentance, for the intercession of grace, so too, the process in Weir's films of exposure to otherworldly, dark, or Aboriginal forces, which is followed by psychological breakdown and then some form of reintegration, has a necessarily therapeutic and religious dimension (even at *The Last Wave*'s end, David has come to some terrible, but nonetheless necessary, realization). In this respect, there seems to be some divine plan at work leading us to greater awareness, precisely the idea that many of Weir's films promote.

As Jung observes,

> We know of course that without sin there is no repentance and without repentance no redeeming grace, also that without original sin the redemption of the world could never have come about; but we assiduously avoid investigating whether in this very power of evil God might not have placed some special purpose which it is most important for us to know. . . . [T]he encounter with the dark half of the personality, or "shadow," comes about of its own accord in any moderately thorough treatment. This problem is as important as that of sin in the Church.[113]

For Jung, as for Weir, these are not just philosophical concepts but emotional truths, dramas played out repeatedly in every individual's life in the process of becoming one's self. "What the symbolism of alchemy [which Jung sees as strongly related to Christianity] expresses is the whole problem of the evolution of personality . . . the so-called individuation process."[114] With this insight in mind, we can see that Weir's films, which repeatedly focus on crises of identity, can be viewed as essentially religious dramas of personal discovery; and regardless of whether these dramas culminate in irresolution (as in the girls' disappearance in *Picnic at Hanging Rock* and Truman's passage into a new realm in *Truman Show*), apocalypse (the destruction of Sydney in *The Last Wave*), emotional bonding (Guy and Jill's relationship in *The Year of Living Dangerously*), emotional separation (the leave-taking between Book and Rachel in *Witness,* and Keating and his students at the end of *Dead Poets Society*), or synthesis (Max's psychological regeneration in *Fearless*), they are nonetheless all concerned with the yearning for some sort of union with forces greater than one's self that may justifiably be deemed spiritual.

All of Weir's films can be seen as descents into the unconscious, encounters with death. Additionally, in one sense or another, Weir's films often involve a night journey that results in some form of enlightenment. Mythologist Joseph Campbell defines the night journey in the following way: *"A hero ventures forth from the world of common day into a region of supernatural wonder: fabulous forces are there encountered and a decisive victory is won: the hero comes back from this mysterious adventure with the power to bestow boons on his fellow man"* (italics in original text).[115]

We can see this structure of descent or passage into an unfamiliar realm present in many of Weir's films. Arthur's late-night journey toward the dysfunctional town of Paris in *The Cars That Ate Paris*; the schoolgirls' trip to the rock in *Picnic at Hanging Rock*; David's descent into the sewers in *The Last Wave*; Frank and Archie's passage into the hellish miasma of war in *Gallipoli*; Guy's evening walk through a poor section of Jakarta in *The Year of Living Dangerously*; the students' evening trips to the cave in *Dead Poets Society*; Truman's retreats to his basement in *Truman Show*—all qualify as night journeys that act as preludes to self-knowledge.

In Weir's films a descent into an underworld rather than journeys into a delightful realm are more common (although this realm may initially appear delightful, as in the picnic to Mt. Macedon at the beginning of *Picnic at Hanging Rock*). Moreover, it is clear that the journey does not have to take place at night; the "night" aspect may be figurative, suggesting the traveler's initial ignorance of what is to come.

Any "decisive victor[ies]" in Weir's films are predominantly psychological in nature; indeed, the whole hero myth is clearly a projection of an internal journey, a descent into the unconscious, a confrontation with the uncanny or repressed. The issue of whether or not the night journey hero bestows benefits on his fellows parallels a distinction (derived from critic Robert Winer) that I will sonn discuss: that between witnessing and bearing witness, between seeing and then acting on what is seen, between keeping to one's self the insights gained as the result of an experience or communicating them to others.[116] In this respect, of all Weir characters it is *Fearless's* Max who comes closest to the Campbell prototype of the hero, since, after an extraordinary event, Max helps a significant number of people.

The hero's night journey can be read as the period during which one dreams.[117] Although Campbell conceives of this journey in terms more sanguine than those that might be used to describe the journeys in Weir's films, the essential structure is nonetheless quite similar.

> The first step [of the hero's journey], detachment or withdrawal, consists in a radical transfer of emphasis from the external to the internal world, macro- to microcosm, a retreat from the desperations of the waste land to the peace of the everlasting realm that is within. But this realm, as we know from psychoanalysis, is precisely the infantile unconscious. It is the realm that we enter in sleep.[118]

When Campbell goes on to talk about one of the benefits to be gained from the night journey, the wisdom to be gained from dreams, he might just as well be describing the psychological movement of many of Weir's characters.

> [A]ll the life-potentialities that we never managed to bring to adult realization, those other portions of ourself, are there [in the dream realm]; for such golden seeds do not die. If only a portion of that lost totality could be dredged up into the light of day, we should experience a marvelous expansion of our powers, a vivid renewal of life. . . . Moreover, if we could dredge up something forgotten not only by ourselves but by our whole generation or our entire civilization, we should become indeed the boon-bringer, the culture hero of the day. . . . [T]he first work of the hero is to retreat from the world of secondary effects to those causal zones of the psyche where the difficulties really reside, and there to clarify the difficulties, eradicate them . . . and break through to the undistorted, direct experience and assimilation of what C. G. Jung has called "the archetypal images."[119]

The writings of Northrop Frye are also helpful in understanding Weir's films. Frye describes one of the prime aspects of comedy in the following way: "the movement from *pistis* to *gnosis*, from a society controlled by habit, ritual, bondage, arbitrary law and the older characters to a society controlled by youth and pragmatic freedom is fundamentally, as the Greek words suggest, a movement from illusion to reality."[120] What we have here is an apt description of the structure of both *Dead Poets* and its thematic and structural predecessor, *Picnic at Hanging Rock*. In each film, young people are trapped within a society (represented in microcosm by an educational institution) that is ruled by a series of repressive qualities: habit (uniform dress as well as an obsession with canonical writings); ritual bondage (the binding of *Picnic's* Sarah; the paddling of *Poets'* Knox); arbitrary rules of behavior (the insistence on seemly conduct in both films, each of which features a teacher telling students to stop acting unruly); and, most significantly, the tyranny over the young by older characters whose restrictiveness is opposed by the presence and actions of younger, more humane and sympathetic characters (Mademoiselle de Poitiers in *Picnic;* Mr. Keating in *Poets*).

In each film, the illusion of socially absolute values is, for a time, dispelled, but via different mechanisms. Since it is improbable that the girls in *Picnic* (unlike *Dead Poets*' students) would act rebelliously against their elders, their emancipation is achieved by virtue of an outside force operating on them: the sexual-magnetic influence of the rock (which also affects one of the adults as well, Miss McCraw). *Picnic*'s Bertie and Sarah are freed from the restrictive effects of unknown parentage (both are relegated to subsidiary roles, Bertie as servant, Sarah as victim of prejudicial attitudes) by near-deaths or death: Bertie and Michael become closer as a result of the girls' disappearances.

Frye's observation that in many comedies "there is the same movement from normal world to green world [a world within which life and love 'triumph . . . over the waste land']"[121] and back again"[122] invites comparison with Campbell's description of the structure of the hero's journey. Additionally, the "green world" journey involves an entrance into a realm with which, as I have pointed out, the hero's journey also intersects: the realm of dreams. Frye states, "The green world has analogies, not only to the fertile world of ritual, but to the dream world that we create out of our own desires. This dream world collides with the stumbling and blinded follies of the world of experience."[123]

In Frye's view, then, dreams are representations of our wish to make the world conform to what we want. For Frye, as for Jung and Weir (for both of whom fertility often seems to be construed as self-knowledge), dreams express a reality more significant than the one available to us through empirical experience, precisely the notion proposed via the *wayang* shadow play in *The Year of Living Dangerously*.

Campbell and Frye's observations also function as descriptions of Weir's role as a filmmaker: to journey away from conventional representation, "dredge up" elemental images, and then communicate them to the audience. As Campbell notes, "[The hero's] solemn task and deed therefore . . . is to return then to us, transfigured, and teach the lesson he has learned of life renewed."[124]

This responsibility is drawn attention to by critic Robert Winer, who places great emphasis on the distinction between witnessing and bearing witness, which he regards as "the same as that between taking in and giving forth, between passive registration and active testifying."[125] Viewing this distinction as equivalent to that between seeing and acting, one realizes how often this structure appears in Weir's films. *Witness*'s Samuel moves from merely seeing McFee commit a crime to identifying him as the perpetrator, an act that represents a somewhat regrettable movement into the adult, corrupt world represented by

John Book.[126] *The Last Wave*'s David progresses from inert anxiety to a seeking after truth; The Plumber's Jill retaliates against Max's intimidation; *The Year of Living Dangerously*'s Billy Kwan repeatedly draws attention to a problem he verbalizes at the film's beginning: "what, then, is to be done?"; reacting to Allie's offenses, the two older brothers in *The Mosquito Coast* begin to rebel against him, and so on. In all of these cases, Weir seems to be telling us that we not only need to achieve a synthesis of our conscious and unconscious promptings (which in the films are usually represented by opposing characters, thus cluing us in to the figurative approach to characterization that many of the films exhibit) but must pass beyond awareness to an application of our new knowledge (indeed, we may also regard Weir's filmmaking as the director's way of "bearing witness" to his realizations). While not in any sense implying political or social involvement, Weir nonetheless encourages us to respond to the behest that new awareness virtually mandates some form of personal, pragmatic change. As Søren Kierkegaard writes in *The Sickness unto Death*, "to have a self, to be a self, is the greatest concession made to man, but at the same time it is eternity's demand upon him."[127]

Weir has quite distinct thematic concerns, but he is reluctant to be singled out as having a prominent "signature." Although in early films such as *Picnic at Hanging Rock* and *The Last Wave* Weir employed a great many stylistic devices (whose use he freely acknowledges)[128] such as slow motion, gauze shots, and heavily stylized soundtracks to communicate his themes, he subsequently claimed to repudiate this approach in favor of what he refers to as a more 1940s, invisible mode of directing.[129] However, Weir doesn't really seem to have changed his method of directing so much as changed the way in which he views it. The overt stylistics of the early films, which Weir now seems to find embarrassing, have yielded to an aesthetic approach in which serving the needs of the film's story comes before pleasing the director's taste for stylistics. In this respect, Weir's 1986 comment on the different visual style of *Witness* seems quite appropriate. Noting that *Witness*'s look "comes very much from Flemish and German paintings,"[130] Weir comments, "it's a case of using one's talents to serve the idea rather than imposing a style overall."[131]

Weir does, though, feel awkward being singled out as a creator. After completing *The Year of Living Dangerously*, Weir commented that

> I *am* looking for ways to force change on myself. I am trying to drop stylistic aspects, to remove myself further from the film, to allow other influences to come in, to find a fresher approach, and to not become too predictable. I'm looking for a way to eliminate, to simplify, to rely on fewer tricks and gimmicks, and in a way I've been trying to do that for years.[132]

Yet as one can note both from the extremely strong influence that Weir had on *Year*'s script[133] and, doubtless, on the film's visual design, he has not dropped all stylistic effects. I believe that what we're really seeing in Weir's comments on his role as director is a combination of a desire to widen his films' appeal by making his work more generic; an impulse to avoid being hampered by categorization (Weir has said, "I think style can become inhibiting to a long career");[134] and his characteristic shyness in response to his role as a powerful directorial force. In a 1983 video interview produced by the Australian Film, Television, and Radio School, Weir seemed a bit uneasy when answering questions about his work; it's also well known that he does not like to grant interviews, another sign of a desire for anonymity on both a personal and artistic level.

Interviewing Weir for *Film Comment*, critic Pat McGilligan asked the director about his reluctance to be identified through his films.

> *McGilligan:* You seem so resistant to any definition. I bring to you examples of motifs in your work: of intuition and madness, of underlying social consciousness, of "lost" individuals transforming themselves in a clash of cultures— and you say, "Partly accidental, partly coincidence."
>
> *Weir:* Totally. I was thinking the other day, "Gee, that would make an interesting film . . . ," some short story I was reading, then I thought, "Oh no, it's another thing of a person going into a foreign culture. . . ." So I decided I can't do that.
> McGilligan: Why do you frown at it?
> *Weir:* It's too obvious. Also, I like to feel I'm more private than that. I don't take any pleasure in interviews because, like a lot of public entertainers, professional entertainers, absurdly this contradiction exists for me of wanting to stand up and get applause while at the same time wanting to retain privacy.
>
> But as the number of pictures build up, someone with a head on their shoulders can fairly easily sit down and form a portrait of the person who made them. That's not unreasonable.[135]

Thus, it isn't stylistics that Weir resists so much as what he regards as the danger inherent in being typed as a specific kind of filmmaker.

As Weir notes in an interview for *American Film*, "I do think you begin to see something of yourself in your work and it can make you uncomfortable." But then he expands the concept by stating, "and self-conscious."[136] Once again, we see Weir expressing a desire to retreat into the mystical concept of the completely intuitive artist. In many respects, Weir seem to be right about himself. For example, *Green Card*, which was consciously crafted for actor Gerard Depardieu, is his weakest film. Alternatively, when Weir works with a strong script dealing with action and ideas, as he does in *Witness* and *Fearless*, a film project can produce in him what he means to produce in his audiences: a sense of "wonder,"[137] a quality that apparently delivers both filmmaker and audience from self-consciousness.

In the 1970s, while making a documentary about an Australian potter, Weir interviewed Shiga, a Japanese pottery maker working in Australia. According to Weir, Shiga feels that

> there was no art, it was all craft. He talked about how the great potters didn't sign their pots because it was considered a vanity to do so; how their pots were utilitarian objects . . . how you make each one to the best of your ability—using *Head, Heart, and Hand*—which is what I called the documentary—in perfect balance. How you should never think about making a work of art because you would be punished if you did. That the gods choose when to touch your hands, and you will never know when that may be. You must keep working, and every now and then, when the gods do touch your hands, out will come this wonderful creation. It was so fundamentally opposed to the European idea of, simplistically speaking, the artist-as-God.
>
> I loved his approach. Here were movies—which were items to be used and consumed in your daily life and then thrown away. When I returned to feature filmmaking, the emphasis for me was clearly on craft, and to forget about the artistic propaganda trip that I felt had been perpetrated.
>
> For a long time I had been asking myself: Is film a craft, or is it an art? . . . The result of these conflicting thoughts over the years was that craft was the correct emphasis for me. Because I found myself happiest in the Hollywood tradition, and I needed to find a healthy attitude toward what I was doing.[138]

While acknowledging the role of inspiration, then, Weir is nonetheless attempting in his work to sculpt his films (in a consciously un-self-conscious way) and then have the art emerge out of his attention to functional detail. Perhaps as a result both of the director's interview with Shiga and of the year when he left feature filmmaking and studied classical cinema (1978),[139] Weir's work has tended to become less *obviously* stylized. The feature films produced after 1979 (*Gallipoli, The Year of Living Dangerously, Witness, The Mosquito Coast, Dead Poets Society, Green Card, Fearless,* even the self-reflexive *Truman Show*) mix craft and art, design and inspiration more successfully than Weir's earlier films.

All of Weir's films are stories about an individual attempting to achieve some sort of reconciliation between conscious activity and unconscious yearnings, reality and dreams—in essence, between the body and the spirit, the flesh and the word. As I observed earlier, the films trace a gradual progression from intellectual to emotional dramatizations of these themes. By the time of *The Year of Living Dangerously,* Weir has finally found the intervening force that makes possible a reconciliation of contrary tendencies, and to which I previously drew attention: love, a quality that is either proffered and received (as in *Year*); reluctantly refused (Book's spurning of Rachel in *Witness*); passed on (Keating's legacy in *Dead Poets Society*); achieved, but with melancholy results (the final parting of Georges and Brontë in *Green Card*), or desired and possibly embraced (*The Truman Show*). The yearning for an integrated life, for a return to a prelapsarian existence in which one's self and one's world exist in harmony, is often realized in the latter part of Weir's cinema. In its most satisfying manifestation, in *Fearless*, spiritual integration involves the repudiation of intellectual ways of dealing with alienation (the academic attitude represented by the psychiatrist Perlman and the lawyer Brillstein) in favor of an approach that sees grace, which leads to psychological healing, in the form of people helping one another.

Weir's tale about finding a stone carving that he knew he was going to discover, a tale which became the basis for the story of *The Last Wave*, is instructive.[140] The way that I read this anecdote, the story that the stone had to tell (namely, the lesson about precognition that Weir derived from its discovery) was there, waiting, before Weir found it, just as the best of his films, which speak directly to our most primal urges, tell us stories that, to return to a concept discussed earlier, we *re*-cognize as already familiar. These films, which have power because they contain elements that are either lodged, unacknowledged, in our subconscious or that we've seen before in our dreams, provide us with clues to action that we already possess. Viewed and then integrated into both the conscious and subconscious realms, Peter Weir's films telescope back into our awareness, becoming dreams within our own life dreams from which we wake only when we leave the theater.

CAR CRASH DERBY

The Cars That Ate Paris, Weir's first feature currently available for viewing, is a modest film that has a subtle charm. Although it is by no means a major work, and sometimes seems to be a collection of half-realized ideas, it is nevertheless similar to first films by other directors, such as Orson Welles's *Hearts of Age* (1934) and François Truffaut's *Les Mistons* (1957), in that it shows the artist struggling with his craft and moving toward the thematic and visual ideas that will subsequently become his major concern.

Cars is a film about Arthur, who is phobic about driving as a result of his killing an old man with his car, and who is on a trip with his brother George. When George sees strange lights one evening on the road outside the town of Paris, Australia, he loses control of his car and trailer, which skid off the road, killing him. That the accident was intentionally caused by some of Paris's denizens subsequently seems clear, especially given the frequency of crashes near the town and the manner in which Parisians, using warning lanterns, reroute cars off the main road and onto perilous byways.

Arthur is taken in by the town's mayor and encouraged to stay; but when he realizes that the town seems to profit from the local crashes, he leaves, having apparently overcome his fear of driving.[1]

Commenting on the gestation of the film's idea, Weir stated,

> I was driving through France, and I'd been diverted off the road by some road-works and I thought: why did I follow those directions? I seemed to be wandering through very strange little villages. Later I was in England and I saw a paper with the headline "Shotgun Shooting In East Cheam" and below, in a tiny little paragraph "15 Dead on the M1", and I thought, well, if you're going to kill someone you kill them in a motorcar accident, not with a shotgun. So I sat down in a hotel . . . and wrote the story.[2]

Yet there's another element to the film, the notion of intentional deceit lead-ing to murder and pillage. As Weir notes,

> I was always intrigued by the idea of the Cornish pirates early in the last century who moved a light at night so that ships would crash on the rocks. They would then go down and loot the ships. And so I thought of a town that had once been famous for gold and then for pastoral industry. They were failing, and the town closed up. Then, with true pioneering spirit, according to the mayor, by tacit agreement the people set up a trap on the road into town where they would catch the cars, take them to town, and by night cannibalize them. It was just a simple little entertainment, a little allegory.[3]

If we respond to Weir's suggestion and read the film as an allegory, it be-comes a comment not only on repressed desires (a concept that forms the basis of numerous classic horror films)[4] and a small town harboring a horrible secret but also, as we will see, on the manner in which an obsession with consumer-ism and machines turns one into a consuming machine.

Weir peppers the film with absurdist bits of business that work at odds with the grim atmosphere that he is creating. On the road during the day, Arthur and George pass three men who for no discernible reason seem to be trying to load an animal carcass into the trunk of their car. Outside the Paris hospital there is a man swathed in bandages like a mummy, who, despite a serious injury, is working on the hospital sign. The hospital doctor, who apparently experiments on crash victims, and who uses a power drill to perform lobotomies, adminis-ters a word association test to Arthur by having him look at various photo-graphs: a tree, a television, a house, and so forth. Among the photos, though, are not only pictures of car crashes—which the doctor insists that Arthur eu-phemistically refer to as "accidents"—but also pictures of maimed victims. Arthur—who is already feeling disoriented, and who is clearly disturbed about the death of his brother, his being in a strange town, and the unusual behavior of the people whom he meets—reacts to the photos with dismay. At this point, the doctor pauses and then, completely ignoring Arthur's reaction in a comic example of exaggerated medical indifference, muses dreamily, "Sometimes I think it's a pity I never became a professional photographer."

The opposition early in the film between its comic tone and the grim car crashes testifies to the director's fascination with contradictory elements. At one point, one of Paris's residents rather comically uses a toy car to illustrate the manner in which George and Arthur's car had crashed (the man, who is very serious about his demonstration, is careful to have the little car slowly roll off the edge of a papier-mâché cliff). Like the first half of Carol Reed's *The Third Man* (1949), *Cars'* first half keeps the nasty and depressing aspects of death at a distance via the insouciant behavior of its characters, darkly conceived though they might be. The old woman lovingly polishing a hubcap; the operation on a crash victim that involves surgical-gowned hospital attendants removing the man's shoes and watch; the men in the local pub listening to a car radio spewing out music—all of these elements contribute to *Cars'* whimsicality. In a similar black-humor vein, when Arthur inquires at the hospital about the condition that his brother was in after the crash, the orderly, Darryl, blithely replies, "You ever seen a bloke with a foot up his nose?" And when Arthur tells the mayor the story of the accident that traumatized him, the mayor rather calmly comments, "Yes, these old pedestrians are a real problem, aren't they?" The statement is disorienting both for Arthur and the audience. Arthur is looking for validation of his guilt. The mayor ignores Arthur's obvious unease and shifts responsibility for the accident onto the victim. Neither Arthur nor the audience expect this reaction, which runs counter to the empathetic response one would normally expect. But perhaps that's the point here: Paris is a town full of the abnormal and unexpected. It's a place that takes advantage of motorists' trust: in this case, in the form of the warning lights that are supposed to lead you away from danger, not into it. The Parisians' vampiric delight in death is disorienting, especially since most of them look so "normal."

Equally troubling is our inability to divine just what the mayor's motives are. Does he want Arthur to remain in Paris so that he won't inform the outside world what's going on there, or does he truly want him to become a member of the community because he likes him? There's no way to tell. What is clear, though, is that the scenes of domestic life at the mayor's home, virtually all of which take place in the living room, are shot in such a way that the atmosphere of the room, with its low ceiling and the sound of the radio dimly playing in the background, seems stuffy and cramped. Yet it's into this kind of milieu—one rife with repression, unspoken secrets, and meaningful glances (the significance of which is unexplained)—that the mayor wants to incorporate Arthur.

As it will in Weir's subsequent feature, *Picnic at Hanging Rock*, the landscape assumes significance in the film, although the treatment of the landscape in *Cars* is somewhat different from that of *Picnic*. Where in the later film the outback represents nature as both threat and supportive system, in *Cars* the landscape is decidedly dangerous. Despite the idyllic view of Paris that Arthur and his brother perceive on their way to the town, Paris is ultimately revealed as a homicidal community with none of the redeeming qualities of *Picnic at Hanging Rock's* outback. As Brian McFarlane notes,

A deceptively sleepy town nestling in the hills, [Paris] seems, but increasingly, one realizes, it is an inescapable death-trap for anyone trying to get in or out. . . . Weir's vision of the country town is a long way from [Australian] poet Kenneth Slessor's affectionate evocation of it: "Verandas baked with musky sleep / Mulberry faces dozing deep / And dogs that lick the sunlight up / Like paste of god." Weir is interested in the possible horror behind the verandas; for him, the mulberry faces are only pretending sleep, and the dogs are more likely to be licking up blood.[5]

Although in terms of scope *Cars* is clearly a small film, Weir attempts to widen its thematic scope by satirizing the manner in which contemporary civilization has transformed the automobile into a near-divine device with animalistic power, a quality present in the growling noises and suggestively potent, painted-on teeth that characterize the cars of the town's youth.[6] In essence, the town's youth are rapaciously eating the old (at the film's end their cars begin to knock off pieces of town buildings) in a mirror image of the manner in which the town "devours" travelers who come too close to its borders.

Paris's destruction mirrors the debilitating wasting away that comes from the town's insularity. However, the town's self-enclosure is threatened by two "outside" characters, Arthur and the itinerant minister Ted Mulray, the latter of whom—despite the thinness of his characterization—represents ethical considerations that before his appearance have been missing from the film. When Arthur approaches Mulray, apparently wanting to talk about his post-trauma guilt, the mayor senses a potential threat to the town's homicidal industry. After pursuing Arthur into the countryside in his car, the mayor takes Arthur aside, proposing that Arthur become his surrogate son as a way of keeping him within a family structure, the oppressive qualities of which act as a microcosm of the town's claustrophobic aspect. "There are things that close family members don't do," says the mayor. "They don't talk to outsiders like Ted Mulray. They keep themselves to themselves"—in essence, they work at continuing the repression of normal reactions of guilt and shame in favor of the conspicuous consumption of material goods (hence the mayor's wife's fur coat, a souvenir of a car crash, which she euphemistically refers to as an object obtained "second-hand"). The notion of culture clash resulting from the intrusion of an outsider into a self-sustaining, hermetic environment is a quality characteristic of Weir films such as *Picnic at Hanging Rock, The Last Wave,* and *The Year of Living Dangerously.* Additionally, the presence of hidden knowledge in *Cars* anticipates the elements of the unknown in many of Weir's films. Unlike most of Weir's protagonists, though, *Cars'* Arthur is invited into a fraternity of knowledge but ultimately refuses to remain within it, partly because Paris's secret is too horrible and accurate a reflection of his culture's deadly obsession with automobiles, partly because membership in this fraternity mandates remaining within the town's claustrophobic confines.

Limitation is present not only in the film's theme and scope but also in its approach to characterization. The only two notable characters in the film are Arthur and the mayor, the rest of the townspeople being at best shadows. Along with the film's thematic emphasis on insularity, what the paucity of characterization and emphasis on only two characters suggests is that if Arthur remains in town, he will eventually start to become a cipher like the mayor, who is nothing more than a bland, smug, distilled version of a stereotypical British provincial. When one of the hospital's discharged "veggies," Charlie, shoots and kills Mulray (he does so because, like Paris's other young people, he doesn't feel that he's receiving his fair share of spoils from the accidents), the film can no longer ignore the consequences of the town's behavior. This incident, along with the torching of one of the cars of the town's youth (the night before, a group of young drivers damaged the mayor's front yard, in the process rather comically slicing in half a ceramic figure referred to as "the mayor's aboriginal"), triggers the film's final actions. The youth finally rebel. Discussing the young people's revolt on the night of the Paris Founders Ball, the mayor is told that "the cars [are] upset over the burning." The identity between humans and their machines has become complete.

It's also on the night of the ball, primarily as a result of the breakdown of social controls, that the submerged part of Arthur's character re-emerges. As in other Weir films, in *Cars* "the return of the repressed"[7] is characterized by having the original personality respond to imminent change first with fear, then with passionate desire as the characteristics of the alternative self are gradually embraced (a movement repeated in the actions of the middle-class character of Jill in *The Plumber*). By the time that Arthur, under the mayor's prompting, repeatedly smashes a car into Darryl's vehicle, his cathartic merger with his former aggressive self is complete and he is cured of his phobia. After murdering Darryl, Arthur stands next to the bloody corpse and says, "I can drive." Arthur is reborn, although this rebirth only returns him to another realm filled with repression, one dominated by the chrome-plated materialism of a world ruled by automobiles, which function as symbols of displaced sexual aggression.

In many respects, *Cars* seems to anticipate elements from *Fearless*. Each film centers on a traumatized crash survivor, although unlike *Fearless*'s Max Klein, Arthur (whose spiritual crisis seems to be of slight concern to the film) is a guilt-ridden individual before his film's action begins. Moreover, unlike Max after the plane crash, Arthur does not re-enter a presumably sane society but finds himself in the midst of a world that is a perverted version of his own psychology, in which greed has replaced guilt as a response to destruction. Yet in each film, the mechanism that delivers the protagonist from his post-crash psychology is the same: an essential repeat of the disaster that caused his trauma. Max replays his initial helplessness in the plane; at *Cars'* end, the circumstances surrounding Arthur's brother's death (as well as the killing of the old man whom Arthur hit) are reinvoked when Arthur kills Darryl. Arthur has thus taken on the personality traits of the town's youth who, via destruction, escape from repression.

The split between civilization and the outback is not only present in the contrast between the relatively civilized highway and the anarchic town of Paris but, more pronouncedly, in the distinction between the behavior of Paris's two generations, the adults and the children. The youths' rebellion brings the law of the jungle into the streets of Paris where, in the mayor's unintentionally comic words, this murderous town, which prospers by victimizing passersby, is striving to make it "a safe place for people to park." In this respect, at the film's beginning Arthur, as a result of the trauma he's been through, seems to mediate between the two groups. Disoriented and depressed, Arthur is incapable of being a member of the adult or youth community. Throughout the film, Arthur moves uneasily between these realms, accepted by and entering into neither, trying to accommodate the mayor by not protesting against the awkward request for adoption into a family that we're never convinced he likes, but failing as well to establish any rapport with the youths whom he encounters in the streets, who treat him with contempt. And though he tries to repudiate the town by leaving, Arthur even fails in this endeavor when, nearing the town limits, he comes up against a gang of cars that growlingly revs its engines when he approaches. Arthur's withdrawal from driving suggests that he is quite similar to the Caucasian characters we meet in Weir films such as *Picnic at Hanging Rock* and *The Last Wave* who, like Arthur, are brought into contact with an outback civilization that either unlocks or challenges their repressed attitudes and contradicts their view of reality. It's probably safe to say that it isn't just the guilt over the death he caused that's haunting Arthur so much as the fact that the accident seems to represent an example of (perhaps unintentional) belligerence of a peculiarly perverse sexual kind, which makes Arthur feel tremendously uncomfortable. Indeed, throughout the film Arthur seems extremely sexually restrained. In the one scene in which there is any hint of sexual potential, during which he is alone with the mayor's ambivalently solicitous wife, Arthur fails to evidence any degree of sexual personality. Indeed, the entire atmosphere of the mayor's home is characterized by a complete lack of emotion and empathy—thus the mayor's barren marriage and deeply traumatized adopted daughters, who are the children of car crash victims. There's a wonderful scene in which Arthur, like a prepubescent adolescent, plays on the floor with the mayor's daughters while the mayor sucks on his stubby pipe and reads his newspaper; given the arrested development of his emotions, Arthur seems to be the perfect person to fit right into the mayor's family unit.

During a little talk that they have, the mayor suggests that Arthur give up trying to cure himself of his phobia (thereby indicating that the town, like a community of the undead, thrives on pathology) and enter into the unhealthy spirit of keeping unpalatable personal secrets hidden, among which are the pleasure in murderous aggression made possible through driving and the (unacknowledged) desire on the part of the townspeople for bloody revenge against a society that compels people to conform to the need for automobiles, items which the Parisians both covet and despise. This aspect brings up one of *Cars'* most interesting elements: a critique of Western culture's obsession with automobiles. This obsession is so intense as to constitute a fetishism that can be viewed as sexual longing pathologically metamorphosed into a desire for material things. For the residents of Paris, cars are icons of industrialism and consumption; their significance as both a means of transportation and a source of used parts (which the townspeople trade for food and other goods) is secondary. Indeed, the notion of transportation receives no prominence in the film; only Arthur (and, briefly, the itinerant minister) are significantly linked with cars as transportation via the way that they enter and leave the town. One might question why there is such a great stress in *Cars* on automobiles when they almost never go anywhere (even the town's youths seem to only drive around in circles), yet the answer seems obvious: in *Cars* automobiles represent stasis, not movement, especially stasis as an analogue for ethical and spiritual inertia (thus the significance of Arthur's being designated parking superintendent: in his job he is only responsible for cars that don't move, an appropriate position for a man afraid of driving). The town is clearly trapped within a moral realm that seems frozen beyond change. The only time that the residents of Paris become demonstrative is when they act out their hostility against cars by destroying them, not just ripping them apart when they're brought into town but also igniting them (during the riot at the film's end, the adults set fire to a local teenager's car as well). In fact, unbeknownst to themselves, the townspeople not only seem to hate cars but progressive civilization as well; Paris's citizens appear to be intentional anachronisms judging by their archaic manner of dress and housing and their repeated emphasis on small-town values. As a symbol of industrialization and mechanization, then, cars come to signify the present, which the Parisians loathe and fear. And as the cross-cutting between shots of surgical procedures and townspeople disassembling cars suggests, the Parisians also view the human body as anathema, something to be torn apart and reduced to its essentials: thus the profusion of brain-dead "veggies" in the hospital, who are the result of pointless experiments that nonetheless succeed in keeping people "simple" in the asexual, anti-industrial way that the townspeople prefer.

Even for the audience, cars assume a significance quite out of proportion to their real importance. Contemporary Western culture is filled with advertisements that attempt to transform cars into romantic devices that promise to unlock a world of sexual adventure and delirious acceleration. The film's opening sequence, which features a young couple going for a supposedly idyllic drive in the country, emphasizes advertising's emphasis on glamour, sex, consumption (here evidenced by cigarettes and Coca-Cola) and romance, qualities associated with what is, after all, little more than a simple excursion in a moving piece of metal. The way that this sequence is represented—with low-quality romantic music, adoring couple, and clichéd loving glances— makes it serve as an embodiment of commercialism that testifies to an enervation of basic impulses which throughout Weir's work functions as a key attribute of white, middle-class civilization. Despite its rough edges, then, Cars contains in microcosm many of the themes with which Weir will deal in his subsequent work.

Although Weir regards Cars as "a black film that was too vicious,"[8] the film is, rather, quite appropriately conceived. What Weir has done in Cars is to take traditional Australian themes and parody them through exaggeration and perversion. Thus, mateship appears in the form of the film's destructive gangs of youths; ockerism is represented in the persons of unusual characters such as the mayor, the doctor, and the hospital orderly (who is also a member of a youth gang); and simplicity of motive and action, qualities that in Weir's films are usually associated with Aboriginal experiences, appear in the persons of the hospital "veggies." As with all successful satires, Cars holds up a mirror to its subject, revealing the imperfections in society that are normally hidden by custom and accommodation.

The film's dispassionate tone is a corollary for the absence of affect in the town's residents, who have adapted to technology by becoming emotionally catatonic. Indeed, Cars' ambience (which is partially a result of its limited budget) seems to be the result of Weir's desire to create a tawdry atmosphere to reflect the moral poverty of the town's residents. The sense of ethical and spiritual dislocation that we perceive in Cars is complemented by the film's repeated awkward framing and rough editing; the latter quality frequently takes the form of a shot's being held too long, abrupt cuts away from a scene, and scenes being juxtaposed with little regard for continuity.

The primitive aspect of Paris becomes an analogue for a poorly realized desire for a return to Eden, a desire that is opposed to the rowdy aspects of the town's teenagers, who through threats are attempting to push Paris into the latter half of the twentieth century (indeed, these two strains can be seen in the contrast between the progressive nature of the youths' cars and the old-time outfits that the other residents of Paris wear to the Founders Ball). Although most of the town's youth, hidden inside their cars, are anonymous, their cars have been modified so that they appear to have human faces, a rebellious attempt to assert individuality in opposition to the homogeneous nature of the town's older residents. And though the mayor refers to the teenagers as being lazy and in need of work, it's clear that despite their destructiveness they represent the only vital element in the film.

Most of Weir's films deal with the intrusion of an stranger into a community that is held together by ritualized behaviors and attitudes. Often, this individual appears as an anomaly to the community, in that he or she not only represents either a perversion or regression of values but also acts as a reminder to the community of how different from them he or she is or how far from their primal values they have moved. In *Cars* Arthur is an outsider who is simultaneously atavistic (he cannot abide cars and is out of synchronization with the "progress" that they represent) and more ethically advanced than the residents of the town in which he finds himself, for whom, apparently, no awareness of the strange relation between them and cars exists. Arthur recognizes cars as machines that can cause destruction; but the residents of Paris have, unwittingly, sublimated their fear of the car and transmuted this fear into neurotic covetousness. Paris is a town in the middle of a religious, and homicidal, chrome age.[9] As the automobile's victim, the only one of the crash survivors who has any memory of how he got to Paris, Arthur functions as the audience's surrogate, not only as a representative of the automobile-dominated era in which we all live but also as an individual inquiring into how the town became the way it is. The intensity of his simultaneous repulsion from and attraction to cars embodies our own conflicted attitude toward them.

Unlike many of the other integral communities in Weir films (e.g., the "character" of the outback in *Picnic at Hanging Rock*, the alternative society of the Aboriginals in *The Last Wave* and the Amish in *Witness*, the student members of the Dead Poets Society, all of whom are guardians of an organized community's secrets), Paris's enclosed status doesn't protect natural, enviable values but rather repellent ones. The community in Paris is more akin to the nightmare world of *Witness*'s "cult" (to use Deputy Commissioner Schaeffer's words) of rogue cops who are devoted to destruction as a means of self-aggrandizement.

The mayor is given a somewhat uncharacteristic speech in which the effect on society of automobiles is captured.

> Let's be blunt, Arthur, you've got two dead men on your conscience. You've also got this fear of driving. You know, here in the Paris hospital, in the Bellevue ward, we have people who don't even know their own names. No, it's true. It happens in hospitals all over the country, all over the world—accidents, brain damage, and sometimes they haven't even got a mark on their bodies. People who can't handle the shock, people like you. Not very pleasant, is it? But that's the world we live in, the world of the motor car.

Yet at the film's end, this placid little world that feeds off violence starts to break down as the youth wreak vengeance against the town and begin to destroy it. By the conclusion of *The Cars That Ate Paris* there's no longer any "safe place to park" because there's no town left.

2

DEADLY DÉJEUNER

The intentions of *Picnic at Hanging Rock,* Weir's faithful adaptation of Joan Lindsay's popular novel, are clear from the film's opening title, which informs us that the story to be told concerns the disappearance of a group of schoolgirls at Hanging Rock.

> On Saturday 14th February 1900 a party of schoolgirls from Appleyard College picnicked at Hanging Rock near Mt. Macedon in the state of Victoria.
> During the afternoon several members of the party disappeared without trace . . .

The key point implied in this title is that no one has ever been able to determine what happened to these young women. The film's predominant, announced characteristic, then, is one of intentional mystery, not in the service of vagary but as an encouragement toward an awareness of what Weir conceives of as the natural tension between the material and spiritual realms. Simultaneously, *Picnic* informs us that the boundary between these realms is at times so fragile as to make it difficult to affirm the one while denying the other for very long—that, in fact, the realm of the mysterious repeatedly infringes upon that of the real, defying attempts to explain it rationally. Weir insisted in an interview that he was not primarily concerned with the film's supposedly sexual subtext: "I was never really interested in that side [sexuality] of the film. I didn't see it as part of its theme."[1] Nonetheless, it's hard to deny that the film's depiction of a clash between the empirical and spiritual realms parallels the conflicts between its portrayals of repressed and expressed sexual behavior as well as the opposition between the personality of characters such as the school's headmistress, Mrs. Appleyard, and the mathematics instructor, Miss

McCraw, who tend to deny sexual forces, and those of some of the schoolgirls, who seem to be yearning to act on their desires.

Yet it's in the very nature of the repression that we also get a hint of the larger theme with which the film deals. Since repression involves suppression of psychological and mythological qualities in favor of culture-dictated values, it represents a tearing asunder of a natural continuity between perception and impulse on the one hand and understanding and action on the other—essentially, the rending of a whole consciousness into artificially segmented parts. In this respect, Weir's comment that he was only interested in the film's sexual subtext as part of a greater scheme of awareness ("For me the grand theme was Nature, and even the girls' sexuality was as much a part of that as the lizard crawling across the top of the rock. They were part of the same whole; part of the same question")[2] does not contradict his previous assertion so much as place it in context. The statement implies that what Weir is working toward in all of his films is a restoration of a sense of awareness that accepts all things as part of existence. What appear to be violent and disturbing events in the director's films (e.g., the disappearance of the girls in *Picnic*) actually represent an attempt on the part of natural forces to reestablish a sense of order. Read in this way, the film's denouement, with Mrs. Appleyard dead and the school (presumably) disbanded, becomes a return to normalcy.

Most writers on the film have commented on the sense of irresolution that characterizes it.[3] Certainly, this aspect, a quality with which I will deal later, is a significant part of *Picnic*'s aesthetic texture, but it is obviously not the film's main attribute. If it were, why would Weir announce the irresolved nature of the disappearances so blatantly at the film's beginning, which would cause the ensuing film to act as little more than a foregone example of what has already been asserted? Instead, we must step a bit away from the mysterious disappearances, if only for a while, in order to discover the film's central concerns.

Although the opening title tells us that it is the first Saint Valentine's Day of the twentieth century, Weir immediately thrusts us into the actions and trappings of a school and milieu that look as though they haven't acknowledged the passage of time at all. The sense of stolidity at Appleyard College, which is about to be challenged by the events at the rock, is made apparent in the camerawork of the film's opening shots. Like the incongruous, British-oriented school set down in the Australian bush (Joan Lindsay refers to the college as "an architectural anachronism"),[4] the camera at first is stationary, unaffected, a quality that is then challenged by a slow dissolving of images into one another as though the change in images were part of some natural process. Indeed, throughout the production, Weir is heavily reliant on the visuals to supply not only significance but diversion: having virtually no story to tell, Weir must count on the sense of atmosphere to communicate the majority of the film's meanings, which, as is customary with the director, deal with doubles, repression, and social and sexual displacement.

Many of the film's attributes derive from the genre in which it is working. Commenting on the period film in Australia, critic Graeme Turner notes that these films qualify as

> a particular sub-genre: films set in the past, foregrounding their Australianness through the re-creation of history and representations of the landscape; lyrically and beautifully shot; and employing aesthetic mannerisms such as a fondness for long, atmospheric shots, an avoidance of action or sustained conflict, and the use of slow motion to infer significance.[5]

Yet it's obvious that the other films that Scott Murray, who uses Turner's quote, cites as sharing these characteristics are quite different from Weir's film in intention and execution.[6] Neither Ken Hannam's *Sunday Too Far Away,* with its gritty realism, nor Fred Schepisi's *The Devil's Playground* (1976) and Gillian Armstrong's *My Brilliant Career* (1979), partake of the overt lyricism and explicit fascination with the unknown that Weir's film does. It would perhaps be better, then, to view *Picnic at Hanging Rock* less as a period film than as an investigation into metaphysics that uses a period setting as the basis for its dramatics.

I will begin by concentrating on the film's sexual aspect. In addition to the romantic overtones of the date on which the film's opening events take place is the fact that the holiday stems from the actions of two third-century priests whose martyrdom led to conversions to Christianity. The disappearance of some of *Picnic's* schoolgirls occasions a comparably violent shift in perspective.[7] Additionally, it is relevant that the entire school, with the exception of a gardener, a handyman, a maid, a driver, and an all-female staff of teachers, is made up of postpubescent young schoolgirls. Thus, sexual potential is everywhere. The fact that the school is a preparatory institution implies that its students are poised on the brink of self-realization, thereby opening up the story to the possibility of change. Like the precipices that they encounter at the rock, the girls seem ready for a shift or fall, and the placement of the action on a day commemorating the death of a martyr to a religion that emphasizes love makes the voyagers candidates to be similar martyrs to passion. Despite the affair between the school's handyman and its maid, the atmosphere at the college is similarly poised for a change, especially given the powerful sublimation of desire inherent in the girls' playing at love by sending valentines to each other, evidence of a constraint that corsets the girls' emotions as stringently as their bodies are reined in physically, while their behavior is similarly drawn in, in accordance with Old World behests that they at all times act with decorum.

The girls are thus compelled to experience a violent split between their emotions and activities; they do little but quote love poems and fantasize about idealized romantic encounters. The only depicted passion at this point is that between Sara and Miranda (as ineffectual a love as the one we see later: Irma's fixation on Michael).[8] Sara's idealization of Miranda goes beyond a schoolgirl crush to suggest in its intensity a characteristically Victorian longing for a spiritual union beside which even sex would be inadequate. These girls—one dark-haired, one blonde; one orphaned and virtually destitute, the other from a nuclear, well-to-do family—make up only the first of many counterpart pairs in the film. Yet what may be Sara and Miranda's most significant quality is the class to which each girl belongs. Sara is lower class; Miranda is obviously upper middle class. The split between them hints at the social critique that becomes one of the film's central concerns, especially given the way that only the lower-class characters are granted forthright sexual expression. Yet since we know that it's only by virtue of its period setting that such archaic distinctions are made possible, *Picnic* by its very nature contains within it the seeds of its own destruction in a manner comparable to the way that the conscious forces in the film, those allied with mathematical precision, order, and rationality, must inevitably yield to the unconscious, which is associated with freedom of action. In essence, the power of the rock, which is based on forces that cannot be either measured or explained, is fated to predominate in the film: by stopping the quaint watches that try to measure out that which is timeless, by frustrating the guardians' attempts to have the students take a "safe" excursion on the rock when what the girls really want is to break loose and be free, by wreaking havoc upon those members of the party who are either too ethereal (Miranda) or too idealistic (Marion) to be left undisturbed, leaving behind only the most mediocre of characters (Edith most prominently).[9]

The notion of time as a human rather than natural construct is one of the film's major themes. It's not just the influence of the magnetically oriented rock on the timepieces of the driver and Miss McCraw that suggests the vanity of humans attempting to take the pulse of the universe. This aspect is also present in the ticking of the clock in Mrs. Appleyard's office, with its heavy intimations of fatality and doom, a sound that has its corollary in the sounds of the search party slapping sticks together when searching for the girls, which is itself a duplication of the sounds made earlier by Edith, who rapped a stick against the sides of the rock as the girls wandered off onto it, a similarity that suggests a collapsing of different time schemes, a quality that *Picnic* repeatedly employs.

Opposition, which is the governing principle in the film's first half, arises from the clash between many paired concepts: the school's outdated, Old World conservative values versus the wildness of its surroundings; male versus female; the antagonism between civilization and nature (emblematized in the image of the picnic cake with ants crawling across it); the clash between idealized as opposed to actual sexual relations; the conflict between the attempt to measure universal forces (Miss McCraw's desire to survey the rock mathematically) as opposed to the ungovernable power of the rock itself, which is beyond all of these tendencies. What predominates, though, is the ineffable, unclassifiable power of natural forces.

One of the reasons why Weir concentrates so much on natural surroundings in *Picnic* is not only to contrast them with the staidness and artificiality of behavior encouraged at the college, but also to establish a uniquely Australian "feel" to the area in which the college is located. Brian McFarlane quotes "Australian poet and literary critic" Chris Wallace-Crabbe: "One way to escape the European ghosts that lean over one's shoulder and jog one's pen is by paying careful attention to the facts of immediate environment: the artist can forget mistletoe and oak in his observation of paperbark and pepperina."[10]

In a sense, then, one of the many subjects that Weir explores in the film is that of the Australian national identity, which, judging from the indeterminacy of the film's events, is characterized by confusion resulting from the conflict between the British origin of many Australians and the influences occasioned by the country's remote location and its native Aboriginal culture. Equally important is the film's view of nature, which is conceived of as both inviting and threatening. As McFarlane notes in a statement that echoes the tenor of Mrs. Appleyard's warning to the departing girls, "a picnic in the Australian bush is an idyll that should be undertaken cautiously: the landscape may look passive from a distance but up close it may be fraught with danger for the uninitiated."[11]

The association of the Aboriginal realm with the forces of nature is not only a characteristic of later Weir films such as *The Last Wave;* it is present in *Picnic* as well, since Hanging Rock is situated near Mount Macedon, which is regarded as sacred by Australia's Aborigines. What *Picnic* cites, then, without actually including them, are the dark "others" who emerge in subsequent Weir films; their presence in *Picnic,* which is exaggeratedly Caucasian in conception, is made manifest both by their virtual invisibility in the film (there is only one Aborigine in *Picnic,* who is seen in a very brief shot) and their association with the rock. As a consequence, the journey into the outback, which is also tradi-tionally considered an Aboriginal domain, becomes a confrontation with the symbolic dark realm that the materialistic and empirical whites in Weir's films so fervently attempt to deny through their eccentric rituals, garden parties, re-pressive education, and suppressed longings. Thus, *Picnic*'s coachman, Bertie, who at times seems a bit too obviously a representative of lower-class primal forces (he appears to be an innocent version of *The Plumber*'s Max), inadvert-ently highlights the sexual repression of his counterpart, the upper-class Michael, by pointing out that whereas both of them are physically attracted to the schoolgirls on whom they spy, he gives voice to his desire.

Those who come in contact with the rock either disappear or return mute about their experience: silent like Irma,[12] reticent like Edith, dazed like Michael. It's almost as though, like the film's watches and clocks,[13] the youths have had the delicate balance of their internal mechanisms disturbed. The trip to the rock is repeatedly identified with some sort of venture into an untamed, virtually Edenic region, an aspect present in the shot in which a lizard, in the midst of a lovely oxymoronic image that combines wildness and refinement, moves past the exposed arm of one of the recumbent girls. Yet the area around the rock is conceived of by repressed humans in negative, postlapsarian terms: thus Mrs. Appleyard's warning that the region is redolent with "venomous snakes and poisonous ants." However, the key statement about the trip is, again, Mrs. Appleyard's when she says that she expects the girls to avoid "any tomboy foolishness in the manner of explorations, even on the lower slopes," a comment that not only links daring and aggressiveness with a male-associated impulse (from which the school presumably protects the girls) but also implies through its use of the phrase "explorations on the lower slopes" a tentative in-quiry involving the genitals, a notion that lends to the trip a hint of a sexual adventure into the unknown—in essence, a loss of virginal innocence.[14]

In fact, the film dramatizes a very significant kind of anxiety concerning the girls' trip. Given the Aboriginal association with the rock, Mrs. Appleyard's trepidation about the excursion can be read as a fear of miscegenation: the dis-appeared girls are spirited away into the rock's dark crevices. As a result of the trip, the dark-haired Irma, the only girl to be recovered, who returns to the school in a dress whose red color is sexually suggestive, finds it impossible to effect a union with a white, fair-haired male. She may, indeed, be physically "in-tact," but in a psychological and, perhaps, moral sense, she is tainted. Bias that is both racial and class-based applies to Irma's counterpart, Sara, who is also dark-haired, and who is singled out for punishment because she rejects traditional white culture in her refusal to memorize the poem by Felicia Heymans, preferring instead her own, passionate verse. Cursed by the combination of her dark hair and poverty, she cannot hope to be integrated into the school's upper-class white society. Like Neil in *Dead Poets Society*, also characterized as an outsider, she decides that in response to the abuses that she is compelled to suffer, suicide is her only option.

The presumptuousness of the attitude that humans are meant to rule over and be served by nature rather than live in harmony with it is strongly related to the hubris of characters like Mrs. Appleyard and Miss McCraw, and it is clear that the inability to completely dominate some of the girls, especially the shy and virtually wordless Sara, frustrates some of the college's staff to such a degree that they become sadistically abusive with regard to her. Their major attempts to subdue the girl, either through trying to have her memorize poetry, denying her food, or binding her to correct what they feel is her reprehensible stoop, smack of a desire to subdue willful forces that becomes a corollary for these women's attitude toward nature, thus identifying the girl with universal forces.

Miranda's statement that "everything begins and ends at exactly the right time and place" might also seem to be part of this continuity of presumptuousness were it not that its underlying intention is to express that there appears to be an order to the universe that somehow seems appropriate, a statement that links up with Marion's observation that the upper-class Fitzhuberts, also picnicking in the park region (though their formal dress and stiff demeanor make them seem woefully out of place in the natural surroundings), "surely must be fulfilling some function unknown to themselves." However, through its insistent depiction of a breakdown of temporality and causality, and its repudiation of the necessity of functionality (all of which are humanly derived concepts), *Picnic* makes it plain that, occasionally, events don't have any readily apparent meaning; they just happen. Thus, despite the statement by the wife of the local policeman Sergeant Bumpher that "people just don't disappear . . . not without good reason," the fact is that sometimes they do.

Indeed, in *Picnic*, not only time and causality but propriety holds no sway. Three of the wandering girls inadvertently prepare for their assignation with the rock by removing some of their unnatural constraints: in an implicit embracing of sexual freedom, shoes and stockings are left behind. Reputedly, Miss McCraw ascends the rock without her skirt; similarly, after Irma is found, she is not wearing her corset. The significance of the loss of these pieces of clothing, the latter especially, is clearly sexual: along with a heavily sugared diet (e.g., the

Valentine's Day cake), tight attire was one of the dominant causes in the early part of the century for the delay of sexual maturity among young women, diet and dress inhibiting the onset of menarche.

Less successful in the film is the friendship that arises between Bertie and Michael, which is meant to duplicate that between Sara (who is Bertie's sister) and Miranda, but whose convincing aspect is subverted by the awkwardness of its conception. The split between the sexual attitudes of the classes had already been shown in the contrast between the girls' repression and the sexual expressiveness of the school's maid and handyman; it wasn't necessary to repeat it in the distinction between Bertie's ribald comments and Michael's embarrassed glances at the girls. More effective are the discontinuities that the two young men's stories introduce: Bertie incognizant of his sister's presence at Appleyard College, Michael unable to recall precisely how many of the girls he had seen. Reliable information, then, seems impossible to obtain in mysterious circumstances or places. To frustrate our attempts at rational explanations, Weir fills the film with intentionally inexplicable events: How did Michael get the torn fabric of one of the girl's dresses in his hand? Why do Michael and Bertie have so much difficulty ascending the rock? Like the virginity of the returned girls, the mystery of the film remains "intact." At *Picnic*'s end, when Weir disturbs conventional chronology by repeating the shots of Mademoiselle de Portiers and Miranda waving to each other but reversing their original order, he also reinvokes one of the film's most interesting shots. When they had first reached the vicinity of Hanging Rock, Miranda had climbed down out of the carriage and unlatched the park gate. As she did so, a group of parrots started screeching and flew up into the air. Weir dissolves between shots of the flying birds, which first seem to fly in one direction, then another, and shots of Miranda. When he brings back a shot of Miranda from this sequence at the film's end, he freeze-frames on her turning away after waving goodbye. With the back of her head to the camera and her hair flying away from her head, she herself seems like a winged creature (very close to the "angel" that Mademoiselle de Portiers had called her) about to take flight out of the mundane universe and into a mysterious, dream-like realm in which she becomes one with the unrepressed forces that underlie all of *Picnic*'s action.[15]

The film's only major drawback lies in the fact that it encourages us to draw a connection between the girls' disappearance and the abusive actions of Mrs. Appleyard, suggesting that the collapse of the school and Mrs. Appleyard's subsequent death are the karmic result of the headmistress's stern behavior toward some of the girls, Sara in particular. Such a conception, while it may satisfy the audience's desire to see some form of justice meted out, introduces an element of suggested causality, thereby violating Weir's apparent intention to demonstrate that the film's events are beyond explanation. Indeed, in one version of the story that was under consideration for scripting, Mrs. Appleyard's journey to the rock and eventual suicide were to be depicted, a literalism from which Weir wisely withdrew. Unfortunately, the film retains the events, albeit in narration.[16]

One of *Picnic*'s overriding qualities is the emphasis on the camera's privileged view, by virtue of which it functions as a curious but, ultimately, morally disinterested outsider, regarding incidents and characters but not intruding upon them. Early in the film the camera, in the persona of a detached detective, establishes the tone of the film's latter half, which is that of an investigation, one not involved with inquiring after objects (as in *The Last Wave*) or examining photographic renderings (as in *The Year of Living Dangerously*) but rather merely observing a series of conditions for which Weir refuses to provide any explanations. (Indeed, Weir and Joan Lindsay decided to not even discuss with critics whether or not the events on which the book and film are based actually occurred.)[17] Repeatedly in *Picnic*, we either see characters (who are often hidden) staring at others (as when Michael and Bertie surreptitiously watch the girls) or experiencing unique visions (e.g., Miranda's sight of Sara, a dark silhouette against a bright sky, standing on the school balcony). Perhaps more intriguingly, we tend to catch characters at visually unusual moments. In these shots, which draw attention to themselves by virtue of a camera placement that, with regard to sight lines, is notably artificial, the camera eye is placed on axis for the audience (in order to render an image for us) but off axis if we consider the image that the character being filmed would be seeing. Thus, at one point, Miranda, who is sitting in front of her large mirror, is also positioned in front of a small oval desk mirror. In order to have Miranda's face appear in the small mirror for us, though, Weir has to set up the shot so that the sight line for Miranda is off axis for her character. Consequently, what Miranda would actually see if she glanced into the small mirror would not be herself but the camera—the mechanical, dispassionate other—looking at her.[18] The audience is thus placed in an unusual, ambivalent state of mind, at once inside the film's fiction (when we ignore the situation with the sight lines) and outside it (when we are aware of the ploy Weir is compelled to use to achieve his shot). As a result, we experience a disturbing simultaneity of contradictory forms of awareness, just as many of the film's characters do when they cannot reconcile the girls' disappearances with what they know of "reality."

Similarly, later, on the rock, when the four ascending girls pass by a fissure, the camera (looking out at them from within the rock, and thereby embodying the point of view of the rock's inner presence) is once again directly implicated, this time as voyeur, perhaps no more so than when, after the first three girls have passed by the camera and before Miranda walks by, the speed of the images perceptibly slows,[19] thus abruptly pulling us out of the dream-world fiction of the film and into an awareness of the mechanical realm that makes such an effect possible.[20] This doubling of awareness presages the doubling of comprehension at the rock, where the apparently indifferent stone actually houses an ethereal force that makes itself manifest in dream-like images, the tone of which will reappear in films such as *The Last Wave* and *The Year of Living Dangerously*.

Picnic's overt acknowledgment of the filmmaking process prepares us for the other doublings that occur later in the film that, like the previous ones achieved through mechanical means, make reference to two worlds operating simultaneously. At one point, Michael, cued by looking at a swan, envisions Miranda (whom he sees in an internal revery).[21] Bertie begins after many years to once again think about his sister after being prompted by dream images (which, unknown to Bertie, foretell her suicide) that he says are seen through a kind of haze. (This quality not only alludes to the yellow gauze filter through which the entire film was shot[22] but also refers us back to Michael's ruminating on the mystery of the girls' disappearance while staring at Irma through the netting that surrounds her bed, both gauzy elements acting as objective corollaries for the ghostly atmosphere that separates the material from the dream/subconscious/repressed world.) At these junctures, we experience along with the characters the feeling of simultaneously being in the material and dream realms, both of which are operating within the context of the larger dream that is the film. Neither Michael nor Bertie, though, is able to recognize that their dream-like or literal dream images are attempting to speak to them; their ignorance of the reciprocity between the conscious and unconscious realms is as great as Sara and Bertie's incognizance of their proximity (Appleyard College is quite close to the Fitzhubert estate, where Bertie works). The implication being made here is apparent: to increase our awareness of events that are often vital, we must allow commerce between the conscious and unconscious spheres. Failing this, we are fated to experience the sense of loss and separation that characterizes so much of the film.

When Michael begins to think about a swan while Sergeant Bumpher is questioning him, Weir dissolves from a view of Michael's face to the image of the swan, then cuts to a shot of Michael looking at the surface of a lake. This last shot, though, takes place at an entirely different time, during one of his uncle's picnics. These three shots manage to make a number of significant points: Michael has somehow intuited the connection between Miranda and a swan that is made concrete in the porcelain swan Sara has placed on her dresser in front of Miranda's photo (the girl has, in essence, built a shrine to her lost friend), a fact that testifies to the film's repeated insistence on a form of communication among people that transcends physical boundaries. Moreover, by cutting to a view of the lake without first establishing where (or precisely when) the shot is taking place, Weir collapses the conceptual distance between disparate times and places, thus encouraging us to minimize the usual distinctions that we make regarding the location and chronology of events, a quality typical of the manner in which we often experience things in a dream.[23]

The character in the film who seems most allied with the dream realm is Miranda. Although her early, ambiguous statement to Sara that "you must learn to love someone else apart from me . . . I won't be here much longer" seems prescient in light of her later disappearance, the girl's attitude toward life is clarified through her quoting Edgar Allan Poe's poem "A Dream Within a Dream," two lines of which she incorrectly recites at the film's beginning.

Miranda states, "What we see, and what we seem, are but a dream, a dream within a dream"; yet Poe's lines read, "*All* that we see or seem / Is but a dream within a dream" (emphasis in original).[24] Although Miranda adds an additional "dream" to emphasize the rhyme, the major significance of the change that she makes derives from a further modification that subtly alters Poe's meaning. Poe's poem is a response to the torments that occur when one parts from a lover. The poem's speaker consoles himself about the loss of his love by asserting that to lose something as apparently substantial as love should not be painful, since everything, including love, is dream-like and therefore fleeting. The poem, which is in two stanzas, moves from an initial assertion about dreams that provides a modicum of consoling certainty to a final line in which the tone shifts from the categorical to the inquisitive: "Is *all* that we see or seem / But a dream within a dream?"

Unlike the poem's speaker, Miranda feels comfortable with her view that life is doubly abstracted. For her, the things that we see, and the people whom we seem to be, are a dream within a dream. This powerful dream state does not represent to her a condition of anxious unreality but one of super-reality that makes the empirical world seem pale by comparison. Like her previously mentioned assertion about things "begin[ning] and end[ing] at just the right time and place," Miranda's statement from Poe (which is the film's first line of dialogue), coming as it does from the most ethereally beautiful of all the schoolgirls, identifies her as the most appropriate member of the school to be painlessly spirited away by the rock until she is made one with the universal forces toward which she has all along been drawn.

The audience partakes of oneiric feelings as well. Through the camera as inquiring presence, we become dream-like observers of otherworldly events; and later, when the action moves to the ascent onto the rock, the camera itself seems to swoon under the magnetic influence of the rock's towering presence. This effect is most notable not only in the pivot-pan shots of the rock but in the 330-degree pan that Weir uses as the girls are ascending the rock and during which, for the majority of the pan, he shifts attention away from the girls, at once invoking the natural context within which the girls are moving as well as drawing attention, after the pan is complete, to the progress they made while the camera was off somewhere else, taking in the landscape. Like Mademoiselle de Portiers, so strongly affected by her high regard for Miranda that she has a Botticellian vision of the girl, the camera itself has been overcome by the incongruity of these beautiful young women set down in the middle of the outback.

During the picnic, when Miranda gazes through a magnifying glass at a flower, the notion of the investigation of a natural mystery asserts itself. As in so many other Weir films (*The Last Wave, The Year of Living Dangerously*), characters, intentionally or otherwise, sift clues for answers. (Thus the statement of the gardener, who shows the handyman a natural wonder [the apparently intelligent movement of a mimosa], that some mysteries don't have answers, precisely the stance that the film takes.) In a sense, though, Weir does provide some form of response to the obsessive inquiring that the film is constructed to provoke. On the rock, Edith, despite promising not to, starts complaining about being tired and hating the ugliness of the surroundings, to which Marion says, "I wish you'd stop talking for once," by which she seems not only to be replying to Edith's whining but commenting on the inappropriateness of any kind of speech while on the rock, since the area's overpowering sense of just "being" easily dwarfs the power of language to express its existence. As in *The Last Wave,* we're meant to understand that language is incapable of doing anything other than providing a pale simulacrum of only part of the world—that it is, in Platonic terms, a shadow of real things, indeed, a shadow of shadows, since all that it can do is attempt to establish some sort of relation between what we perceive (which is itself partial and shadowy) and how we communicate it.[25] There's no solution to the mystery in *Picnic* precisely because it's inappropriate when dealing with nature to expect it to reflect a human conception of reality. In *Picnic*'s view, the mystery is not the girls' disappearance so much as the strangeness of the attitude that there must be an explanation for every-thing.[26] As Weir notes about the film's lack of a traditional ending,

> My only worry was whether an audience would accept such an outrageous idea. Personally, I always found it the most satisfying and fascinating aspect of the film. . . . I did everything in my power to hypnotise the audience away from the possibility of solutions. . . . There are, after all, things within our own minds about which we know far less than about the disappearances at Hanging Rock. And it's within a lot of the silences that I tell my side of the story.[27]

It's precisely in these special silences, the portions of the film in which dialogue is absent and images and sound prevail, that *Picnic* tells its tale. The film's emphasis on sights and sounds elevates these aspects to a primacy of meaning, so that Marion's request that Edith stop talking becomes the equivalent of John Cage's behest to sit quietly and listen to and watch the world.[28] Rather than frustrating audience desires, *Picnic* remolds them; we should have no more trouble accepting the film's refusal to provide answers than we should in suspending our disbelief and assigning credibility to its characters, both responses being, to a degree, unnatural and illogical.

It has been suggested that in *Picnic* as well as in *Gallipoli* and *Dead Poets Society* there is a repressed homosexuality in operation.[29] The suggestion seems a misreading of the films that stems from a literalizing of the personal affinities among the characters. Only a reductionist response could make possible the view that closeness among characters of the same sex has a homosexual rather than sororal or fraternal element. Instead, what Weir is dealing with in these films are notions of emotional and psychological bonding. Indeed, it's a violation of Weir's entire attitude to allow these kinds of bonding to collapse back into the physical realm that they so obviously oppose. Rather, what *Picnic at Hanging Rock* manages to do via its distant, gauzy gaze is to push aside the veil between the material and spiritual spheres and, having done so, communicate through its director's ambiguous, ethereal images a clear intuition of the incorporeal realm.

NOTES FROM UNDERGROUND

In one sense, *The Last Wave*—which tells the story of a white lawyer, David Butler, who, in defending some Aborigines against a charge of murder, comes to some disturbing revelations about himself—might seem a logical outgrowth of *Picnic at Hanging Rock*'s obsession with mystifying the viewer in order to create an unsettling atmosphere. The difference in the method that Weir uses to create this effect, though, is striking, for where *Picnic* intentionally withholds information, *The Last Wave* inundates the audience with images and dialogue that are meant to produce an otherworldly effect. Whether or not this effect is successfully achieved, it's clear that the director is here branching out in terms of audience appeal and stylistics. Indeed, although the film is set in Australia, the personality crisis that its protagonist undergoes might just as well take place in any Western industrialized nation; and the manner in which *Last Wave* links up with a similarly apocalyptic film such as *2001: A Space Odyssey* (1968) is instructive.

According to Weir, he conceived of the film as the result of a serendipity.

When I was in Europe I wanted to go to Tunisia because, after Pompeii, the next best preserved Roman city is there. So we were driving there, and stopped for a walk, and I was suddenly seized with this strange feeling I was going to find something. I even saw what I was going to see. And there it was, on the ground, a carving of a child's head. I brought it home and I thought about it for ages afterwards. What *was* that experience? *Why* did I see the head in my mind before I saw it in actuality? And then I started to think, what if a very rational person—a lawyer, say—had had the same experience? How would he cope with it? And that was the beginning of *The Last Wave*.[1]

The Last Wave is concerned with concepts typical for Weir at this juncture in his career: culture clash; the exposure, through excessive circumstances, of an insular individual to unfamiliar forces; the return of repressed elements; and the function of shamanism and magic, especially as regards their relevance to someone from white, Western society, the rationalist basis of which tends to deny any alternative views. Additionally, the film takes as one of its central interests the reading of evidence as a significant activity, a quality that was present in *Picnic,* but only marginally so, since the only evidence available to those characters trying to explain the schoolgirls' disappearance was a red cloud, a torn piece of lace, a missing corset, and the fact that two of the picnickers' watches had stopped, none of it useful in solving the mystery of the disappearances.

Like *Picnic, Last Wave* is certainly concerned with a mystery, but only insofar as this becomes the justification for an inquiry into a cultural obsession with signs and symbols and their decoding—or conversely, whether or not the culture in question, through a combination of indifference and presumed sophistication, has lost interest in symbols, depleting their significance to such a degree that this quality reflects the enervation, and heralds the imminent death of, that culture.

As Carl Jung makes plain in *Man and His Symbols,* there is a significant difference between a sign and a symbol.

> [Man's] . . . language is full of symbols, but he also employs signs or images that are not strictly descriptive. Some are mere abbreviations or strings of initials . . . others are familiar trademarks, the names of patent medicines, badges, or insignia. Although these are meaningless in themselves, they have acquired a recognizable meaning through common usage or deliberate intent. Such things are not symbols. They are signs, and they do no more than denote the objects to which they are attached. What we call a symbol is a term, a name, or even a picture that may be familiar in daily life, yet that possesses specific connotations in addition to its conventional and obvious meaning. It implies something vague, unknown, or hidden from us . . . thus a word or an image is symbolic when it implies something more than its obvious and immediate meaning. It has a wider "unconscious" aspect that is never precisely defined or fully explained . . . as the mind explores the symbol, it is led to ideas that lie beyond the grasp of reason.[2]

As this discussion proceeds, I will show that in *The Last Wave,* one of the primary distinctions between the white society that David represents and that of the Aborigines for whom he acts as a lawyer is the distinction between a logocentric, sign-oriented culture, and one that places a greater emphasis on symbols and images than on verbalization. As Jung observes, the significance of symbols derives from a profound area of meaning, that of dreams and the unconscious, whereas, he implies, signs exist exclusively within the conscious realm.[3] This distinction—which parallels the one between Aboriginal and white society, and which appears in virtually all of Weir's films in either concrete or symbolic form—is exemplified when two Aborigines, Chris and Charlie, come to David's house and see his wife Annie's painting. Charlie (through Chris's translation) comments that the painting is "very nice," a polite response that is almost certainly a linguistic veil for the fact that what Charlie had really meant is that Annie's graphic image is a sign, not a symbol, and is therefore essentially meaningless. The fact that the painting is an awkwardly realized depiction of a frog suggests how little understanding of the natural world's significance white culture has, especially in contrast to the powerful and naturally based Aboriginal images present in the film. According to *The Last Wave,* Sydney is constructed over the ruins of Aboriginal sacred places; as a result, white culture has symbolically attempted to disavow the symbolic significance of Aboriginal culture, not only crushing it under the materialistic weight of its cars, people, and buildings but relegating it to a subterranean existence in the city's sewers, the repository for waste products that are involved with bodily functions that are traditionally hidden and denied. (In this sense, the film functions as a strong precursor of a theme made more concrete in *The Plumber.*) In essence, then, the whites in *Last Wave* are attempting to deny their primal attitudes by keeping them trapped within a symbol of the subconscious.[4] However, in the film these forces from the unconscious, long-repressed, rise back up to the surface and wreak destruction.

Predominantly, the film's Aborigines are associated with nature and darkness, rain and disasters. Natural elements and the notion of destruction are present from the film's very beginning. After a shot of two Aboriginal children running down a road on which they are passed by an automobile, a symbol of mechanical culture, we see an Aboriginal man looking up and pointing to the sky. This scene is followed by one at a school where the students, most of them white, don't seem to be taking any heed of the weather, an ignorance that suggests that unlike the Aboriginal man, they have lost the capacity to be prescient about nature, a notion that is emphasized throughout the film. Weir then gives us a shot of another child tolling a bell, a symbolic gesture that not only prefigures the prophetic role that Chris and Charlie will assume but which also inadvertently heralds a shift in the weather. Thunder is heard (although no clouds are seen), a white child finally realizes that something is wrong (it's November, when rains almost never occur in Australia), and there is a sudden downpour. After the children are hurried inside, and are somewhat patronizingly told by their teacher that what they are witnessing is nature at work, the rain turns to icy hail. One child is cut by broken glass from a shattered window, and the children's initially amused response turns to terror, precisely the progression from interest to panic that David undergoes as the film progresses.

One of the ways that Weir maintains a successful ambiguity in the film is by concentrating on action and images that at first seem to have nothing to do with the story. At one point, Weir zooms in on a British Leland car, only vaguely intimating that there is some connection between the leopard on the car's logo and the film's story. The car logo, as well as the bus poster for the Tayonga Zoo, which features two chimpanzees, not only demonstrates how white society appropriates the power and significance of animals and turns them to commercial account but also highlights the society's use of natural images as nothing more than superficial signs instead of meaningful symbols.

Alternatively, Weir's imagery in the film is made up of symbols, among the most effective of which are the early shots of water, which, as a result of various stylistic effects (slow motion, unusual events or sounds accompanying our views of water), have an almost dream-like aura that suggests a collapsing of what Weir regards as the artificial barriers between waking and sleeping awareness, the conscious and unconscious realms. As we will see, these images have a virtually surrealistic force. Thus, the shot of a man under a clear plastic umbrella bending over a water fountain in the midst of a rainstorm, which seems somewhat absurd and contradictory (the man reaching for water in the midst of plenty), succinctly communicates the tension between the spigot (a man-made object meant to restrain or divert water) and a natural force, the rain, that is simultaneously available in its unrestrained form. The image is made more compelling by its affinity with the essential elements of the shot of the spigot outside David's house, which drips during a violent rainstorm; apparently, this man-made bulwark against water's pressure cannot stop the force of the water any more than the flimsy awareness of David's conscious mind can prevent the repeated intrusion of visionary episodes. Again, we're prepared for the eventual conflict between white civilization and natural phenomena that is one of the film's primary concerns.

Weir was canny in casting Richard Chamberlain in the part of the lawyer who, through his contact with Aborigines and disturbing dreams and visions, comes to understand that he's not just the complacent middle-class man he thinks he is but is also a prophet who is destined to foretell the doom of the civilization of which he is such a well-integrated part. Like Keir Dullea in *2001*, who plays a character similarly representative of the society in which he is placed, Chamberlain is a bland, weak, and emotionally repressed actor who seems as successful a visual embodiment of white culture as any director could hope for. (Pauline Kael noted that when he needs to express feeling in the film,

all that Chamberlain does is "quiver . . . his lips to connote sensitivity . . . contract . . . his nostrils for apprehensiveness and pull . . . in his cheek muscles for
ineffable sorrow").[5] In contrast to the Aborigines, whose fervor reflects the
powerful influences at play in the film, Chamberlain seems like a pale outsider
in the midst of forces that he can neither control nor understand.[6]

Although Chamberlain's David seems ineffectual, he is nonetheless the re-
cipient of impressions that no one else seems capable of receiving. Just as, later,
out on the street, Chris will "feel" David watching him without turning around
to visually verify his impression, when David is having dinner with Annie and
their daughters, he senses that there is something wrong in the house, although
no one else in the room seems aware of anything untoward. The camera, which
views the family group through an archway—a vantage point repeated later in
similar circumstances that establish the icon of a symbolic portal or window
through which so many of Weir's characters perceive a corollary universe—
slowly snakes forward toward the actors (all of them very carefully positioned
in a neat pattern, one parent and one child on either side of the table, David and
Annie at opposite polarities) while, in a complementary movement, a gather-
ing puddle of water gradually traces a path down the house's staircase. In essence, what we see in this scene is that, as in Andrei Tarkovsky's *Solaris* (1972),
it seems to have begun raining inside the house (the children's denial of having
left on the upstairs bathtub tap, which David offers as a possible explanation
for the flooding, seems genuine enough). When David goes up to the bathroom and opens the overflowing tub's drain, his hand, seen from underwater,
lingers over the drain hole; David is apparently fixated on the force that is
drawing the water down into the Sydney sewers, the repository of the Aboriginal civilization into which he will soon be drawn by a similar, but this time apparently inexplicable, pull.

In a scene with elements of pursuit and camera placement that seem an
homage to *Vertigo* (1958), David, in his car, follows Chris through a city street.
As David looks through the glass barrier of the car's windshield, his vision is
suddenly obscured by a tar-like substance that falls from the sky, an example of
nature frustrating his attempt to maintain a "clear," rational view of events as
he plays out the role of Western-style detective, searching for empirical clues to
what is happening to him. Along with David, we can't be sure of what we're
seeing. Later, Annie—looking at David through another of the film's portals—
sees him standing in the foyer, dripping wet. *Last Wave's* preponderance of
dream-like images makes it unclear whether David is actually there or if she's
seeing him in a vision.

A death is the first dramatic event in the film, the one that becomes the motivation for David's becoming involved with the Aborigines. An Aboriginal man named Billy steals some tribal artifacts; his punishment is murder by a death stick wielded by the film's Aboriginal shaman, Charlie. As explained by the white coroner, though, Billy's death was caused by his heart simply stopping (this despite the fact that the coroner remarks on how healthy Billy was).[7] Yet a policeman to whom the coroner is talking (who seems fixated on holding his fingers under some running water) seems to think that Billy could just as easily have died from drowning. Since the coroner cannot explain why Billy died, and since the policeman's theory seems somewhat plausible (he notes that the coroner once told him that it takes only a cup of water to drown a sheep; presumably, half that amount could drown a human as well), what we seem to see here is an example of an event's meaning being determined by the assumptions of the culture in which one is raised. The coroner and the policeman never assume that there could be a tribally based explanation for Billy's death; they explain the man's death scientifically.[8] We are thus reminded of Weir's belief that one's opinions mandate one's view of reality, not the other way around.

As in *Picnic at Hanging Rock*, Weir isn't above intentionally perplexing the viewer about what is going on in the film. Billy is seen asleep at a table in a bar over a place mat that has classic symbols on it. The scene begins with the sound of a drum that sounds tribal but turns out to be played by a white member of an Irish band. Yet despite this collapsing of white and Aboriginal culture in what seems to be something of a joke, the rest of the images and references in the film are without humor. Unfortunately, such seriousness at times seems pointless and pretentious. The coroner says "there's something about this [Billy's death] that seems strange"; the statement seems clichéd, as does David's saying about the Aboriginal defendants involved in Billy's case that "they're keeping something from me."

More successful, because it takes on elements of dream-like representation, is the manner in which Weir blocks scenes and creates images. At one point, David is in his house puzzling over the visions he's been having. Weir shoots from the outside of the house about ten feet away, with the camera looking through a window. The window is the central one of three, thereby enclosing David not only within the window's frame but within the larger frame of the surrounding windows, bracketing him symbolically just as he is hemmed in by the distressing circumstances within which he finds himself, which have the characteristic of a puzzle inside of a puzzle, a dream within a dream. Additionally, in this shot the winds cause the fronds of three plants that surround the window to not only further enclose David but to sway, their finger-like fronds pointing toward him, a symbol of nature accusing him for his ignorance and indifference to the natural order of which the Aborigines are such an integral part.

The first character to move out of David's dreams and into his reality is Chris. After falling asleep at his study table, David dreams of Chris holding out to him a ceremonial stone. Weir places the camera in the same spot for the shots of David actually asleep at the table and seeing himself asleep at the table in his dream. (David not only dreams that he is dreaming but, during the dream, he dreams that he wakes up, thus not only blurring the distinction between the dream/non-dream realms for the audience as well as for David,[9] but also visually communicating a continuity between the two realms that David cannot as yet accept.)[10] When David meets Chris for the first time, Chris enters through a barroom's door after briefly letting his right hand linger over the door frame's opaque glass, lending a dark, visionary quality to the part of him that held out the dream symbol to David in the first place.

As we might expect, when Chris and Charlie come to David's house for dinner, David and Annie are ill at ease. When David shows the men his family album, we realize that he is reacting to an unconscious prompting to explain his point of origin, his tribal source, very possibly in response to an unconscious awareness that, like many Australians, he is a member of a society made up of displaced individuals. In one photo, the three wavy lines carved into a rock over the head of his mother's grandfather match those that David will see in one of the Aboriginal stone carvings in the sewers, suggesting that his assignations with the Aborigines were fated to occur. It also seems likely that David becomes involved with Chris and Charlie because he has a need for contact with a culture like that of the Aborigines, which, dating back to the last Ice Age, has the longest continuous cultural history in the world.[11] When asked why there are so many "anthropological symbols and images" in his films, Weir remarked, "I think probably just living in [white] Australia, which has such a recent history. It's really a trauma that the country's still going through, this dislocation from Europe, with a complete severing of roots. There's no real consciousness of where you came from."[12] In essence, David is being encouraged to contact his cultural, psychological, and anthropological source. Despite the film's anxious aspects, it tells a story about an antidote to the anomie that results from a lack of cultural history.

Chris tells David that dreams are "a way of knowing things . . . dream is a shadow of something real," illustrating this point by tilting a light and casting the shadow of his hand across David's face. But what Chris means by "real" isn't the same as what David understands by the term. For Chris, the real exists within the realm of the subconscious, while for David at this point, the real equates with the empirical world of Western-based things. Yet since the dreams that David has continue to bridge the gap between these two realms, we're repeatedly encouraged to negate this distinction. Just as David must descend below the city's surface into its sewers in order to contact the essence of the Aboriginal culture, so too must he move beyond what he sees in his dreams and visions into a realm in which these images become, not just the subterranean, unconscious realm of reality, but reality itself. Indeed, through a Jungian contact with "the dark half of the personality, or shadow,"[13] which for David is achieved via his relations with the Aborigines who represent this realm, David comes to an appreciation of his true identity, an appreciation toward which he is also encouraged by Charlie's repeated question to him in a subsequent scene: "who are you?"

If *The Last Wave* were no more than a film about a character who, as a representative of white culture, has (in Chris's words) forgotten "what dreams are,"[14] it would be slim fare indeed. Instead, we can start by reading the film as a gloss on the decoding of signs and symbols, with obvious relevance to the act of both creating symbols in the process of filmmaking and the activity of decoding them in the process of viewing films. It's clear from *Last Wave* that after his initiation into a culture rich in symbols, David, despite his realization of his buried identity, is no better off than before—that he is, perhaps, worse, since he has passed over from being incognizant of symbols to being obsessed with them, thus suggesting that any type of fixation, even one as apparently healthy as a concern with meaning, is pathological. The warning applies equally well to Weir's films in two ways: in a possible example of his conflicted attitude toward filmmaking, Weir seems to be telling himself not to become too obsessed with creating stylish images (a lesson he only consciously realized in 1978), while at the same time he's telling the audience not to read too much into the images he creates. We are again being encouraged to be as Weir would like to see himself: predominantly appreciative, not analytical. (As Weir said of the visuals in *Picnic at Hanging Rock,* "what interested me [was] . . . the way hair fell on the shoulder, images—just pictures.")[15] As we have seen, though, it is unlikely that Weir can successfully repudiate programmatic intention. If he truly had no intention, if life for him was all appreciation and no intellection, he would be unable to function as a filmmaker.

As Weir has noted about *Last Wave,* "my interest itself lies in those unknown areas, not so much in finding neat endings. There are no answers; there is no ending."[16] As a result, we might regret Weir's inability, because of budget restraints, from filming *Last Wave*'s conclusion as he wished. For David's vision of the final, apocalyptic wave that heralds the end of the latest cycle of creation and destruction, Weir wanted to actually flood some Sydney streets.[17] Yet given the surrealistically unparseable images that we already have, such as the pedestrians drowning in a crosswalk (one man, whom David had glimpsed in an earlier scene, is seen underwater still grasping the potted plant he'd been carrying previously) or David's car radio spewing water (both apparent announcements of the great wave that will engulf Sydney), we get a sense of otherworldly visual power, while the alternation between enervated expository scenes and forceful images successfully communicates the film's theme of the profound distinction between the word and the symbol.

Weir gives the speech about David's alter ego, Mulkril, to Vivean Gray, an actress who in her parts in *Picnic at Hanging Rock* and in *Last Wave* is associated with steadfast rationality. In *Picnic,* Gray's Miss McCraw viewed the trip to the rock as an inconvenient excursion exposing herself and the girls to (in Mrs. Appleyard's words) "venomous snakes and poisonous ants," and, with similar ironic distance, regarded her stopped watch with wry amusement. In *Last Wave,* Gray returns as Dr. Whitburn, an archivist who delivers a speech about Aboriginal culture and the significance of the stone that David had dreamt about.

This expository scene is virtually de rigeur in mysteries and science fiction films; in films such as *Psycho* (1960) and the original *Invaders from Mars* (1953), such scenes not only provide information but also comment on the pretentious rationality of scientific authority figures, none of whom ever seems capable of satisfactorily accounting for the mysteries to which we've been exposed. In the present scene, Weir has Gray speak in precisely the same flat, unemotional voice that Miss McCraw used in *Picnic*. She tells David that the Mulkril are a race of spirits from the East who bring sacred objects with them. "A Mulkril has incredible premonitory dreams that appear at the end of a cycle when nature has to renew itself," she says, going on to note that this cycle culminates in some sort of apocalypse such as an earthquake or flood. Whitburn then identifies the dreamtime, the realm from which David's visions emanate. "There's the realm in which you and I operate," she says, "and then there's the dreamtime, which one meets in dreams." The last statement seems, perhaps, intentionally truistic and self-enclosed, until we realize that it implies the cocoon-like structure of meanings, one enfolded inside the other, that informs the entire film. Just as the shell of David's white personality eventually breaks open to reveal who he really is, so too does the shell of mystery around the dreamtime need to be broken through in order to confront the unmediated nature of dreams. Similarly, just as David must descend below the city's surface into the sewers in order to directly contact Aboriginal culture, so too must he move beyond his vague response to his visions and dreams in order to contact the primal basis of reality. Writing about *The Last Wave,* the critic for *Positif* referred to this movement as "the progressive elucidation of a mystery," an intriguing term in that it implies that what David is doing is metaphorically casting the light of awareness into that part of his soul that has formerly been conceived of as being dark.[18] In fact, though, it seems that what David is doing is bringing into his life a proper kind of awareness that views the dark and the light as equally necessary in order to make his existence more complete. In other words, David is approaching that blending of opposite qualities that seems to be embodied in the previously mentioned image of Chris's black hand tilting David's dining room light onto the lawyer's white face as he tells him about dreams.

In *Last Wave,* the intellectual blankness of white culture is present in the form of David's ascetic, fine features. When out at David's stepfather's house, both David and his bleached blonde wife seem to almost leach into the sunlight. Yet it's into bright scenes like this one (and the schoolchildren scene at the film's beginning) that notions of darkness intrude. David's discovery while at his stepfather's of his repressed dreams, and the storm at the film's beginning, introduce troubling components. In each scene, natural elements (dreams, the storm) act as reminders of a kind of cosmic justice against the attempts of white society to pave over those forces of passion, desire, and a direct relation with nature that are associated with the subconscious. In *Last Wave,* as in *The Mosquito Coast,* nature seems to be paying whites back for their offenses against it.

The significance of David's white vagueness may be explained by going a bit deeper into some of the actions in which Weir involves David, many of which concern some form of "otherness." The parking garage attendant shows David a vegetable that David regards as exotic. David's father reminds him that when David was a child, he used to have nightmares about his body being stolen. David is extremely reluctant to become involved with the tribal murder case, preferring the safe anonymity of white tax law. In one scene, David is at a party with a group of other white people who are wearing masks. Toward the end of the film, part of David's self-realization involves him staring at a white mask of his own face. Weir seems to be suggesting that David is a man who throughout the majority of the film sleepwalks during a nightmare of denial, repeatedly resisting his role as a visionary in much the same way that Weir resists his own (ironically opposite) tendency: to intellectualize his own visions.

Concentric circles of confusion and misunderstanding, puzzles within puzzles, dreams within dreams, dominate the entire film. Thus, the shot of the three concentric circles[19] that Charlie paints on an overhanging rock ledge during the opening titles sequence dissolves to a shot of the outback landscape, an effect that not only casts a magical Aboriginal influence over all of the film's succeeding action but also presages the magical dissolve (derivative from the opening of *Picnic at Hanging Rock*) in *Last Wave's* post-titles shot, in which identical horizon shots photographed under different weather conditions are superimposed on one another, a visual multiplicity that anticipates the doublings of action, image, and character (e.g., David and Chris as counterpart dream seekers) that permeate the entire film. Repeatedly, events double themselves, not only in duplicated scenes (e.g., David twice returning to his house and being greeted by his daughter, a repetition of action that signals his growing inability to break out of the loop of confusion between the day and dreamtimes that actually signals a healthy movement toward a blending of the two realms), but also in dreams either being repeated or anticipating other dreams that anticipate events that may be real, imaginary, or dreamed. When David dreams that he sees Chris outside his door, standing in the rain and holding out a ceremonial stone to him, the image occurs later in the film in an apparently non-dream sequence. I say "apparently" because it isn't clear at times which events in *Last Wave* are actually occurring and which are dreamed or imagined. Aside from the trial and, perhaps, the Sydney law office scenes, it's difficult to tell which scenes in the film are, in the traditional sense, real. Yet even this statement, which implies a distinction among scenes, seems suspect. Are the daytime scenes, or the ones that take place in the evenness of indoor illumination, more real than those that occur in chiaroscuro or darkness, or do we just think so because as members of Western culture we're conditioned to trust more in things that we see and are suspicious of things that happen in the dark?[20] In commenting on the arbitrary way that we designate what is acceptable, Weir has observed that, for example, the terms "occult" and "mysterious" carry with them implicit value judgments about reality that are overlooked in conventional conversation. It should be apparent that, as Weir notes, "we've only chosen to see the world in a certain way; it's by common agreement that these things are so. It's why we laugh at foreign tribes who paint their noses red, or something. They laugh at us because we wear sunglasses. It's what we all agree upon."[21]

An additional perspective on the film's assertion of relativity with regard to "reality" is provided by Jung, whose commentary returns us to the notion of circles within circles as a way of further elucidating *The Last Wave's* iconography. In discussing the notion of the unconscious, Jung writes:

> I differentiate between what I have produced or acquired by my own conscious effort and what is clearly and unmistakably a product of the unconscious. Some-

one may object that the so-called unconscious mind is merely my own mind and that, therefore, such a differentiation is superfluous. But I am not at all convinced that the unconscious mind is merely my mind, because the term "unconscious" means that I am not even conscious of it. . . . . There is only one condition under which you might legitimately call the voice [heard in dreams] your own, and that is when you assume your conscious personality to be a part of a whole or to be a smaller circle contained in a bigger one.[22]

In this sense, the concentric circles that Charlie painted, which are also present on the rock that Chris holds out to David (the same rock that David uses to kill Charlie), embody one of the film's prime meanings: the circles tell David that his unconscious dream promptings (one of the circles) are not only related to his conscious self, but are attempting to speak to and (in a Jungian sense) modify his conscious self (another circle).[23] Were he only to properly decode his dream images, then, David would not be so lost. Unfortunately, David does not understand what place in his understanding dreams occupy.

In one sequence, David, after walking through his house (a sequence shot in barely perceptible slow motion, an effect that signals the scene's unusual aspect), goes to his front door and stands in the doorway while frogs drop from the sky. (Has Annie's painting of a frog prompted this image?) The rain of frogs, a plague similar to the falling petroleum, is merely one of the dream-like portents signalling imminent disaster. Weir uses slow motion in apparently factual scenes as well, as when David is conversing with one of the Aborigines. According to Weir, in these scenes he intercut views of a character speaking, which were filmed at normal camera speed, with reaction shots of David filmed at 120 frames per second.[24] The effect, as in the previously mentioned sequence, is barely appreciable, yet it strongly hints at the temporal and perceptual displacement that David is experiencing as he is repeatedly exposed to a culture whose view of time and reality is wildly out of synchronization with his own. Here, as in many of *Last Wave*'s scenes, visual technique becomes the prime bearer of meaning, an appropriate quality in a film in which the white, logocentric character's view of the world is being questioned and undermined. Essentially, what David is being urged toward is a view that, as in Weir's story about discovering a rock carving that he knew he was going to find, makes no distinction between the visionary and empirical realms. Thus, when Weir told actor David Gulpilil (who plays Chris) the story of his prescient experience regarding the stone carving, Gulpilil replied, "So what? What's unusual about it? Doesn't it happen to everybody?"[25]

Toward the film's end, in the underground cave, David, staring at the mask of his own face, not only views his priestly other self but, in the struggle with

Charlie (which he had earlier intuited), also confronts his missing father. At the point of recognizing the parent whose absence he resents, he kills him, an act that not only makes possible a kind of rebirth but also presages David's final eruption out of one sewer of misconceived self-perceptions and into another. At the film's end, when he is beached like detritus, spewed out of a pipe like the literal garbage that strews the sand, David first attempts a ritual washing away of his dark nightmare world, but discovers that he cannot do so. As David looks out to sea, the early morning sky darkens and destruction, as an anteced-ent to renewal, seems imminent. After the purge of the film's preceding events, the cycle starts over in the form of a tawdry apocalyptic vision that is as artificial as the white civilization whose destruction it heralds.

One of the deadly cars toward the end of *The Cars That Ate Paris*

Picnic at Hanging Rock's Miranda (Anne Lambert) during her climb up the rock

Sara (Margaret Nelson)
and Mrs. Appleyard
(Rachel Roberts) in *Picnic
at Hanging Rock*

A fateful wave goodbye:
Picnic at Hanging Rock's
Mademoiselle de Portiers
(Helen Morse)

Chris (Gulpilil), David (Richard Chamberlain), Charlie (Nandjiwarra Amagula), and Annie (Olivia Hamnett) during their disturbing dinner in *The Last Wave*

A sensibility in flight from itself: David with his wife, Annie, in *The Last Wave*

The invasion of the home: Jill (Judy Morris) and Max (Ivar Kants) in *The Plumber*

Uncle Jack (Bill Kerr) and Archie (Mark Lee) in *Gallipoli*

Gallipoli's Frank
(Mel Gibson) and
Archie

An uneasy foursome: Guy (Mel Gibson), the Colonel (Bill Kerr), Billy (Linda Hunt), and Jill (Sigourney Weaver) in *The Year of Living Dangerously*

Reportage in the midst of political turmoil as practiced by Billy and Guy

Guy and Jill in *The Year of Living Dangerously*

The protective embrace: Samuel (Lukas Haas), Rachel (Kelly McGillis), and John (Harrison Ford) in *Witness*

Voyeurism and terror: *Witness*'s Samuel

Evanescent bonding: *Witness*'s Rachel and John

Desire, skepticism, envy, and rage during a presumably restful moment: Rachel, John, and Daniel (Alexander Godunov) in *Witness*

Inevitable separation number 1: *Witness*'s Samuel and John

Inevitable separation number 2: Rachel and John in *Witness*

WATER PRESSURES

The mild sexual suggestiveness of *The Cars That Ate Paris* reappears, but in an ominous and far more sophisticated form, in *The Plumber*, which was originally produced for Australian television and later released theatrically. Shot in 16mm during a three-week period, the seventy-six-minute film may very well be the most compact statement that Weir has yet made on the relation between civilization and savagery.

The nature of the plot makes it obvious that what is being played out in the film is a kind of invasion, a figurative rape. A plumber, Max, arrives to fix the pipes in the bathroom of a young married couple, Jill and Brian. Although there doesn't seem to be anything wrong with the plumbing, Max keeps returning to the couple's flat while only Jill is there, increasingly insinuating himself into Jill and Brian's personal and sexual relationship. (Weir refers to the repeated meetings between Max and Jill—whom he obviously feels are the film's most important characters—as "fatal encounter[s].")[1] Complementing the fact that Max is an invasive presence is the plumber's indeterminate status: he constantly changes his story about who he is and what he has done in the past (at one point, Max claims that he had been in prison for rape, a story he later denies).[2] Whether he's toying with Jill in order to play on her vulnerability and naïveté (as he says at one point he is) or whether he's genuinely equivocal is also unclear so that, as is characteristic of Weir's work at this period, neither the characters nor the audience can clearly grasp what is happening in the film. Along with Jill, then, we are thrust into a region in which we are cut loose from the normal assurances of episodic certainty.

Some things are clear, however. Brian, for example, is a very weak character. The nature of his sexuality is characterized at the outset as he's seen reaching for a bottle of hair tonic toward the end of his shower. In response to Max's later query, Jill comments that her husband's hair is thinning, an obvious sexually linked quality that vividly contrasts with Max's thick and copious hair. Additionally, Jill and Brian's sexual relationship never seems demonstrative; both are apparently quite repressed, always behaving in a safe and prescribed way. Brian is too caught up in his work as a nutritionist to pay much significant attention to Jill; Jill, working on her master's degree in anthropology, having quit academia to work at home, seems, in Max's words, to be suffering the bored life of a housewife.

Jill comes from a sheltered background, a fact that is made clear when Max refers to her "posh" schooling and her correct pronunciation. Recognizing Max as a sexual force gives the scene in which Jill shames him by correcting what she obviously regards as his working-class pronunciation added significance and points us toward the film's essential meaning. A passage from Toni Morrison's *Playing in the Dark* is quite useful here.

> We need to explicate the ways in which specific themes, fears, forms of consciousness, and class relationships are embedded in the use of Africanist idiom; how the dialogue of black characters is construed as an alien, estranging dialect . . . how Africanist language practices are . . . used to . . . reinforce class distinctions and otherness as well as to assert privilege and power; how it serves as a marker for illegal sexuality. . . .[3]

Substitute the term "working-class Australian" for Africanist and we have a succinct and incisive description of *The Plumber*. Max is quite clearly the "other" in the film: he represents direct (and, for Jill, threatening) sexuality; his sensibility involves attitudes, actions, and reactions that often seem strange or distorted (some of this quality may be attributed to the fact that the film, without resorting to exaggerated point-of-view shots, is predominantly told from Jill's perspective), all in response to a sense of inadequacy catalyzed by Jill and Brian's smug, insular, upper-middle-class, white-collar lifestyle. In essence, Max is nothing less than an Aboriginal presence, as much, as I will point out, as the warrior who invaded Jill's tent, and who perhaps, like Max, reacted negatively to the patronizing aspect of the supposedly objective, distanced information-gathering in which Jill and Brian were engaged. Like the black presences in *Picnic at Hanging Rock* and *The Last Wave*, Max insinuates himself into white society and disrupts its quaint, annoying orderliness. We can also divine Weir's presence in the film: he summons Max as the dark genie in order to cause chaos. The manner in which this chaos is ultimately resolved, though (Max's vanquishment), represents white Australia's treatment of its Aboriginal population, who were victimized by atomic bomb testing on their land, used as cheap slave labor, and preyed upon sexually. Aboriginal culture's shocked reactions to these and other racist abuses are testified to graphically in the pictures of the desolate urban Aborigines that David's wife looks at in *The Last Wave*.

The Plumber's characters are not aware of their attitudes toward dark characters, though; they are as dumbfounded by Max as they are obtuse about everything else in their stereotypical lives. Ironically, this lack of prescience extends to Max as well, whom Weir conceives of as being clearly out of his element. None of the characters properly reads the signs that would indicate what was about to happen to them. Brian can't see that for career considerations, it would be wise to not mention his theories to some visiting health officials; Jill is unsure whether Max is playing with her or not; Max is unaware that this apparently repressed, middle-class woman he's toying with has successfully dealt with primal characters before and, in response to his aggression, will manipulate him back into the sewer-like prison to which, judging by the later appearance of a man who seems to be his parole officer, he will be returned. Like the workmen in Sam Peckinpah's *Straw Dogs* (1971) who believe that they can taunt the film's presumably defenseless young married couple, David and Amy Sumner, without risking retribution, the blue-collar character in *The Plumber* suffers for unleashing in his victim the repressed, subconscious impulses that he represents.

On a conscious level, Jill believes in equality among the classes, a notion as artificially grafted onto her lifestyle as the posters and accoutrements from primitive civilizations with which she and Brian have adorned their student apartment. There's more than a hint at patronization in Jill and Brian's attitudes, both of them supposedly interested in Aboriginal cultures but actually exploiting them, advancing themselves through their "scientific" work. When Brian mentions that he's doing research on the debilitating effects of junk food use among tribesmen, the statement acts as both a comment on the manner in which civilization has corrupted tribal culture[4] as well as the manner in which the Aboriginals have been impoverished at the expense of well-paid whites like Brian.

Jill participates in this attitude in other ways. At the film's beginning she tells a story about being on a research expedition. One night, a Bitu sorcerer came into her tent and began chanting. During this experience, Jill had to sit absolutely still; after a while, unnerved by the experience and not knowing what to do, she picked up a bowl of goat's milk and threw it in the man's face. Aside from the characteristic Weir juxtaposition of solemn ritualizing and black humor response (something also present in the scene between *The Last Wave's* Charlie and David in Charlie's apartment when Charlie starts chanting and David looks at him dumbfounded), what is significant about the story is not only Jill's aggressive behavior but also the fact that while telling the story, Jill re-creates the act of picking up the bowl of milk by slowly raising her hands over her head in an inadvertent mimicry of some ritualistic activity. Later, during the meditation class that Jill and her friend Meg attend, the same kind of gesture is employed, with similarly little spiritual significance. Thus, neither the civiliza-tion of the Bitu nor the Eastern culture to which the meditation technique al-ludes has much relevance for these bored, middle-class white Australians. (To emphasize the point, Weir has one of the meditation class participants rudely cough during the session; later, after the class, Meg lights up a cigarette while extolling the class's healthy effects.)

Perhaps we can begin to get to the heart of *The Plumber* by discussing the nature of the plumber's trade, which is never explicitly discussed in the film. The only activities that we see taking place in Jill and Brian's bathroom are people showering (one of Brian's guests from Geneva says that he has to use the bathroom but he's never seen doing so). We're shown the shower stall and sink but never the toilet. Thus, in keeping with the story's emphasis on society's "civilized" tone, the room's excretory functions (its initial and primary pur-pose) are buried in the film, as is the other primary class of forbidden human functions, the sexual ones. Although there are shots of Jill's underwear hanging in the bathroom when Max arrives, and a glimpse of an illustration from the *Kama Sutra* on the bathroom wall, direct acknowledgment of life's sexual as-pect is strongly repressed in *The Plumber.*

Opposing this tendency, though, is the way that Weir frames certain shots. Max is first seen only from the waist down, and there's a complementary shot of Jill and Max when Max reaches down to get his tools out of his bag: each character's genital area is pointedly accentuated. Max asserts an explicit equiva-lence between mechanical and human plumbing (one that mirrors the conti-nuity between mechanisms and human bodies proposed in *The Cars That Ate Paris*) when he says of the plumbing in Jill's bathroom, "your pipes, if you'll pardon the expression, are buggered." Although Max's use of the phrase "if you'll pardon the expression" is meant to convey a politeness apparently in-tended to distract the listener from the sexual allusiveness of the words that are to follow, it's nonetheless clear that his plumbing reference hints not only at sex but an unorthodox type of sex: anal. When he goes on to tell Jill that "all your pipes are too small," it's difficult to believe that he's not commenting on Jill's vagina and it's never having been spread wide enough by what, it is implied, must be the small penis of her husband. When Max finishes his statement, Weir cuts to a shot of Jill's troubled eyes, thereby revealing that Jill is beginning to slowly apprehend the hostility behind Max's ambiguous assertions.

Max seems to be conscious of the metaphoric aspect of his work. "It's what you can't see that counts in plumbing," he says, and this statement seems to refer not just to the hidden aspects of his symbolic trade, the dealing with devices involved with excretion, but also to a whole range of repressed ideas and feelings, from sexual deviance and homicide to other "uncivilized" qualities such as revenge, deceit, overt hostility, and passion, forces that through his ministrations he unintentionally unleashes. What Max also unwittingly highlights is a meaning based on a pun that is inherent in the title of his trade. "Plumbing" can refer not just to metal pipes or bodily passageways but also to delving into the depths of a given utterance or situation, a peeling back of the traditional layers of polite commerce that civilization uses to ensure the propriety of actions and statements. Indeed, as in Weir's previous film, *The Last Wave,* in which the Sydney sewer system served as a metaphor for the realm of the subconscious, dark side of human awareness, so too in *The Plumber* is there a fixation on going below the surface of things in order to properly "read" events. The conflict between the Western empirical approach to reality and that represented by the Aboriginal is most strikingly introduced through the film's least vital character, Brian. Brian's work with Aborigines is based on a Western approach to nutrition. Nevertheless, he believes he has discovered among the Aborigines the reappearance of a nervous disorder called *kuru,* which apparently results from eating the brains of an ancestor, presumably in order to pass on his knowledge, but which also causes communication of the bacterial disorder from which the eaten person was suffering. One of Brian's colleagues disparages his theory, remarking that Aboriginal behaviors have passed out of existence. "Ritual cannibalism no longer exists," Brian's associate says. Like the opposed arrows seen on the pipes (that appear under the name of the actor who plays him), Brian is characterized by two opposing tendencies. He vacillates between accepting his colleague's view and believing that what he is seeing is a return to traditional tribal patterns of behavior. It's clear, though, that the characters in *The Last Wave* and *The Plumber* who hold that tribalism is dead are merely deluding themselves. In Weir's films, tribalism and what it represents, subconscious behaviors, is often shown as re-emerging.

Like *The Last Wave*'s Aborigines, Max is not only allied with water but represents a similar kind of symbolic, subconscious force. Max simultaneously catalyzes the re-emergence of repressed attitudes and brings to the surface antagonisms between Jill and Brian that have to do with the conflict between Brian's placing a priority on his research and Jill's indecision concerning whether she should be an academic or subordinate herself to her husband and be a homebody. Moreover, Max represents virtually barbaric and unalloyed attitudes toward sexual expression (via his repeated innuendoes) that this good little academic couple, whose marriage seems without passion, have repressed. Just like the Bitu warrior in Jill's story, Max propels Jill into action. The Bitu comes into Jill's tent; Max invades her apartment. The Bitu chants to Jill; Max sings her a song, during which Weir cuts to a photo of an Aboriginal warrior. In the original version of *The Plumber*'s script, the story about the Bitu involved the warrior's exhibiting his erect penis to Jill;[5] as previously noted, Max insistently makes thinly veiled references to Jill's sexuality. Jill's response to what she regards as the warrior's threatening presence (she throws the bowl of milk in his face) causes him to break down crying. (In Weir's early version of the story, the Aborigine "was so humiliated that he defecated on the floor,"[6] an action that not only strengthens the connection with Max's trade but further allies the film with the Sydney sewers of *The Last Wave*.) Jill resorts to a similar response with Max, whom she recognizes as another male armed with a weapon-like sexual organ. After upbraiding him with his bad diction and shaming him in front of Meg, she plants her new watch in Max's van, causing him to be arrested and break down screaming at her.

Max seems to consistently act in a devious way. Although Max usually enters Jill and Brian's flat by the front door, when Jill, upset by his disturbing sexual and social innuendoes, denies him access to the apartment by the usual route, Max enters via the crawl space in the ceiling. Like a bad dream that keeps recurring despite one's efforts to suppress it, he reappears in Jill's supposedly secure realm, dropping down into the bathroom after having used what he refers to as the "tradesmen's entrance," a phrase that not only links up with Max's explicit criticism of how a former employer had treated him like nothing more than a lowly laborer, but which also serves as a reference to illicit lovers ("backdoor men") and anal sex.

In one scene, Jill disrobes before showering and, without expecting to, finds Max in the bathroom. In this scene, it's just as though Jill has been raped, since Max has invaded her most personal space, her bathroom, and, having entered unannounced and without permission, has literally invaded the "body" where she lives. Jill's reaction to this event (she later withdraws into sleeping a great deal) mirrors that of *Straw Dogs*' Amy, just as the obtuseness of Brian's response to his wife's anxiety is similar to that of *Straw Dogs*' David. Neither woman can adequately communicate to her husband what she is feeling, not because of a lack of articulateness, but because of each man's refusal (which is partially a function of their privileged social status as males) to accept that his wife is in jeopardy. (Jill tells Brian at one point, "it makes you tense having someone in the house like that; you just wouldn't know about it.") As a result of the previous, albeit unacknowledged, degree of alienation between the married partners in each film (a problem exacerbated by the intrusion of lower-class characters), the woman, already made to feel somewhat inadequate by her academic husband (whose career is allowed to take precedence over hers), slowly becomes more and more estranged from her former perceptions, among which are her view of her husband. Nevertheless, after the violent acts that culminate each film—the assault against the farmhouse in *Straw Dogs*, the arrest of Max in *The Plumber*—the invading characters are vanquished.

The ironic point in both films is that despite what we might first expect, it isn't the more uncivilized characters who exhibit the most bestial reactions but the intellectual, supposedly more conventionally socialized ones. As *The Plumber* progresses, we realize that Max is wrong in thinking that he is more in touch with primitive feelings, with the crude facts of existence, than the well-behaved people whom he meets. When these civilized types become aggressive, their actions far outstrip those of which the apparently more rudimentary character is capable. In one scene, Jill puts on a recording of what sounds like a Bitu warrior chant; the stark primitivism of the sound startles Max, whose delusion is that he is a primal man; without realizing it, Max retreats into the bathroom as though he's being exorcised, compelled to return to the source from which he came.

It has been suggested that Max may not be the completely manipulative character that he appears to be, a reading that would mandate that we view him as both threatening and engaging; that if he appears evil, this reaction may be ascribed to Jill's unbalanced state, a function of her insecurity regarding her homebound role.[7] When casting the part of Max, Weir eventually hired Ivar Kants because none of the other actors tested for the role seemed capable of projecting both menace and charm, the latter quality apparent to Weir in what he referred to as Kants's "smile [and] . . . cheery grin."[8] Granted, Max does *seem* charming, at least to Meg and the building superintendent; yet both of these women also refer to Max's overt sexuality, Meg stating that the plumber's presence in Jill's apartment makes things seem daring, the superintendent saying that Max is "overpaid and oversexed." Yet neither woman's home is being rudely invaded as is Jill's, and for an unjustifiably protracted amount of time. Even if we grant that Jill's uncertainty about her sexuality and career skew her perceptions, it's nonetheless clear that Max drags out the repair work (if any was ever needed), with no apparent motive other than to continue coming to Jill's apartment.

Weir relates that when dubbing the film, the projectionist told him, "God, I know that type of woman—the stuck-up bitch! She deserves everything she gets!"—a quote offered by M. Kinder, one of the film's reviewers, in defense of *The Plumber*'s supposed ambiguity.[9] Kinder goes on to note that women have had the opposite response to the film, seeing Max as a clear threat.[10] It seems likely that despite Weir's view of Max as an equivocal character, the plumber is a manipulative and unbalanced individual who initiates a provocative series of power plays with Jill and, in effect, authors a scenario whose end he simply could not foresee. The game that Max plays with Jill is not pleasant for her; indeed, Max's game, in which Jill does not want to participate, ignores her right as an individual not to be coerced. (Max's game-playing also mirrors the blindness to Jill's feelings exhibited by Brian.) Despite the director's pronouncements about Max, it should seem clear that the plumber's character hardly partakes of the usual Weir ambiguity.

Jill's response to Max's actions is to construct her own scenario (albeit a completely fictional one) in order to defend herself. By the time she has arranged her hair, dressed in fancy clothes, and put together a candlelight dinner for Brian, she has not only already put her watch in Max's van but has also equalled the plumber in primal cunning. When, presumably having been tipped off by Jill, two policemen arrest Max for having stolen the watch and he looks back at Jill, Weir reprises the warrior chant on the soundtrack. Ironically, in response to his own teasing, the person whom Max conceived of as a powerfully suppressed woman has, like many of Weir's characters, discovered the primal basis of her personality. As payback for Max's manipulations, Jill has unleashed her pent-up resentment against him. Earlier in the film, Brian had described some New Guinea tribesmen who eat the testes of dead warriors to increase their fertility; similarly, Jill has (figuratively) castrated the plumber and, apparently, appropriated his power, turning it against him while hiding behind a mask of innocence that mirrors the feigned boyishness Max had exhibited in front of Meg and the building superintendent. At the end, watching while Max screams out "You set me up, you bloody bitch!" she regards him with a look of feigned pity and real wonder that cannot hide from us her feelings of triumph and satisfaction. In the film's last shot, Jill, her head cocked quizzically to one side, looks down at Max, who is floors below her. Their "proper" symbolic positions have been restored, with the victimizer now become victim. Max is well on his way to being returned to the figuratively underground location where white society prefers that its essential desires (especially those as blatant as the ones that he represents) be housed, and is capable of only helplessly staring up at the warrior woman whom he has inadvertently brought into being.

5

THE DEATH OF A NATION

In *Gallipoli,* Weir heavily relies on C. E. W. Bean's official history of Australian participation in World War I[1] and Bill Gammage's book *The Broken Years,*[2] both of which are acknowledged in the film's credits. Moreover, *Gallipoli* is the least stylized of Weir's films. The director obviously intended much of it to have an almost documentary-like feel. To achieve this end, the film is extremely attentive to historical detail. In fact, a comparison between the film and photos from the Gallipoli campaign shows how many factual details Weir has incorporated into the film, from the way that the soldiers dress, to the scenes of men strung out across the sand in front of pyramids, to the flies covering the stale biscuits that the soldiers eat.[3]

It might be helpful at the outset to sketch in the political situation within which *Gallipoli*'s events take place. Historian Kenneth Jackson notes that the Gallipoli campaign "was conceived by Winston Churchill, then the first lord of the Admiralty, as an easy way both to knock Turkey [a German ally] out of the war and to open the way to the Black Sea and Russia."[4]

Churchill's scheme failed, though, when British battleships met fierce resistance from Turkish "shore batteries on the Gallipoli peninsula and minefields in the Dardanelles."[5] As a result,

Churchill and his advisers decided to take Gallipoli by invasion and thus open the sea route to [Istanbul]. The invasion was a disaster from the start. The British landings at Cape Helles stalled a few miles from the tip of the peninsula, while the Australians and New Zealanders were even less fortunate. They landed at the wrong place and spent the next eight months clinging to a narrow beachhead under the guns of tenacious Turkish defenders. . . . [T]he stalemate continued through the spring and early summer of 1915. Finally, the British decided to make new landings closer to Istanbul at Suvla Bay in early August. To confuse the Turks and prevent them from moving in reinforcements, the British commander-in-chief ordered his Australian and New Zealander forces to launch a series of frontal assaults at ANZAC Cove.[6]

The most infamous of the incidents at Gallipoli took place on August 7, 1915, when a battalion of Australian soldiers was ordered to assist the British in their battle against Turkey by assaulting Turkish trenches at what was referred to as The Nek. Gammage's description of the area near The Nek is of great help in properly appreciating the strategic situation in which the soldiers found themselves.

The Nek was a ridge 50 yards wide at the Anzac line, narrowing to about 30 at the Turkish front. The opposing trenches on it were about 20 yards apart, and at least five Turkish machine guns covered the intervening ground. Four lines of the light horse, each of about 150 men, were to seize the enemy front line and the maze of trenches and saps behind it. . . . [T]hey would be preceded by a naval and artillery bombardment, and were to attack at two minute intervals.[7]

Historian John North's description of the physical layout of the area is equally telling. North quotes Bean, who says that the machine guns were "on inaccessible spurs on either flank." In North's words, the attack was "a frontal assault of a degree of madness unexcelled in any theatre of war: to attempt it—as [Bean] remarks—was 'like endeavoring to attack an inverted frying-pan from the direction of its handle.'"[8]

Despite the fact that the assault was considered virtually suicidal from the beginning,

The light horsemen were eager and confident, for this was their first great battle, and they expected to break from the interminable trenches into the open. Sick men hid or escaped from their doctors to be in the charge, and every man was impatient to emulate the Lone Pine attack they had watched the evening before.[9]

The heavy bombing of the Turkish trenches before the Australian assault was supposed to debilitate the Turks. Unfortunately, the shelling ended seven minutes too soon, giving the Turks time to regroup and return to the trenches. As Bean observes in *Anzac to Amines,*

For some reason that may now never be discovered—probably an error in timing watches—this shelling suddenly ceased when the watches of the Light Horse officers only showed 4:23—that is, seven minutes before the attack; and when, at 4:30, Lieutenant Colonel A.H. White of the 8th Light Horse gave the word 'Go,' and, followed eagerly by the 150 men of the first line, scrambled from the deep trenches, there burst out within three or four seconds from the Turkish trenches, packed with men, such a torrent of rifle fire, growing quickly to a continuous roar, as soldiers can seldom have faced. . . . Except those wounded whom bullets had knocked back into the trench, or who managed to crawl a few yards and drop into it, almost the whole line fell dead or dying within the first ten yards. . . . [T]hree or four men reached the Turkish parapet.[10]

Gammage's description of the assault is even more detailed.

At four on the afternoon of 6 August the artillery began a gentle bombardment. It intensified early on the 7th, but at four twenty three A.M., seven minutes before time, it ceased. The light horsemen stood still in the silence. In the enemy trenches, soldiers cautiously emerged from shelter, lined their front two deep, fired short bursts to clear their machine guns, levelled their rifles, and waited. At four thirty precisely the first line of the 8th Light Horse leapt from their trenches. As their helmets appeared above the parapet, an awful fire broke upon them. Many were shot, but a line started forward. It crumpled and vanished within five yards. One or two men on the flanks dashed to the enemy's parapets before being killed, the rest lay still in the open.

The second line saw the fate of their friends. Over their heads the Turk fire thundered undiminished, drowning out any verbal order. In front the slope was shot bare of foliage. Beside them lay dead and wounded of the first line, hit before they cleared the trench. But they waited two minutes as ordered, then sprang forward. They were shot down. The 10th Light Horse filed into the vacant places in the trench. They could hardly have doubted their fate.[11]

A personal testimony makes the tragedy even more poignant.

You can imagine what it was like. Really too awful to write about. All your pals that had been with you for months and months blown and shot out of all recognition. There was no chance whatsoever of us gaining our point, but the roll call after was the saddest, just fancy only 47 answered their names out of close on 500 men. When I heard what the result was I simply cried like a child.[12]

As it appears in Weir's film, then, this event's tragic nature is not a distortion of the facts;[13] and though Weir's dramatization of the event makes it seem that virtually all of the soldiers involved in the assault were killed, this isn't much of an exaggeration. The defeat was so overwhelming that it is generally regarded as the worst military loss in Australian history.

Despite the fact that the word "Gallipoli" conjures up for Australians images of battle, battle scenes occupy a very small part of *Gallipoli*. Like Lewis Milestone's *All Quiet on the Western Front* (1930), Weir's film prefers to let the impending war scenes hang like a pall over everything that comes before them.

And like *Chariots of Fire* (1981), which it seems to anticipate, *Gallipoli* uses a sports competition as an analogue for a race against time and death.[14] Indeed, the Turkish trench toward which the blindly patriotic and optimistic young Australian soldiers rush, as though it were a finish line, does represent an end point, but one with a decidedly grim outcome.

The film prepares us for the collapsing of the military and civilian spheres from its very beginning. Weir's innocent protagonist, Archie, is faced by a stern man (whom we later learn is his uncle) who is in military garb and is training him for a race. The man uses a starting gun much like the one that the Australian Colonel Barton uses later in the film to signal the beginning of the final assault. *Gallipoli* means to draw a connection between competitiveness in sports and in war. However, the analogy is only meant as a reflection of Archie's point of view. Sublimely unanalytical, Archie regards the Gallipoli campaign as a wondrous event. Unfortunately, Archie's ambition is typical of many young men. There's an idealized, irrational response to the call of fife and drum, an example of which we see early in the film when, at the height of Archie's triumph after winning an amateur race, a recruitment parade comes by. Patriotic attitudes are present as well in the newspaper headlines of the war story that, in a symbolic move, Archie has placed in the middle of a book on sports, indicating thereby that the conflict will interrupt his devotion to personal fulfillment. The headlines mention "baptismal fire, splendid gallantry, magnificent achievement," qualities on which Archie obviously seizes and by which he is attracted; he thus overlooks the deadly implications involved with baptismal fire, and seems to ignore the part of the headline that makes it clear that the battle being waged is "fierce." Periodically throughout *Gallipoli,* we see characters talking about the war as though it were something glorious. There are numerous references to notions of mateship, of camaraderie, of groups of friends joining up at once, not only implying that the groups should be kept together regardless of where they're headed but suggesting that allegiance to one's friends is somehow a microcosmic representation of allegiance to one's country. Yet even if this were so (which it does not seem to be), there's no attendant implication that any Australian owes fidelity to a cause that is almost exclusively British. It's precisely on examples of such foolhardy romanticism that Weir focuses.

Despite the fact that Archie is too young to enlist, his uncle allows him to transfer his enthusiasm from the sport of running to what a recruiter at the racing grounds refers to as "the greatest game of all." But then this war, like any war, is no game; it's more like the Trojan horse that the recruiting party uses to attract volunteers, which is intended to stand in for a real horse but in fact, especially for the Australians, functions as a symbol of a campaign with no inner substance. Later, when Archie and his new friend Frank are in the desert on their way to enlist, Frank (who has stated, "[it's] not our bloody war; it's an English war") asks Archie why he wants to join the army, to which Archie replies, "so that the Germans won't be here next." After this remark, the camel driver who's with them, who has not heard about the war, looks around at the vast desert and says, "and they're welcome to it," making it clear that the boy's justification is mighty far-fetched. The stories about the Germans nailing cats to church doors are clearly propaganda manufactured to create public support for what would otherwise be a fairly unpopular cause.[15] Nonetheless, even Frank joins up, if only to stay with his friend. Weir thereby demonstrates that where for Archie competition is more important than life, for Frank, it's mateship that compels him to join a cause that is clearly both perilous and pointless.

If we read *Gallipoli* as a comment on both the Gallipoli campaign and the war in Vietnam, the film's significance expands. The Vietnam war occasioned a certain degree of enthusiasm in the United States, as did the Gallipoli campaign in Australia. However, just as some Americans thought that the Vietnam war was unnecessary, some Australians felt that the Gallipoli campaign was pointless, while others wanted no part of it at all. (Even a patriot such as Gammage is compelled to observe that "between January 1912 and . . . June 1914, 28,000 boys or their parents were prosecuted for avoiding the call-up.")[16] As one might expect, political justifications for each war were promptly trotted out. Yet the American justification for the war as a stopgap against communism is the same as Archie's saying that if Australians don't fight, the Germans will be in Australia next. There was very little reason for American involvement in Vietnam or Australian involvement in Gallipoli, but appeals to feelings of blind patriotism and stories about supposed atrocities kindled people's enthusiasm. What we see here is nothing less than the usual Weir split between thought and feeling.

Interestingly, while Weir tries to play on our emotions in the film, he also wants the audience to react intellectually, coolly, with regard to the dramatized calls to arms. In *Gallipoli,* we actually take both sides in the characteristic Weir duality, at once intellectually distant and emotionally engaged. Yet at the film's end, we react with both pity and outrage at such a waste of life, all in the service of a cause that in retrospect, which is the vantage point of the film, doesn't really seem that important. This point of view is aptly characterized by historian

Peter Liddle. "In the entire campaign it is difficult to select an assault more cru-
elly futile than that at the Nek. . . . [T]he attack might serve as a microcosm of
the appalling futility of warfare, and trench warfare in particular. . . ."[17]

During some war games, Archie and his friend Frank meet again after being
separated, and are so glad to see each other that they forget they're supposed to
be playing at being enemies. Seeing them laughing together, an officer says,
"what do you think you're doing? This is supposed to be warfare." The officer's
statement does more than berate Archie and Frank for what he considers to be
frivolous activity; it also inadvertently implies that despite the fact that the war
game is supposed to be real, these men have no personal animosity against one
another—no more so, actually, than they do against the Turks whom they'll
soon be fighting.

Racial hostility (a cultural blindness that some of the men have brought with
them) is merely another fiction encouraged in the soldiers.[18] As Weir demonstrates, it's precisely such divisive notions, which separate people into opposed
categories so that "others" (in this case, dark "others" such as the film's Egyptians and Turks) can be despised, that make wars possible. This attitude trans-
mutes fear (the usual reaction to the unknown or uncanny) into hatred, which,
Weir reveals, in wartime is nothing more than fear armed with a weapon. The
kind of rivalry that we see between the British and the Australians, the officers
and the men, the infantry versus the light horse, are examples of similar kinds
of antagonism. The encouragement of animosity against "foreigners" is played
upon to maintain a status quo of alienation, which masks the actions of governments that profit from divisiveness among common people and seek to destroy all allegiances except those to the state and the party. Only the Australian
Colonel Barton, alone among the film's officers, risks his life along with his
men. The rest of the officers seem to stay comfortably ensconced far from the
lines of battle.

A racial aspect of which the film makes no significant mention is the then-
current Australian attitude toward Germans. All that we hear of this element is
Archie's repeating a piece of racist propaganda. Yet in Australia during the war,
Germans were treated horrendously.

> By October 1914 most German nationals in Australia were interned, and most
> citizens of German origin or extraction were subject to social, economic, and legal
> bars. Some patriotic Australians demanded more. . . . Australian Germans were
> beaten up, spat upon, dismissed from jobs . . . their homes were stoned, their
> property destroyed, their children forced to leave school. The law, the courts, the
> trade unions, and the universities discriminated against them . . . worse was to
> come for citizens of German blood in Australia.[19]

Instead of confronting this issue, Weir displaces it onto the racist attitude of the Australians against the Egyptians, whom the Australian soldiers see as fiscally deceitful and sexually compromised. He does, though, focus on the issue of class, from the early question that Frank asks Archie about the light horse ("They only take toffs and farmers . . . ?"); through the remark of Snow, one of Frank's friends, after Frank has been transferred to the light horse ("Infantry not good enough for you, mate?" with a sneering pause before the last word); to the statement of the otherwise egalitarian Colonel Barton that the ball into which Frank and Archie insinuate themselves is for officers only. What Weir is mostly communicating through these class distinctions, though, has less to with conflicts among the Australians than with those between the Australians, who represent egalitarianism (although anyone conversant with the treatment of Aborigines in Australian would know this representation to be false), and the British, who are portrayed as the embodiment of class snobbery. Yet this aspect of the film also dramatizes the ambivalence that Australians feel as both British-influenced individuals (at home, for example, Archie's uncle reads to the children from Kipling, "the great author of Empire")[20] and as outcasts from the British empire. The divided political allegiance of many Australians is in one respect a symptom of personal anxiety about their identity. Thus the film's emphasis on appearances, how one looks to others: Frank checking his uniform in a mirror before entering the ball, Archie's concern with how it will look if he doesn't join up, the whole premium placed on mates sticking together in the face of forces that threaten group solidarity.

It's precisely in its restraint that *Gallipoli* is notable. The film started out with a much grander design, but was reduced in the scripting process until eventually it primarily focused on the actions of only two men.[21] In doing so, *Gallipoli* simultaneously manages to elevate Archie and Frank to symbolic status as (respectively) the typical callow Australian youth and the sentimental scoffer, and to personalize the film so as to make Archie's death that much more affecting and Frank's survival that much more ironic.[22] Weir notes, "As it's been said, by a British soldier marching toward the front line in France, 'We marched forward toward the transmutation of our personalities.' They [the survivors of Gallipoli] did not come back the same men."[23]

More particularly, though, Weir sees in the "transmutation" of Frank's personality a shift in the national character of Australia, away from innocence (present in the person of Archie) and toward a skeptically detached, bitter realism—essentially, a loss of idealistic dreaming. In Archie, the only man whose death is focused on,[24] we're supposed to see the demise of Australia's naïveté, a loss that, it is implied, is a prerequisite to maturity.[25]

When interviewer Kathleen Tulich asked Weir why he compared *Dead Poets Society* to *Gallipoli,* Weir replied, "In the sense of youth and spirit, and the fragility of physical and moral danger—moral in the sense that you knew that the Frank Dunne who comes back to Australia is very different to the one who went. A new type of cynicism had entered society."[26]

Although Weir seems in this quote to be overlooking the element of hopefulness in the boys' tribute to Keating at *Dead Poets'* conclusion, his point about *Gallipoli* is still well taken: like *Dead Poets, Gallipoli* dwells on the evanescence of youth and life within the context of a war between the older generation and the younger.

While one might regret that Weir has not presented us with a personalized epic—as did David Lean in *Lawrence of Arabia* (1962)—we can still appreciate the film's economical use of its resources. If the viewer focuses on *Gallipoli's* battle scenes, one notices that there are not many actors in them; as in the shoot-out at the end of Sam Peckinpah's *The Wild Bunch* (1969), in which a relatively small number of Mexican actors managed to take on the roles of a great deal of men, *Gallipoli* uses its resources economically.

Gallipoli is Weir's favorite among his films, primarily because, as the director implies in a *Film Comment* interview, it is his "least personal" work.[27] Yet Weir's assertion that *Gallipoli* is the film that has "the least to do with me, really,"[28] seems to conflict with his statement that the film's subject has an especial significance for Australians.[29] Yet if we view Weir's former statement as a reference to the film's predominantly straightforward mode of representation, a quality in marked contrast to his work in his previous feature films,[30] we can appreciate the meaning behind Weir's remark. It would seem that in *Gallipoli* Weir intentionally played down most of his overt stylistic effects for two reasons that have nothing to do with his oft-stated desire to achieve an "invisible" style. Weir probably believed that his film, about which he obviously had very strong feelings, would reach a wider audience if it seemed more impersonal.[31] Additionally, Weir apparently felt that attention-diverting stylistics similar to the kind he had used in films such as *Picnic at Hanging Rock* and *The Last Wave* would compromise the perception of the historical significance of the film's events, especially since Gallipoli holds such an important place in Australian culture.[32] Indeed, as Weir puts it, "Gallipoli, for us, marked the birth of a nation. In fact, we celebrate it each year."[33]

To a significant extent this national holiday represents identity achieved through a repudiation of British elitism. In this respect, the function of the film's British officers has a special significance. Weir has stated,

My feeling, and the feeling of the veterans we spoke to, was very clearly not anti-British. It was anti-British *officers*. The larger issue [in the film] is not the anti-British viewpoint. . . . [T]he men [at Gallipoli] had observed this British leadership, had begun to realize that they were going to be used, and this created a developing sense of one's Australian-ness. . . .[34]

Kenneth T. Jackson contends that *Gallipoli*'s pro-Australian emphasis results in what amounts to a severe misrepresentation in one of its crucial scenes. The film makes a point of asserting that while the Anzac (Australian and New Zealand) soldiers were under threat of being fired upon, British soldiers were drinking tea on a secure beach, as though to imply that the British did not actually engage in much combat. This "fact" probably derives from Gammage, the only historian to make this assertion.[35] Jackson points out that actually, "the British suffered twice as many deaths as the Australians and New Zealanders combined."[36] A more damning condemnation of the British occurs during the scene in which a character referred to as Colonel Robinson orders the Anzac force to attack (and later, to attack again despite the fact that the first attack has been murderous) even though the shelling of the Turkish troops has ended many minutes earlier. Robinson's character is quite obviously based upon British Field Marshall Sir William Birdwood, whom both North and historian Christopher Pugsley identify as the man who ordered and sanctioned the attack on The Nek.[37]

However, according to Jackson, the man who actually ordered the assault was not British but Australian.[38] Despite the fact that the sources that Jackson cites in his article do not support his claim, it nonetheless seems that Jackson is correct.[39] Although I believe it is quite clear that Birdwood ordered the attack, it was Birdwood's brigade commander, the Australian Colonel Antill, who insisted, despite the slaughter of the first two assault groups, that, since marker flags had been seen in the enemy trench, the next wave of soldiers must attack as well.[40]

Pugsley confirms this analysis.

The Light Horse attacked in four waves. It should have been stopped after the destruction of the first wave but the Australian brigadier on Russell's Top insisted that the attack continue. . . . The attack was suicidal and should never have been ordered. Birdwood and the Australian staff of the 3rd Australian Light Horse Brigade must bear the brunt of the blame.

Pugsley also makes it clear that the British were nonetheless made to take the blame for the assault order. "It was [British Major General Sir Alexander]

Godley whom the Australians identified as the villain, and The Nek was renamed by the men, 'Godley's abbatoir.'"[41]

Even if the fictional Colonel Robinson is supposed to be Australian, one would be hard pressed to tell it from the film. The character's haughty demeanor and accent certainly make him seem British. Weir, though, contends that the character should be recognized as being Australian. "Despite his uniform being that of an Australian officer, some audience members assumed, wrongly, that he was British. Perhaps it was his English sounding accent, or simply the desire to blame someone else for the needless deaths that followed."[42]

One wonders, though, how many people could have successfully identified this character's uniform. If Jackson, a professor and chairman of the Department of History at Columbia University, thought that the character was British,[43] one probably shouldn't be surprised that viewers less familiar with the details of the Gallipoli campaign have made the same mistake. Thus, albeit unwittingly, *Gallipoli* continues a tradition of misrepresentation that favors the notion of Australian martyrdom at British hands.

Here's the crucial scene as it appears in David Williamson's screenplay. Robinson is talking to Frank, who has given Robinson a message concerning the devastations of the first assault.

> *Robinson:* Tell Major Barton that the attack must proceed.
> *Frank:* I don't think you've got the picture. They're being cut down before they get five yards.
> *Robinson:* Our marker flags have been seen in the Turkish trenches, so the attack must continue at all costs.[44]

In the way that the film places the blame for the tragedy on the British, it reflects Gammage's viewpoint. In a passage that includes the tea-drinking reference, Gammage makes it clear that for him, the pointlessness of The Nek assault represents the tragedy of the entire war in microcosm. "[The men] went bravely to a worthless end. . . . [A]ll the tragic waste of the Great War was contracted into their passing, for as they died the English troops at Suvla [a bay close by], plainly visible from The Nek, were making tea."[45]

However, the film does show that while members of the command were positioned far from the fighting, Australian officers took part in the battle. Major Barton, for example, resolves to die with his men, a decision that has an historical basis in the actions of the real Lt. Colonel A. H. White. Gammage quotes White, "who led the first line and was killed less than 10 yards from the Australian trench,"[46] as saying, "'Boys, you have ten minutes to live, and I am going to lead you.'"[47]

Weir's didactic purpose in the film is to emphasize that the Australian spirit of resistance to unjust wars, an attitude to which Frank gives voice, began during the Gallipoli campaign.

> There hasn't been much awareness of history in our country. For instance, there've been no films made in Australia about Gallipoli, no great novels, no great poems, or paintings.[48] So in the late Sixties and early Seventies, when our country was torn in half [over Australian participation in the Vietnam War], there was no recalling of the last time our country was torn in half, over the conscription issue in 1916–17.[49]

Correlating this attitude with contemporary Australian filmmaking, Weir then notes that, "the films now being made in Australia are giving Australians a view of themselves that they've never had before, a feeling of context and of special separateness."[50] Thus, *Gallipoli* becomes a political document that comments on the present, an aspect that makes sense of the use of Frank, the reluctant joiner, and Archie, the exuberant adventurer, as character types representing attitudes about what forms patriotism should take. The film's point, of course, is that Archie's enthusiasm is primarily a function of his credulity, with the resultant implication that blind allegiance to any cause, military or political, is wrong. The birth of the Australian nation, then, becomes not only the act of its declaration of independence from British influence but also a simultaneous refusal to unreflectively participate in any movement, a classic case on a national scale of repudiating one's parents as a step toward individuation.

As with Vietnam, many of the men who returned from the Gallipoli campaign became extremely introspective and sullen, refusing at first to talk about their experiences. Weir refers to the veterans to whom he spoke while preparing for the film as "a silent generation," men who told him that "they had never discussed the things they were talking to us about."[51] The experiences that these veterans shared with Weir related not only to camaraderie but to horror, to confronting (and, later, recalling) human slaughter on a monumental scale. We know how few of the men in the Gallipoli campaign survived; for those who did, the event represents a confrontation with an unpleasantness that is much more profound, because more real, than the disturbing, otherworldly confrontations in previous Weir films such as *Picnic at Hanging Rock* and *The Last Wave,* in which encounters with the dark unknown seem pale and intellectualized by comparison. Perhaps it's the realistic basis for *Gallipoli* that makes it so significant to Weir, who is here dealing with actual, not fictive or figurative, events that require a directness of presentation.

One critic refers to the film's images as having a "picture book flatness," as though this aspect might be a fault.[52] Yet this characteristic seems an asset to the film; like some of the images in *The Wild Bunch*, which exhibit a lack of depth that Peckinpah and cinematographer Lucien Ballard intentionally created in order to reproduce a quality that they had seen in the Mexican Revolution war films that they had viewed,[53] *Gallipoli* uses pictorial flatness to suggest that the events we're watching are drawn from the past, and that the full dimensionality of these events can never be completely recovered. This aspect is only one of the film's visual assets. Weir works hard to create scenes that seem expansive yet virtually empty: one thinks immediately of the wide-open feelings of the scenes at Archie's parents' ranch, the broad backdrops at the race course, the sense of vast space during the desert crossing (one of the film's most dramatic and affecting shots comes when Frank slides open the door of the stock car in which he and Archie have been riding and there is nothing to see but the sand and light of the desert), and the Australians' playing soccer near the pyramids. These scenes give way not only to the dense Egyptian market sequences but also to the crowding in the trenches (which hampers Frank's ability to return in time with the message to delay the next Anzac assault), aspects heralding the beginning of the downward spiral toward the inescapable destruction that awaits most of the Australian soldiers. This shift from the idyllic to the horrific is present as well in *Gallipoli*'s underwater swimming scene, which functions as the representation of a descent into what initially appears to be a safe region of the unconscious.[54] One day, some of the soldiers go bathing in the nude. Under the water's surface, the young men float as though in a wish fulfillment of the desire to be weightless and free, to be returned to a protective womb. Even when bullets first begin to shoot past them, the bullets seem harmless, since their velocity is considerably slowed down by the water. But, as in many dreams, an ideal state is accompanied by real-life anxieties and details: in an action that presages the slaughter at the film's end, one of the boys is wounded. The dream has vanished.[55]

At the film's end, in a strikingly conflicted iconography, when Archie begins to make his great run toward the Turkish trenches, he first passes numerous dead bodies, and then breaks free. Exhilarated and alone, he is once more, as in his barefoot race toward the film's beginning, liberated, out in the open, at no point more so than at the moment of his death, which, despite the allusion to the race-tape breaking, his arms seem to reach out for. Unfortunately, despite the film's successful aspects, Weir has not compensated for his minimized directorial presence with enough dramatic devices to engage the audience. Moreover, much of *Gallipoli* seems derived from such war films as Stanley Kubrick's

Paths of Glory (1957) and Australian director Bruce Beresford's *Breaker Morant* (1980), films that emphasize war's futility and concentrate on betrayals of soldiers by officers. The film also seems wanting in two important respects: we're given no political context within which to place the Gallipoli conflict; and the story's psychological dimension, which would have involved exploring Archie and Frank's motivations more deeply, is never developed. Although politics and psychology aren't a significant part of this intentionally restrained film, they are prominent in Weir's next production, *The Year of Living Dangerously,* in which the director not only branches out emotionally but also returns to the stylistics that are a hallmark of his cinema.

6

PUPPET SHOW

As in the most successful of Weir's films, the meanings of *The Year of Living Dangerously* lie discreetly embedded beneath the film's surface. The film distinguishes itself not only as Weir's only overtly political production aside from *Gallipoli,* but also as a drama whose symbolism, which involves shadows and vision metaphors, is inextricable from its story.

Year highlights the differences among its Indonesian, Australian, American, and British characters as well as the sexual distinctions that emanate from the tension created by having a female actress essay the part of a male. In other words, in *Year*, identities—national, political, and sexual—become blurred, an effect that seems natural in a film set in the midst of a political state on the brink of revolution, a situation that acts as a metaphor for threats against the integrity of one's existence and identity.

Although it is not presented in *Year,* some historical background on Australia's relations with Indonesia may be useful. In 1947—a year in which struggles against colonial rule were prevalent in India, Pakistan, and Vietnam[1]—Australian Minister for External Affairs H. V. Evatt expressed his opinion that Dutch rule in Indonesia was (in historian Robert Lacour-Gayet's words) "worse than the invasion of the Netherlands by Hitler in 1940. . . . [T]he right of a people to self-determination was [Evatt's] reason for supporting the Indonesians against the Dutch."[2]

This is not to say that the Australians didn't have colonial aspirations of their own. "The British government had handed over its part of [New Guinea, namely, its Eastern half] to the [Australian] Federation in 1906."[3] After the First World War broke out in 1914, Australia seized the northern portion of New Guinea, which had been ruled by Germany,[4] thereby putting "an end to

94

the sharing arrangement that she had disliked from the start."[5] Following the war, Woodrow Wilson made it clear that he considered Australian annexation of Eastern New Guinea to be "anathema."[6] However, Australia remained adamant, and in 1922, Article 22 of the League of Nations Covenant recognized the right of "mandate power[s]" to administer what it referred to as

territories . . . which, because of the sparseness of their population or their small dimensions, or because of their nearness to the mandate power, or for other reasons, may be more suitably administered if the laws of the mandate power apply to them as though they belong to that power's territory, with the condition that the safeguards for the protection of the native population be respected.[7]

As Australian prime minister William Hughes put it, the arrangement constituted "a 999-years lease in lieu of a freehold."[8] However, this agreement still left New Guinea's Western half under Dutch rule. Lacour-Gayet observes,

Once the issue of Indonesian independence had been resolved [in 1949], the government in Canberra noticed somewhat belatedly that the new Republic of Indonesia was New Guinea's next door neighbor. The Liberals took a diametrically opposite view on this question to their Labour predecessors'. The wicked Dutch, who had held on to the western end of New Guinea, overnight became the heroes of the hour. The Indonesians, of course, were determined to wrest this last bastion from them. But [Evatt] . . . objected that if the Indonesian claims were met it would only be a question of time, whatever assurances they might give, until they tried to extend their domination to the territories that the United Nations had mandated to Australia.[9]

As a result, the Australian government took the position that it supported the maintenance of Dutch rule in Western New Guinea. "The strategical [argument was] that, even in the nuclear age, New Guinea was still Australia's last line of defense; the political [argument was] that Sukarno had included Communists in his government; the humanitarian argument [was] that it would be intolerable to let the poor Papuans fall into such unworthy hands."[10] Yet by 1962, in what was clearly "nothing but a face-saving device," the Dutch and Australian governments "agreed to hand over the administration of the former Dutch colony to the United Nations."[11] (In May 1963, "the U.N. passed on to Indonesia, under the name of West Irian, the responsibility that had been entrusted to it.")[12]

Given this history, it should be apparent that *Year*'s Australian foreign correspondent, Guy Hamilton, is not in accord with the political attitude of his government regarding Indonesia. Despite his characteristic Australian antipathy toward the smug conservatism of British like the film's Colonel Henderson (a characteristic that to a degree conflicts with Guy's British upbringing), Guy is sympathetic with the struggle for Indonesian independence, and liberal in his dealings with the country's people. As we will see, Guy is as much a stranger to certain aspects of his personality as he is to some of the political attitudes of his country's government.[13]

The Year of Living Dangerously's overriding concern is with the nature of illusion and reality, especially as these concepts dovetail with two important areas in human existence: romantic love and politics. Each of these areas places a great stress on the devising of a feeling of continuity of self in the midst of instability, a continuity that may partially be achieved by relating to someone, be it a lover or a political leader, who is regarded as having a comforting stability of personality and behavior.

Also implicit in each of these areas are concerns involving the nature of commitment and the distinction between individual desires and the ethics of political responsibility. Essentially, the film inquires into how we make political and personal choices, and whether the distinction that we often posit between the political and personal realms is specious in that it denies the necessity of a reciprocity between these areas.

Observing Guy looking at the sights in a market a scant few moments after he arrives in Jakarta, Billy Kwan, Guy's guide, friend, and (eventual) photographer, says in voiceover the next day, "Most of us become children again when we enter the slums of Asia, and last night I watched you walk back into childhood with all its opposite intensities, laughter and misery, the crazy and the grim, toy town and the city of fear."

Billy means that Guy, despite his previous experience as a journalist, is untested and inexperienced like a child, and thereby unprepared for the stark contrasts that he will see between, for example, the expensive lifestyle of the British and the abject poverty of the native Indonesians. Such violent juxtapositions, coupled with Guy's own sense of cultural displacement, psychologically reorient him.

The theme of childhood also brings up ideas about childhood's elemental fears—the uncanny, the repressed, and ghosts and spirits. The childhood metaphor is invoked during the film's opening titles in the *wayang* shadow puppet play, which is being watched by a group of children. Later, Guy goes to Billy's bungalow and sees his *wayang* puppets. After Billy expresses his admiration for Indonesian President Sukarno, he remarks, "The puppet master is a priest." Of course, Billy, who manipulates the puppets and who admires the manipulative

Sukarno, functions as a puppet master himself when he engineers a meeting between Guy and Jill Bryant, a British Embassy official, and steers them into a relationship, to some extent as a way of becoming Jill's surrogate lover. (Indeed, claiming, on a pretext, that he is leaving the city for a while, Billy gives the couple his bungalow to use; unbeknownst to Guy and Jill, though, he lingers outside it when they are making love.) Yet in this complicated world of many masters, Billy is, unknowingly, having his strings pulled as well via his illusions about Sukarno, whom he fails to recognize as a typical politician who is himself manipulated by international political forces.[14]

"They call Sukarno the great puppet master," Billy explains, a man trying to "balance the left with the right." (At the time, Sukarno was in the middle of a struggle between two forces: the communist PKI party and the Muslim generals.) Yet it's Billy's commentary on the *wayang* itself, whose significance must be comprehended if one is, in Billy's words, to "understand Java," that is of the greatest significance in this scene. Billy says,

> The shadows are souls and the screen is heaven. You must watch their shadows, not the puppets, the right in constant struggle with the left, the forces of light and darkness in endless balance. In the West we want answers for everything; everything is right or wrong, good or bad. But in the *wayang* no such final conclusions exist.

For Guy, Billy's speech, whose meaning is obviously very dear to Weir's sensibility, presents him with several new ideas. Billy is obviously attempting to school Guy on the view of reality in Indonesia, which holds that much of what we perceive is illusory. Additionally, Billy is cautioning Guy to avoid being distracted by the actions of politicians and military leaders. Yet although Billy seems to be countenancing a skeptical view of events, he is also inverting the meaning of Plato's parable of the cave, advising focus on the shadows; however, he only does this because in the shadow world of Indonesian politics, shadows, against which we are cautioned in the Platonic parable, are of greater significance, and therefore of more substance, than the actions of people-as-puppets, who themselves lack significant substantiality. In this sense, even the Platonic parable is somewhat inappropriate to the situation in Indonesia, where Guy will be required to pass beyond his former, empirically based consciousness into a realm that is completely outside Western modes of thought that trust in "facts" and "things." In essence, Guy is being told to achieve awareness of himself as a shadow in a shadow play, a dreamer within a dream-like realm who must maintain a consistently inquisitive consciousness if he is to properly understand what he sees and hears.[15]

The three players in the *wayang* whom Billy mentions obviously correspond to the film's principals. Guy is Arjuna, a hero who according to Billy can be "fickle and selfish";[16] Jill is the princess Srikandi, "noble and proud but headstrong," with whom, as Billy points out, Arjuna will fall in love; Billy, whose puppet is raised up by Guy (just as later Guy will raise Billy onto his shoulders), is Semar the dwarf, who "serves the prince." What Billy does not tell Guy, though, is that the character of Arjuna, and the view of reality on which the *wayang* is partially based, to a great extent derives from the *Bhagavad Gītā,* an Indian treatise that, in its dialogues between Arjuna and the god Krishna on the nature of war and reality, bears particular relevance to the situation in Indonesia, where warriors and princes (Sukarno among them) are engaged in what appears to be a elementary struggle for control that, in contrast to the teachings of the *Bhagavad Gītā,* does not lead to understanding but only to power.[17]

In later voiceover, Billy, while typing one of his "reports" on the people whom he meets, comments on his role as manipulator, which is in stark contrast to his role in the *wayang.*

> Here on the quiet page I am master just as I'm master in the darkroom, stirring my prints in the magic developing bath. I shuffle like cards the lives I deal with; their faces stare out at me: people who will become other people, people who will become old, betray their dreams, become ghosts.

The statement contains the plot of the film. The darkroom to which Billy refers is not just a photographic darkroom but also the shadowy world of Indonesia as well as the Platonic cave, where Billy—whose illusion is that he is above all of the film's actions, and who captures so many of the film's major events on film—watches events "develop." The events that develop are those that pertain to himself (he eventually repudiates his other mode, his role as observer, and takes a political stand, thereby essentially "becom[ing] [an]other" person); to Guy, who matures (grows "old") and, in Billy's view, betrays a confidence from his dream lover; and Jill, whose indeterminate role at the British Embassy relegates her to a "ghost"-like realm.

Yet despite the Platonic view of the world as a place of duplicitous impressions, artistic representation can free us. Thus the lesson of the *wayang* that Billy eventually learns: everyone, perhaps most especially Sukarno, is a puppet; we must move beyond shadows into intuited truth, and away, especially, from the greatest arena of illusion: politics. It's through the validity of what one feels, from notions that are essentially preconscious and often (for the sake of day-to-day commerce) repressed, that one approaches authenticity. Billy states, "I don't care about photographs; I care about content. I'm not aesthetically minded,"[18] making it clear that despite his self-delusion about Sukarno, he somehow realizes that the images in the photos he takes (themselves the result of the play of light and shadow) are less important than the significant emotions ("content") to which they can give rise. As both puppet manipulator and photographer, Billy resembles a film director, not only mapping out the actions of the characters under his control, manipulating them as though they are puppets in the service of a script, but also using images to make important points about life and love. In this respect, Weir has a great emotional investment in Billy's character; like Billy, Weir becomes the eyes for a series of passive spectators (the film audience) who, like Guy, are encouraged by viewing images toward a more mature vision of reality. More canny than Billy in that he does not fall prey to the seductive aspect of illusions, Weir puts on a puppet play for us to show us how our dreams, our shadow worlds, can, through filmic shadows, enlighten us.

Guy himself is identified as something of a shadow early in the film. While walking through the market with Billy, he's insulted a number of times, called "capitalist" and "American." Billy advises Guy not to take the insults personally, telling him that he's "just a symbol of the West"—in other words, that to the Indonesians, he's just a type, nothing more than a shadow of a real person (as is Billy, who later in the film, before he enters Guy's office, is seen as a shadow on the blinds). Yet Guy is a shadow twice over, since he doesn't at this point realize that, like everyone else in the film, he is merely a player in the great puppet play. For each character, even Jill (who is possibly a spy, and who is referred to by Guy as a ghost-like "spook," a reference that inadvertently draws attention to the thinness of characterization and action afforded her),[19] substantiality is achieved not through manipulations and politics but through love, precisely the point that Weir will later make in Witness and Fearless.

Vision and eyes, elements also significantly presented in Witness, function in The Year of Living Dangerously as pathways to the inner self, to self-knowledge. Guy is allowed to pass onto the grounds of the presidential residence after a guard looks him in the eyes (as Guy's driver, Kumar, tells him, "The palace guards say they can tell an assassin by the eyes"). In the film, Billy, as he says he will, becomes Guy's eyes, not only as his cameraman but also via the manner in which he interprets the things that each of them experiences. Through his statements and acts, Billy molds the reactions of both the audience and Guy to what they see. By compelling Guy to acknowledge the significance of love and death, the prime moving principles in human existence, Billy assumes the role of the hero who reveals the truth.

At the same time, though, all three of the film's major characters also avoid to an extent the real poverty and pain of the Indonesians. Jill is right when she says of Guy's commentary on a famine in Lombok that it seems a bit exaggerated; as we hear it when Guy plays it back, its descriptions seem inappropriately lush (e.g., "I move as if in a dream through the agony that is famine"). In essence, the nature of this reportage anticipates the metaphoric significance of the injury to Guy's eye (a detached retina): it's horror seen through vision that is detached from emotional candor. The Lombok broadcast becomes the ultimate commentary on media: the broadcast's verbal images are only clichéd reflections of the real circumstances of human suffering and triumph. *Year's* emphasis on eyes naturally links up with the trade of the journalists who are, presumably, reporting what they see. Weir and co-scriptwriter David Williamson extend the notion of sight and seeing to the figurative level, where it symbolizes recognition, as in the lack of recognition of people such as Billy and Guy, who turn a blind eye to events.[20]

Most significantly, the understanding that recognition should bring is missing from certain events, predominantly in Billy's trusting in the false front projected by Sukarno, and in Guy's focusing on getting information about a PKI arms shipment, when in fact the most significant aspect of the information about the shipment, which Jill gives him, is the risk she is taking in communicating it, which she does so that, like her, Guy will have time to leave the country safely.

Despite its insistence on emotional honesty and a continuity between moral sight and self-recognition, the film also dramatizes isolation and alienation, which take shape in the form of the eyes of people in poverty, the longing for each other of lovers, aspects captured in images but only partially understood by Billy, a lonely man who yearns for a close companion ("are you the unmet friend?" he writes of Guy at the film's beginning). Despite his desire for intimacy, Billy also subverts it: his attempts to control people to whom he is attracted, such as Guy and Jill, make it clear that he can't truly be their friend if at the same time he's also trying to pull their strings.

Billy's comment after Guy tells him "you're not a dwarf" seems especially poignant and significant. "That's what I like about you, Guy, you really don't care, do you? Or maybe you just don't see," Billy says. Is Billy referring to Guy's indifference to the suffering he sees all around him or to Guy's indifference to Billy's being a dwarf? If it's the latter meaning, there's a contradiction in Billy's attitude, since he isn't above capitalizing on this condition, as when he crashes receptions from which the hosts are reluctant, because of his stature, to eject him. Yet if Guy does, as it seems, truly see beyond Billy's physical state, this

potential for emotional honesty is perhaps his saving grace, allowing him to finally realize, when his eyes are bandaged and everything for him is literally
darkness and shadows, that what he has all along taken for real—politics and
the manipulation of power—has been an illusion, and that what is most significant are friendship and love.[21] In this respect, it's interesting that when Guy is
lying on the bed, he imagines that he hears part of Billy's gloss on the *wayang*
derived from the *Bhagavad Gītā*: Krishna's statement to Arjuna on sin: "all is
clouded by desire . . . as a fire by smoke, as a mirror by dust—from these it
blinds the soul."[22] The applicability of these words to Guy's current condition
should be evident. Guy's overweening desire for self-aggrandizement as a reporter has obscured his judgment of what is really important: emotional commitment (a similar theme surfaces in *Fearless*). Billy's inadvertently prophetic
commentary makes it clear that Guy's blindness has a metaphoric aspect: it represents a blindness of the soul.

For Guy to attain self-awareness, he must, for the sake of love, perform an act
of sacrifice. As the *Gītā* notes, "This world is in bondage to *karma*, unless *karma*
is performed for the sake of sacrifice."[23] (In this context, the term *karma* is
defined as "'deed,' 'work,' [or] 'action,'" and is used in the Hindu tradition to
mean . . . any action which produces tendencies or impressions . . . in the actor,
which then function as determinants to his future action.")[24] The *Gītā* further
asserts, "some yogins . . . offer sacrifices by the sacrifice itself,"[25] a verse that *Gītā*
commentator Eliot Deutsch interprets as meaning "the offering of oneself as a
'sacrifice.'"[26] An additional commentary by Deutsch on this passage from the
Gītā shows that it is quite relevant to *Year*'s action.

> The term . . . "sacrifice," as used by the *Gītā* . . . does not suggest the giving up of
> something which is otherwise intrinsically good or desirable. . . . [I]t means
> rather the redirecting of one's being away from an involvement with the fruits of
> one's action to an eternal Spirit which is at once in and beyond the phenomenal
> world. . . . [S]acrifice means the turning away from our lower self (of desires, at-
> tachments) for the sake of our higher spiritual self. It means self-surrender for
> the sake of self-realization. It means acting in the Spirit rather than through the
> ego; hence the injunction: "Perform they action free from attachment."[27]

In essence, then, Guy is faced with the dilemma of sacrificing his job as a
reporter for the sake of the "eternal Spirit" of selfless love as represented by Jill,
who hazarded her job at the embassy by telling Guy about the PKI rebellion.
Unfortunately, Guy decides to use the information for a story. In doing so, he
incurs Jill's displeasure and Billy's condemnation. Writing in his journal, Billy
provides the audience with a fine assessment of Guy's decision, which he char-

acterizes in terms whose concern with action as opposed to emotion seems derived from the *Gītā*. "You have changed. You are capable of betrayal. You abuse your position as journalist and grow addicted to risk. You attempt to rule neat lines around yourself, making a fetish of your career and making all relationships temporary lest they disturb that career."

If we read the role of journalist/reporter as standing in for the role of film director, Weir's position becomes plain. Weir wants Guy (as he wants himself) to be emotionally committed to his work as a reflection of, not a replacement for, his emotional commitment to people and the themes in his life that he represents in his "art." In Weir's view, to do otherwise is to separate attitude from action, and thereby be unfaithful to the credo that there should be no distinction between one's life and work. Nonetheless *Year* shows us that the realms of journalism and life are incompatible: Guy must give up reporting in order to live with Jill. Once again, we see Weir trying to meld idea and action, thought and feeling, yet admitting through his films that such a melding is very difficult to achieve. Yet Weir would like to see his characters triumph over occupational and emotional adversity. He has Billy end the journal entry with two questions that focus on the concept of sacrifice for the sake of love, a concept on which, as we have seen, the *Gītā* (which Billy relies on as a basis for existence) places great emphasis. Billy writes, "Why can't you give yourself? Why can't you learn to love?"

Year scarcely shows us the other reporters at work, but we do see how two of them live, and they're a sorry duo—manipulative, selfish, and emotionally cold. In an example of apparent class bias, correspondent Wally O'Sullivan uses one of the locals as a homosexual lover. Similarly, reporter Pete Curtis "buys" a friend for Guy: a dwarf who, as Weir's cutaway shots to a pained Billy make clear, is a perverted reflection of Billy himself. In a subsequent scene, Curtis takes Guy to a cemetery so that they can pick up prostitutes, all the while emphasizing how inexpensive the women are. Despite his emotional callousness, though, Curtis is the only one of the journalists who intuits the actual relationship between Guy and Billy. "Here come Sir Guy and the black dwarf," he says at one point, correctly divining their roles in the shadow play as Billy had described them.

At one point in the film, Billy goes to a hut where a mother and child he's helping to support live. The child is malnourished and sick, thereby exemplifying the country's poverty and the failure of Sukarno's policies. The mother and child drink polluted water, which becomes a symbol of the country's political corruption and the failure of its politics, which takes no cognizance of the common people's well-being. Yet until late in the film, although commenting on death and disease, Billy retains his allegiance to Sukarno, whom he studiously avoids holding responsible for the famine and poor health conditions afflicting the Indonesians. Thus, despite the fact that he obviously has compassion for the woman and her child, Billy is still very much like the reporters: indifferently capturing images, keeping files, making notes. There's no way to explain Billy's blindness to the government's elitism; we can merely note that it's only when something touches him deeply and personally (in this case the child's death) that he protests against these policies. Although, after drawing attention to the poverty in Indonesia, Billy had quoted Tolstoy's question about poverty—"what shall we do then?"—and had subsequently remarked that the woman's deplorable situation "is repeated a million times in this city," Billy refrains until the latter part of the film from taking political action, confining his response to the individual level. "You do whatever you can about the misery that's in front of you," Billy had said. To a degree, this restricted view acts as an indictment of his character and also invites comparison between Billy and Sukarno (or, for that matter, any politician who doesn't respond to the people's needs).

Finally, though, in anger and despair, Billy hangs a banner that reads, "Sukarno, *feed* your people" out of a hotel window from which he is subsequently thrown by some of Sukarno's agents who are provoked by his protest (his death thus seems as much a suicide as a murder). Billy's death is important because it prompts Guy to act emotionally and works to bring Guy and Jill back together. And though the action that leads up to Guy's retina being detached at first seems unmotivated (on his way out of the country, Guy tries to get into the presidential palace), it still works as a final example of the film's vision metaphors and a comment on the emotional detachment that all of the major characters have exhibited. (Indeed, since the injury mandates for a time that both of Guy's eyes be covered, he essentially becomes one of the Platonic cave dwellers, unable to visually distinguish friend from foe, precisely the situation in which he finds himself throughout the majority of the film.)[28] Preparing to board a plane at the airport, he repudiates his role as uncaring reporter by leaving behind his Nagra tape recorder, which the airport security people thread up. The recorder spews out a playback of Guy's radio broadcast on the PKI arms shipment, but now the broadcast, which seems far less important than the consummation of Guy and Jill's love, is first muffled, and then (when the recorder's playback speed goes askew) sounds like gibberish. (In this sense, the film's conclusion somewhat unwisely minimizes the significance of its politics.) In the end, Guy boards a plane, into which he's welcomed by Jill, who embraces him at the beginning of a journey toward the kind of passionate enlightenment to which he'd been blindly stumbling throughout the entirety of the film. *Year*'s emotional reticence for the majority of its running time (a quality that critic Brian McFarlane contends is characteristic of Australian filmmaking)[29] functions as a reflection of its central character's fear of feelings. At *Year*'s conclusion, though, this reticence yields to a closure that emphasizes emotional demonstrativeness.

The film not only posits a continuity between seeing and feeling but also proposes emotional behavior as the standard for judging characters' actions. What eventually distinguishes Guy, Billy, and Jill from the rest of the film's characters is not just their emphasis on vision (Guy reports, Billy photographs, and Jill spies) but their ability to feel love and pain. Critics who were annoyed by *Year*'s emphasis on Guy and Jill's love affair miss its point.[30] There's nothing inherently wrong with turning what some expected would be a predominantly political film into a story about emotional commitment so long as the film remains true to the spirit of the political events that it depicts, especially in the sense that it criticizes politicians for callously ignoring the needs of their country's citizens. The view of these critics disregards the usual Weir insistence that one should attempt to achieve reciprocity between apparently discontinuous realms, such as the political and the emotional, conscious and unconscious, the white and the Aboriginal (present here in the distinction between the Western and Indonesian view of reality). As Weir notes, "to ask why deal with all of those elements [politics and romance] together [in *Year*], why not choose one of them, reveals a view of life and films that is very different from my own."[31] Indeed, if anything, it should be easier to see a connection between Guy and Jill's passion and the passionate politics in the film (since both are easily recognizable phenomena) than to appreciate the relation between the conscious and unconscious realms, which perhaps might require a more academic approach.

When we turn from a consideration of the film's story to its significance as an object that reflects Weir's customary concern with foreign cultures, we find that certain problems in attitude and conception emerge. In this book's introduction I drew attention to the racism in Australian society. As one might expect, as reflected in their filmmaking, other Western cultures have this quality too. In a perceptive article, critic John Powers takes some contemporary filmmakers (Weir among them) to task for what he sees as an unbalanced view of Third World people and politics. After correctly pointing out that many films such as Weir's *The Year of Living Dangerously*, Roger Spottiswoode's *Under Fire* (1983), and German director Volker Schlöndorff's *Circle of Deceit* (1981) seem to capi-

talize on (and thereby patronize) what to us seem the unusual qualities of
Third World milieus, Powers writes,

> We still go there [the Third World] to find the exotic—twilit mosques, fog-
> wreathed jungles, saris and ponchos and fatigues. Other things are different as
> well: Films have moved beyond the obvious stereotypes of particular races to
> imagine a stereotyped, monolithic Third World. Weir's Indonesia feels like
> Spottiswoode's Nicaragua feels like Schlöndorff's Lebanon. The generic Third
> World of the movies now resembles the alien invaders of fifties science fiction:
> The Other has the power to hurt us.[32]

Powers' point is well taken; often, the representation of Indonesia in *Year*
seems characterized by what Powers refers to as "clichéd responses."[33] Moreover, we never become familiar enough with any Indonesian character to determine Weir's real attitude toward them. Ironically, in *Year,* which is a film about
shadows, the Indonesians never achieve substantiality. Where Weir might, for
example, have explored the agony and terror that Kumar must be undergoing
after the failed PKI coup, Weir decides instead to keep the film focused exclusively on Guy's (and, by extension, Jill's) problems. For a film that espouses
sympathy for the plight of the Indonesians, this is a grievous mistake. And
though the film does feature Ibu, the woman to whom Billy Kwan gives money
and advice, her character occupies very little screen time. By contrast, in Christopher J. Koch's novel, on which the film is based, the key scene with Ibu and
the child lasts several pages, allowing for a development of the relationship between Billy and his adopted family, and thereby not only creating identification
with a poverty-stricken Indonesian but also making more credible the depth of
Billy's despair when Ibu's child dies, an act that motivates him to publicly protest Sukarno's policies.[34] (Indeed, Koch makes the connection between Billy's
relationship with Ibu and his changed attitude toward Sukarno explicit:
"[Billy] went to Pasar Beru [the bazaar neighborhood in which Ibu's hut is lo-
cated] to seek not only Ibu, but President Sukarno.").[35]

Other problems with *Year's* characterizations and plotting are highlighted by
comparing the book with the film, which Koch repudiated (he received co-
credit for the screenplay).[36] Obviously, a significant amount of the film's conception was Weir and David Williamson's, not Koch's.[37]

Koch's novel is narrated by a journalist member of the Wayang Bar circle
who is only referred to as Cookie. Although I find Cookie to be an annoying
presence, one can understand why Koch wanted a character who is essentially
outside the book's main action to narrate his story. Since the book stresses inte-

riority—emotion, conflict, and personal decisions—Koch apparently wanted to leaven its subjectivity by using a relatively objective narrator. By doing so, Koch was able to speak through his narrator, thereby including in the book relatively unobtrusive authorial commentary.

Weir takes some of Cookie's observations and uses them as the source for Billy's comments. When Billy talks about childhood's "laughter and misery," these are the words of Koch's narrator. Moreover, Weir appropriates virtually verbatim a great deal of Billy's statements in the book and uses them in his film. Unlike Koch in his novel, Weir wanted us to see *Year* as Billy's story, although one must then question not only whose story it is after Billy dies but also why the film, in contrast to the book, gives us so few insights into Billy's psychology. As with *The Mosquito Coast,* the film does not seem to reflect its narrator's idiosyncratic nature.

Moreover, what the film's Billy says often does not correspond to what we see. His comment on Jill's personality does not tally with the Jill that the film gives us. Jill hardly seems likely to become the "failed romantic" prone to "bitter"[ness]" (qualities that, if anything, seem based more on the book's Jill). Indeed, the film's Jill seems remarkably independent, self-assured, upbeat, and flirtatious.

Some of the disparity between the Jill whom the film describes in words and the Jill whom we see in action is a result of Weir's casting Sigourney Weaver in the role. For one thing, Weir obviously wanted an actress who would complement the attractiveness of Mel Gibson's Guy; he found this quality in Weaver. Yet Weaver brings other qualities to the role as well. Weaver's aura of self-assurance catalyzes her playing of Jill as an initially ironic young woman who is at first emotionally distant.

Physically, Linda Hunt's Billy is almost nothing like the book's Billy Kwan, whose features are distorted; Hunt only matches Billy in terms of size. Billy's unusual physiognomy is an integral part of his personality; despite his claims to the contrary, it accounts in large part for his bitterness, the acerbity of his wit, and his overcompensatory aggressiveness. The film's Billy should probably have conformed to the description Billy offers in the film of a dwarf whom he photographed: "A normal man, normal intelligence, capable of having normal children—but his body is a joke."

Not only does the film lack the book's tension between the normality of Billy's mind and the distortions of his body, but given Hunt's regular features, *Year* also lacks part of the justification for the violent change in Billy's behavior toward the film's end, when he turns resentful and bitter. In the film, the change seems abrupt and, even given Guy's betrayal of Jill's political confidence, excessive and unjustified, whereas in the book, one can see Billy's growing anger not only over Guy and Sukarno's compromises but also over his realization that, as Guy and Jill's affair makes plain to him, he will never live what he considers to be a normal life.[38]

Moreover, by jettisoning virtually all of the book's political background in favor of elliptical references to Sukarno and Indonesian politics, Weir makes it impossible for the audience to enter into the spirit of Billy's disappointment with Sukarno, which in the film seems exclusively based on the president's refusal to alleviate food shortages. Clearly, Sukarno's shortcomings were, as the book makes plain, far more severe than that, encompassing lavish spending on statues of himself and a relentless pursuit of numerous women. Admittedly, the audience has to bring to many Weir films a certain amount of outside data in order to fully understand them, but *Year* is unique in that to even begin to understand the significance of the film's politics beyond the most superficial level (e.g., Sukarno as a compromiser caught between the political left and right) is impossible given the information that Weir's film provides. Not only is there no sketching in of Australia's part in Indonesian politics, but even the barest political details, such as the role of the Moslem right-wing party in Indonesia, are only mentioned in passing or parenthetically (e.g., some wailing in the background of one scene; a brief shot of a mosque's domed roof in another), this despite the fact that it was the Moslem right wing that, along with the army, defeated the attempted PKI coup portrayed in the film.

Granted, as critic John Orr points out, the film does improve on the novel in certain significant ways. It omits what Orr characterizes as an "Ian Fleming sub-plot" involving a Russian spy to whom Guy is attracted, and avoids what Orr refers to as Koch's turning of political allegory into "melodrama."[39] The film also develops the vision metaphor quite successfully. Drawing attention to the way that numerous characters in the film witness Guy and Jill's developing affair, Orr sees *Year*'s use of vision as an external analogue to the interior vision stressed in Hitchcock's *Vertigo,* which also tracks a growing romantic obsession. Orr notes that "Weir's camera focuses on the outward and public manifestations of a private and secret desire."[40] Thus, "[a]s outsiders, the triangle of Billy, Guy and Jill have to keep their eyes open to know what is happening in a situation which changes from moment to moment. But they also watch each other. And the Indonesians watch them, balefully returning their gaze."[41]

Despite Orr's approval of *Year* (even of its political ellipses), I must conclude that in fashioning a new version of Koch's story, Weir has also excised a great deal of the information and action it contains that would have made plausible much of what happens in his film. No amount of cinematic shorthand compensates for this loss. In this respect, reviewers had justification when they complained that in the absence of a coherent and informed political subtext, *Year* tended to look like little more than a love story with a sketchy political backdrop.

Yet there are also benefits that derive from *Year's* focus on its romantic story line. For example, the reporting on the famine in Lombok becomes the first indication of Guy's shift in emotional emphasis, away from restraint to emotional overindulgence; despite the report's element of insincerity, its fervor mirrors the uncontrollability of his desire for Jill. When Jill enters into the spirit of her affair with Guy, she, too, experiences a blending of her emotional and political attitudes, sharing with Guy not only her emotional secrets but one of her political ones as well. Guy's detached retina at the film's end is thus apt, in that it symbolizes his previously misconstruing the intent behind Jill's political confidence by "detaching" his urge to report on the actions of the PKI from the feelings that prompted Jill's act and his love for her. What at first appears to be Guy's unmotivated desire to get into the presidential palace makes sense if we understand it as his unconscious attempt to compensate both karmically (in the sense of a "'law' of moral nature" that stresses the results of one's actions)[42] and sacrificially for making public Jill's secret about the PKI arms shipment.[43] Viewed in this way, Guy's self-willed blindness acts as a commentary on his previous inability to accept how important Jill is to him and functions as a prelude to his development of self-knowledge. Like *The Last Wave*, *The Year of Living Dangerously* tells the story of a central character who through exposure to violent and disruptive forces (the weather in *Wave*, politics in *Year*) moves from safe insularity into a confrontation with previously unknown powers that cause him to see beyond surfaces and into the buried, often repressed essence of himself and events.[44]

Put simply, *Year* views politics as human relationships writ large. The increase in passion between Guy and Jill becomes a corollary for the buildup of fervent resistance to the Sukarno regime by the PKI; and when Guy and Jill's relationship seems to come to full flower, so too does the political situation whose development it parallels. The death of the revolution, which testifies to the failure of compassion to predominate in the amoral world of politics, comes at the same time that the last vestige of emotional restraint between Guy and Jill falls away and their relationship graduates from sexual passion to profound love, to a direct expression of dependence mixed with desire, a movement toward candor reflected in the unmasking of Guy's driver, Kumar, and his sister Tiger Lily as PKI officials.

It's interesting to note that this unmasking, like many similar revelations in Weir's films, is presaged by a series of powerful dream images. One afternoon, Kumar, Tiger Lily, and Guy stop over at an abandoned Dutch villa whose pool, symbolizing ruined colonialism, is layered over with dead leaves.[45] Later that day, during a nap, Guy dreams that he is swimming underwater with Tiger Lily. In the dream, which has more than a bit of sublimated sexuality in it[46] (whereas earlier in the day Tiger Lily has been wearing a black swimsuit, in the dream her suit is a sexually [and, perhaps, politically] suggestive red), Guy attempts to reach the surface; Tiger Lily, though, holds him under. The dream hints at Tiger Lily's deadly potential and suggests her political affiliation, as well as makes it clear to Guy that by being in Indonesia and presumptuously trying to comment on what is going on there, he is not only swimming in unfamiliar waters but has, like *The Last Wave*'s David, descended into subconscious depths of passion and mystery without understanding them. That this descent (which keeps Guy below the level of a conscious awareness of meaning) is represented as murky and enigmatic, associated with water and sexuality, and strongly linked with the presence of a dark "other," pinpoints the connection between the psychological approach of *Year* (which is extended into the realm of politics) and *Last Wave*. After Guy awakens in a cold sweat, dresses, and goes out onto the villa's veranda, he tells Kumar with certainty that he knows he is a member of the PKI. Once again in a Weir film, the material and dream realms act reciprocally. For Guy, the dream has spoken.

In *The Year of Living Dangerously,* Weir has moved from the internal, psychological exoticism of films such as *Picnic at Hanging Rock* and *The Last Wave* to an external exoticism, the landscapes of Indonesia and its political scene, whose respective wondrousness and indeterminacy mirror the philosophical dilemma that his protagonists are facing. The betrayals that the film dramatizes at its end—some reprehensible (Sukarno betrays the populist spirit of the revolution that brought him to power), some unfortunate (Billy feels betrayed by Sukarno)—are balanced by a betrayal that has liberating effects. Jill betrays her embassy trust by telling Guy about the PKI arms shipment, an act that leads Guy to eventually decide that he's made a serious emotional mistake, that he *has* betrayed her trust, a betrayal that he decides to pay for with one of his eyes.

This exaggerated act may be emotionally satisfying only if we overlook its implausibility. Surely Guy's sincerely apologizing to Jill would have been helpful, if not sufficient. And what of Billy's story, and Billy's political transformation?

Why doesn't his death suggest to Guy and Jill that all along they've been using the Indonesians for personal gain, patronizing them for the sake of their careers? After Billy's death the film's political subtext, which was never adequately developed, should have been reinvoked. Instead, *Year* wildly veers away from it, preferring at its end to represent itself as little more than a love story.

One can only surmise that in his desire to immerse himself in the film's emotional content, Weir lost sight of its politics, privileging feelings and disparaging ideas, this despite the fact that there is obviously plenty of emotional potential in *Year*'s political story. This fascinating (and at times frustrating) split in Weir's sensibility will characterize the rest of his films as well.

7

THE EYES OF A CHILD

Witness is about the conflict between feeling and thinking. The love that a Philadelphia policeman, John Book, has for an Amish woman, Rachel Lapp, conflicts with the notion they both have that they can never bridge the gap between their cultures.

In this film, his first American production, Weir chose a story that at first glance seems a radical departure from his previous work. *Witness* is deeply religious and blatantly emotional. Weir had alluded to religion in previous films, but he had never directly portrayed it. Nor had he ever dealt forthrightly with a romantic relationship. Although *The Year of Living Dangerously* featured a love relationship, it tended to treat the relationship rather coolly. Guy and Jill's love affair was chronicled but not romanticized. As for *Year's* love scenes, they were tasteful to the point of curiosity: there was no nudity (save a very brief, unrevealing shot of Sigourney Weaver's bare back) and virtually no embracing. By contrast, *Witness* spends a significant amount of time chronicling the growing sexual attraction between its two central characters. Moreover, the film contains the only instance in Weir's work of frontal nudity.[1] Even if this aspect was included as a marketing ploy, it still represents a radical departure that the director could have resisted. And though *Witness* refrains from showing us Book and Rachel having sex, this aspect can be understood as reflecting both Weir's usual reluctance to be too graphic and the film's desire to leave essential aspects of Book and Rachel's relationship unresolved.

The sexual restraint in Weir's films can almost be read as a form of intellectual embarrassment. Weir has always seemed far more comfortable with abstractions than physicality. In *Witness,* though, he comes as close as I think he ever will to letting himself go emotionally. Like John Book, he seems entranced by the Amish way of life and is almost completely caught up in its sensuous innocence.

A great deal of the film's appeal has to do with the work of cinematographer John Seale, who had never before been director of photography on a Weir film (Seale had been camera operator on *Picnic at Hanging Rock* and *The Last Wave*).[2] We must attribute to Seale the fact that unlike any other Weir film, *Witness* contains notable examples of symbolic framing and camera movement, qualities that not only enhance but at times actually carry the film's meanings.[3]

Another advantage of the film is its well-balanced script, which juxtaposes the Amish with Book, who represents the law. In one sense, Book's morality makes him seem like a symbol of idealized justice. However, although his last name suggests holy scripture, Book's work with secular law contrasts with the higher law, that of the Bible, with which the film's Amish are associated, thereby creating a gulf between Book and the Amish that appears to be unbridgeable. Even the film's title brings up the tension between the secular and religious realms, since witnessing may refer not only to Rachel's son Samuel's watching a murder take place but also to the testimony of someone speaking about his or her devotion to Jesus.

As I noted in this book's introduction, McFarlane and Mayer consider Weir's American films to be superior to his Australian ones by virtue of their melodramatic emphasis. McFarlane and Mayer also point out that *Witness* is far more traditionally crafted than Weir's earlier work. Yet the film's revenge story subplot, as well as the elements involved in bringing its rogue cops to justice, is far less satisfying than the action that deals with Book, Rachel, and the problems arising from their growing affection for each other.

There's a passion at various points in the film that outstrips anything else that Weir has previously done. The barn-raising scene, for example, is very moving. In later films, Weir will achieve similar peaks: at the end of *Dead Poets Society,* when the boys stand in tribute to Keating while the music swells; at the conclusion of *Fearless,* when Max, in tears, feels that he has returned from the dead. In each instance, the scenes invoke powerful feelings, and are accompanied by extremely stirring music. At these points Weir truly seems to have achieved what he says he desires: a movement beyond the distinction between art and craft into a region in which the two have blended, where nothing else matters except the exhilaration that we feel, where emotional coolness has been vanquished by lyricism.[4] These are great moments; they're what we go to movies for.

The notion of being an integral part of one's world is present from the film's beginning. Weir opens the film with a shot of wheat blowing in a field, thereby establishing for us a natural rhythm, which is present in the wind gently playing over the stalks. This rhythm is then identified with the people whom we next see: a group of Amish who are walking through the wheat, which reaches their waists. The image makes it seem that these people, like the wheat, are growing up out of the land. Eventually, Weir uses a head-on shot of the wheat, out of which the Amish, walking up a slope and toward the camera, slowly rise like grain sprouting out of the earth, a shot that suggests a form of rebirth.

The close relation between the earth and the Amish is depicted again in the wooden toy that Daniel, Rachel's friend and suitor, gives to Samuel before the boy and his mother board a train to the city. The toy, which depicts a cow standing in some green grass, concretizes the relation between the Amish and nature: like the Amish, the cow, although visually separable from the land (the cow is white; the grass, green), is ontologically continuous with it, since the toy is made of one piece of wood.

After the funeral of Rachel's husband, we see her in the house of her father-in-law, Eli Lapp, surrounded by a group of women; again, the imagery reinforces the notion of community and also introduces a new notion, one of separation and protection from outsiders. Here, as Daniel, who is obviously attracted to Rachel, approaches Rachel to pay his respects, we see that Rachel is seated within a semicircle of Amish women, whose physical placement at once folds her into the community of Amish as well as keeps her protected within a virtual circle of women, thereby safeguarding her from the intrusions of men.

The action that propels the film forward is Rachel's planned visit to Baltimore with Samuel. At the local train station, Daniel tells the boy, "so, first time to the big city. You'll see so many things." The irony, of course, is that one of the first things that Samuel sees in the city is a murder. Equally important, though, is that the statement is the film's first reference to the notion of sight, which is integral to its symbolic action.

The fact that Weir was called upon to direct the film is the initial example of unsullied vision being invoked. Producer Edward Feldman chose Weir for the film because he felt that Weir, as a cultural outsider, would give the project a new perspective on aspects of American culture such as pastoralism (represented by the Amish) and urban corruption that Americans, acculturated to these qualities, may tend to take for granted. As critic Richard Combs noted in his review of *Witness*, "Perhaps [what Weir brings to the film is] a 'muting' of genre, a simplifying and downplaying of human, action, and mythological elements so that the film emerges, even in its non-Amish sequences, as somehow old-fashioned and innocent."[5]

It's clear, for example, that it takes more than a bit of visual audacity to overtly romanticize the Amish by positing them as such a natural part of the earth; moreover, *Witness's* earth is depicted not as a wasteland but as a source of spiritual fertility and natural continuity. In this sense, Weir's attitude aligns him most strongly with the Amish (Samuel in particular), whose simple lives presumably keep them in tune with the rhythms of nature. At the same time, though, the Amish's strict rules of behavior also rein in many natural human desires. Thus, as in the shot of the Amish women huddled around Rachel, the restrictions on the Amish's sexual longings (especially its women's) are held in check by the community. Eli's later statement that by dancing with Book, Rachel "shame[s] herself" expresses his concern over her apparent abandonment of Amish modesty, just as Book's carelessness in allowing Samuel to handle his gun demonstrates his own blindness to an aspect of Amish life. Yet in a way, through these culturally offensive actions, Rachel and Book are signaling their potential for the physical and emotional bonding toward which they are moving. It is precisely in the blending of their visions of what is acceptable, in this case the acknowledgment of a love that must be affirmed (if not acted upon), that these two characters implicitly invoke the aspect of acceptance and recognition that the metaphor of sight implies.

Primarily, *Witness* deals with two kinds of sight, one literal (which corresponds to the secular realm), one figurative (corresponding to the religious realm). The meaning of literal sight is apparent enough, since it refers to things visually perceived, whether they be Samuel's view of a murder, Book's staring at Rachel (and vice versa), the looks that the jealous Daniel gives Book, and so on. But more important, especially given the film's emphasis on things spiritual, is the inner sight that affords access to the ethical sensibility that characterizes the Amish's actions and Book's integrity. Of course, given the violence to which Book resorts as a policeman, it is suggested in the film that his vision, his judgment, despite its efficacy within the corrupt milieu in which he lives, has perhaps become clouded and faulty. Although it is never made explicit in the film, it is implied that Book gains an important perspective on his former behavior as a result of his stay at the Lapp farm.

Many of the things that Samuel sees on his way to the city and in the train station are new to him, and we tend to see them as he does, through the uncritical eyes of a child. Looking out of the train window, Samuel first sees Daniel in a buggy pacing the train, then a hot-air balloon, to which he waves. During a layover at the Philadelphia train station, he sees a young girl staring at him, and is then intrigued by the sight of a water fountain, which he uses after puzzling over how it works. But innocent sight can lead to problems as well, as when Samuel sees and walks up to a man dressed in what appears to be Amish garb, but who turns out to be an Orthodox Jew. Thus, even untainted vision must be leavened by mature, sophisticated evaluation if one is to avoid embarrassment or trouble. The necessity of this latter aspect is soon demonstrated when Samuel sees two miscreant policemen, McFee and Fergie, murder an under-cover policeman in the station bathroom (the policeman is investigating a drug deal in which these two cops and their superior are involved). After the mur-der, when McFee checks the stalls (in one of which Samuel is hiding), the boy eludes detection by first locking the stall and then scurrying over to one that McFee had just checked, thus using cunning deception, a behavior to which he had never before had recourse, to save himself.

While hiding in the stall, Samuel stands with arms outstretched, braced against the walls in a sacrificial pose; the boy's posture makes significant the other physical postures previously seen in the film, which now, in another col-lapsing of the secular and religious realms, assume a religious significance. When Samuel and Rachel were looking out of the train window, Samuel was at Rachel's side, lower than she, as though his mother were protecting him, an iconography that recalls the way that the Amish women earlier enfolded Rachel. Additionally, Samuel's looking through the train window establishes a link with later views of various characters as they are framed in doorways and windows that assume the dual role of portals leading outward as well as barri-ers hemming people in, an ambiguity that invites comparison with the situa-tion between Book and Rachel, who are attracted to each other but are kept apart by the distance between their two worlds, which is measured in terms of the difference between the secular and religious realms.

In the train station before the murder, Samuel becomes fascinated with a statue, resembling a pietà, of a guardian angel holding up a dead Jesus. The statue, which looms high above the boy, is initially seen from Samuel's view-point, so that, like Samuel's religious upbringing, it seems to have a powerful influence over him. Samuel is then seen from a vantage point over the angel's left shoulder, at once emphasizing his vulnerability as well enclosing him pro-tectively within a half-circle. After the murder (which Samuel views through a portal-like crack in the stall door), Rachel holds Samuel, her arms around him in a pose similar to that between Jesus and the angel, an identification empha-sized by the boy's sacrificial status and the halo-like bonnet that his mother wears, whose points seem like rays. At this shot's beginning, though, we can-not see Samuel and Rachel; our vision of them is blocked by a policeman

whose back is to the camera, indicating the manner in which the two characters' lives will be obscured by the police events that will darkly overshadow
them, and suggesting as well via the policeman's handcuffs how strongly
Rachel and Samuel will become linked to the violence with which the police
are associated.

Before Book enters the scene (which he does through another portal, a
door), he is first glimpsed as a shadow cast on a door's opaque glass, an ominous, death-like image that associates him with the shadow that McFee, looking for Book, will later cast on the opaque window of Book's sister's garage
door. Book is characterized as an ethical policeman, a man whose scruples
even extend to others' lives. (After he criticizes his sister for having a man stay
overnight at her house while her children are there, she tells him to "keep
your holier-than-thou mouth shut.") Yet as Rachel perceives, Book is somewhat insincere when he says that he regrets inconveniencing Samuel and
Rachel. "Sam'll probably have to come back and testify," Book tells Rachel.
"I'm sorry." Rachel candidly replies, "No you're not; you're glad, because now
you have a witness." And though Rachel is, perhaps unintentionally, misunderstanding Book here, taking his statement as a literalism instead of a socially
acceptable but rather meaningless assertion, she's also making it clear that
forthrightness is a quality that she and her people value over everything, and
that Book, mired in a corrupt culture, has lost the verbal directness that might
further distinguish him from his peers.

When he sees McFee's picture in a glass case at the police station, Samuel
reacts with wild-eyed surprise. The reciprocity of glances in this scene anticipates later scenes, also emphasizing sight, that involve meaningful glances between Book and Rachel, which (as with Samuel's glances) carry messages of
discovery. In the present scene, Samuel looks at McFee's photo; the camera,
adopting the boy's psychological point of view, slowly zooms in on the photo.
Samuel then looks back at Book, who is busy on the phone, gazes once again at
the photo, and then, not knowing where to turn, looks in the opposite direction, up at two policemen who seem to loom over him. Samuel then looks back
at Book, who finally sees the boy watching him. The high tension of this moment, in which every look seems significant, is underscored by Weir's gradually
switching to slow motion. Book, seeing Samuel, slowly gets up from his desk
and walks toward him. Reaching Samuel, Book crouches down as the boy
points to McFee's photo. Without words passing between them, Book slowly
covers Samuel's small hand with his in a gesture of concealment (thus encouraging silence as well as establishing a secret covenant between them), nods that
he understands, and then, like Rachel in the train station, protectively puts his

arm around the boy, at once shielding him from the outside and, in contrast to the gesture's use by the Amish characters, enclosing him in a half-circle of deceit. Thus, Book not only assumes the role of a parent figure and protector but also introduces into Samuel's world a further awareness of the necessity of dissimulation.

Protective imagery recurs after Book has been shot by McFee and is recuperating at the farmhouse. Again, Weir relies on purely visual information to communicate dramatic meanings. Rachel is sitting with her back to a wall, watching Book. At one point, she looks at him, and Book closes his eyes, as he doesn't want to have to speak to her. Later when Rachel, still on her vigil, is asleep, Book looks at her. Weir sets up this shot so that a lit oil lamp is behind Rachel, making it appear from Book's point of view as though she has an aura around her torso. But the lamp behind her also casts a golden glow on the wall that rings her head like a halo, a visual motif that Weir will repeatedly employ to remind us of Rachel's beatific nature.[6]

As a Jesus figure pierced in the side (Book has been shot by McFee), Book during his recovery from his gunshot wound falls into a period of hellish torment during which he confronts the demons who inhabit his nightmares (he screams out, presumably to McFee, "I'll fucking kill you"). In these scenes, during which Rachel assumes the role of a guardian angel supporting a wounded victim, she compassionately takes care of Book, at one point tenderly holding his hand while he grimaces in pain. Yet Book also serves as a guardian angel. In the Philadelphia train station, when Samuel first sees Book, the boy is framed over Book's left shoulder just as he was seen over the left shoulder of the angel in the statue. The implicit comparison between Book and an angel establishes a link among Book, Samuel, and Rachel that visually brings them together into something like a family unit.

Vision as a determining factor in decisions involving morality (a quality present in *The Year of Living Dangerously*) resurfaces in a discussion between Eli and Samuel that takes place as they sit at a table on which lies Book's gun, which Rachel abhors (she handles it gingerly, by the barrel, as though it were unclean). Eli is telling Samuel about people who have asked the Amish to serve in the military, justifying the request by telling them, "you must fight, you must kill; it's the only way to preserve the good." But, Eli says, "there's never only one way." When Eli asks Samuel whether he would ever kill someone, the boy replies, "I would only kill a bad man." Eli wants to know how Samuel would determine who was bad. "And you know this bad man by sight? You are able to look into their hearts and see this badness?" Samuel replies, "I can see what they do; I have seen it." Eli's answer makes it plain that he cannot counter Samuel's argument. Indeed, Eli's response sidesteps the entire issue, recommending distance and, essentially, denial as a way of dealing with evil. "And having seen, you become one of them. What you take into your hands you take into your heart. Therefore come out from among them and be separate, saith the Lord, and touch not the unclean thing," at which point Eli looks at Book's gun.

Samuel is now (as Book and Rachel will be later) caught between two worlds. This fact is made clear in his discussion with Eli. Eli advocates distance from the world of violence, a stance that in one respect is no longer available to Samuel, who has recently witnessed a murder. As noted, Eli talks about the inevitability of "tak[ing] into your heart what you take into your hands."[7] Samuel *has* taken into himself what he has seen: the murder, an event in which he took no part, has become part of him. In essence, the boy has experienced a nightmare, a terrible dream of violent death. Returning from the murder scene like a hero back from a recent night journey, Samuel must now learn how to integrate this new experience into his attitude toward life. The way that he does so is by blending Eli and Book's views on violence: Samuel neither withdraws from the deadly confrontation at the film's end nor actively participates in it. Instead, rather than getting Book's gun and using it, as an earlier version of the script would have had him do,[8] he rings the farm's bell, thereby acknowledging that violence must, somehow, be dealt with (thus the boy's statement that, if necessary, he would "kill a bad man").

For all of his trying to fit in, Book is still an outsider on the farm, an aspect evident in the scene in which Daniel comes courting. As Daniel and Rachel sit on the porch swing, Book is seen lurking in the background. Shooting from behind Daniel and Rachel, the camera frames Book in the crook of Daniel's left arm, which he has placed around Rachel and which, like the semicircle of comforting Amish women around Rachel, acts as a protective arc reinforcing the enclosed culture of the Amish and keeping out the stranger, as well as transforming Daniel into an ironic version of a guardian angel, but here a jealous one. However, with just the slightest turn of her head toward Daniel, during which she does not look particularly pleased, Rachel makes it plain that she doesn't welcome Daniel's protective, territorial gesture, as well as signals to Book by this refusal that she prefers his attentions to Daniel's. To make her preference more concrete, in the next scene, Rachel visits Book in the barn, where he is working on restoring the bird house that he knocked down when he passed out at the wheel of his car. Rachel's bringing lemonade to Book (she had also offered some to Daniel), and the playful verbal sparring about Book's "whacking" people, lay the foundation for Rachel and Book's courtship dance to the song "Wonderful World."

Critic Robert Hostetter has objected that throughout most of the film, Rachel's behavior toward Book is antithetical to the way in which an Amish woman would act, that she is too seductive, too forward.[9] (This is precisely Eli's point when he speaks to Rachel after she dances with Book; as he says, "it does not look [right].") Yet there is good reason for Rachel's uncharacteristic behavior, as there is for Book's unusual emotional demonstrativeness: both Rachel and Book have for a time passed into a dream-like, abstracted region, one that occupies a conceptual position midway between the world of the Lancaster Amish and Philadelphia's "English" society, and which is made possible by Rachel and Book's suppressing their awareness that a union between them could actually work out ("what a wonderful world this would be"). Rachel prepares us for this passage into a non-Amish way of life when she argues for keeping the injured Book at the farm, which places the whole community in danger and compels a form of subterfuge that is similar to Samuel's protective behavior in the train station bathroom.

During Book and Rachel's dance, not only is a liberation from the exclusive aspect of their respective cultures temporarily achieved, but intimate physical contact between the couple actually occurs. By singing some of the song's lyrics, Book even goes so far as to declare his love for Rachel. "But I do know that I love you," he sings along. The scene is the most emotionally satisfying that Weir has ever created.

At two points during the dance, it appears as though Book is about to kiss Rachel, but the impulse is subverted by Book's actions, which are delightfully interpreted by Harrison Ford. Book looks at Rachel seriously, moves toward her and then, leaning just slightly to his left, swings her away as they continue the dance, making the avoidance a playful, almost shy, schoolboy move rather than a serious denial (in contrast to his repudiation of Rachel's "offer" to make love in a subsequent scene). Yet the action does have profound meaning, representing as it does Book's implicit realization that he cannot join with Rachel, that the world he comes from is a place apart from hers, thus reorienting him with the police.

This reorientation is affirmed in the next scene, in which Book's corrupt superior, Schaeffer (who is part of the drug deal with McFee and Fergie), insidiously questions Book's partner, Sergeant Carter, about Book's whereabouts. At first, getting no reply, Schaeffer compares the police to the Amish, invoking a false similarity for the sake of his duplicitous argument. "We're like the Amish;

we're a cult, too—a club, with our own rules. John has broken those rules, as you're breaking them now." The rules that Schaeffer is talking about, though, are those associated with collusive lying to protect a group of crooked police; Schaeffer ignores the fact that there's a more important set of rules, those of a higher morality, that transcends the ones he's referring to. This corruption of the idea of loyalty to one's group casts an uneasy pall over the film's proceedings. Indeed, from this point on in the film, positive actions almost always are followed by ominous ones, heralding the ultimate deadly reckoning toward which Book is moving.

After sitting outside on the swing during an incipient lightning storm, Book walks into the house and sees Rachel, who is nude from the waist up, bathing. Rachel realizes that she is being watched and turns toward Book, inviting his attention. Book, though, in a denial that takes the form of avoided glances, can only look down in embarrassment, a gesture with a significance that he explains the next morning: "If we had made love last night, I'd have to stay—or you'd have to leave" (a contention with which Rachel does not agree). Seeing Book look down, Rachel turns her back on him, acknowledging his rejection through her gesture (a movement that will be repeated at the film's end, before they part). The scene's action is rounded out with the next shot, which shows Book in his room, head down, brooding, an image that Weir slowly dissolves onto a shot of the barn, so that for a period of a few seconds, we see a seemingly gigantic Book ominously looming over the Lapp farm, a visual representation of Eli's contention that Book has brought negative forces to the place.

The depressing quality of this brooding aspect seems even more pronounced if we stop at this point to consider how significantly linked in the film apparently disparate forces really are. Writing about *Witness,* critic Robert Winer asserts that Book "takes Samuel into the Philadelphia underworld."[10] Although this statement is true with regard to Samuel's initiation into dark things (the boy is clearly another of Weir's night journey heroes), Winer is somewhat incorrect, since Samuel enters the Philadelphia underworld before Book's first appearance when he sees the undercover policeman's murder. Having witnessed the murder, Samuel (as will his mother later) passes into a realm in which he becomes trapped between two worlds: Lancaster and Philadelphia, which represent the polarities of innocence and experience, ignorance and knowledge, in this case, knowledge of evil.

Winer points out, "Witnessing implies awe, a stance separate from the happening. When we apply the term 'witnessing' to primal scene experience, we are attempting to emphasize the role of the child as a passive, victimized observer."[11] In Freudian psychology, no scene is more primal than viewing one's parents engaged in sex; in *Witness*, the primal scene involves a murder. Are the two situations that different? The link between sex and death, the (implied) creation of life and its destruction, is essential in literature (one thinks of the procreative/degenerative round alluded to in Yeats's "Sailing to Byzantium:" "whatever is begotten, born and dies"). The murder scene that Samuel witnesses not only gives birth to a new consciousness in the boy (an awareness of violent death) but also involves another element of the primal scene: voyeurism. While Samuel watches the murder, the act's perpetrators don't know he's there. Similarly, Samuel's voyeuristic presence is implied during the scenes at the Lapp farm where Book and Rachel are falling in love, a situation that the boy undoubtedly observes, albeit passively.[12]

In the developing relationship between Book and Rachel, Samuel is nevertheless in one respect an active presence: given the fact that Rachel has a child, Book and Rachel's attraction necessarily involves the notion of building a family. Book certainly acknowledges his fatherly role when he gently reprimands Samuel about handling his gun; and the toy that he gives Samuel testifies to his affection for the boy. As a consequence, when Book leaves the farm, he does more than merely part from Rachel; he also causes Samuel to lose another father figure.[13]

Voyeurism is invoked most powerfully at the beginning of the scene in which Book watches Rachel bathing. Yet here, the voyeur's protective barrier, his invisibility, eventually vanishes: the watcher's presence is discovered (indeed, it's clear that Book wants to be seen). The corollary to witnessing that Winer asserts in his essay does not occur in this scene: here, witnessing does not lead to bearing witness, acting in response to seeing. As Book points out to Rachel the next morning, the ethical thing for him to have done was not to act. In this respect, Book's refraining from acting becomes an example of his affinity with the Amish sensibility. As in the town, when roughs threaten the Amish and Eli tells Book to "do nothing," so in the bathing scene, the right thing to do is to turn away, which Book essentially does by gazing downwards, the aversion of eyes an indication not just of refusal of Rachel's invitation to make love to her but, more importantly, of shame. Seeing, therefore, Book judges himself, and, having judged himself wrong, withdraws from the scene.

The downward spiral toward negative events that, after the peaceful interlude at the farm, began with the spurning of Rachel's love continues on the day following her bath. Book, calling the police station from town, learns of Carter's death and, morose over the event, decides to reveal his whereabouts by stepping out of his assumed Amish anonymity and physically retaliating against some youths who are teasing Daniel and the other Amish. After Book's attack on one of the boys, we see a local police car rounding the corner, after which a town resident tells the police about the strange Amish assault. Book has apparently achieved his purpose: the police will report the incident of a rogue Amish, and the information will get back to Schaeffer.

Immediately after the scene in which Rachel runs out to the field to embrace Book, whom she knows is leaving, Fergie, McFee, and Schaeffer arrive at the farm, their car stealthily creeping over a rise[14] in a perverse repetition of the way in which the Amish had seemed to rise out of the field at the film's beginning. When they get out of the car and arm themselves, the men line up as though heading toward a Western shoot-out and begin a slow walk to the farm. The placement of characters and weaponry in this shot (the men arranged in a straight line, the shotguns cradled in the arms of McFee and Fergie, who bracket Schaeffer) seems to allude not only to Fred Zinneman's *High Noon* (1952) but, more specifically, to the march of the remaining gang members through the streets of Agua Verde toward the end of Sam Peckinpah's *The Wild Bunch*.[15] At Eli's prompting, Samuel rings the farm's bell, thereby not only summoning the neighboring Amish but also, to recall Winer's terminology, turning from witnessing to bearing witness. The Amish community appears after Book has dispatched Fergie and McFee. Although the neighbors do nothing more than watch the conflict between Schaeffer and Book, their passive act of watching has an active effect. As Book points out, with so many witnesses around, Schaeffer can't get away with murder; he can't kill them all. Merely by virtue of their numbers, then, the Amish have strength (a notion already demonstrated during the barn-raising scene). The mere act of watching is thus more powerful than Winer imagines it to be. Schaeffer, virtually enclosed within a semicircle of Amish onlookers, is defeated and sinks penitentially to his knees.

In the final sequence, Rachel and Book, both seen in point-of-view shots, take their goodbyes. Rachel stands in the farmhouse doorway, framed in a soft golden light; Book stands just outside the doorway, the road that is to take him away forever winding out behind him. Like other important scenes in *Witness* (the film's opening, the undercover cop's murder, the barn raising, during the latter of which Maurice Jarre's music begins with a passage that echoes the beginning of the Pachelbel Canon), this one is without dialogue. When Rachel admits to herself that Book must indeed leave for good, she half turns away from him, as does Book from her. Rachel then smiles slightly and turns further to leave; Book does the same. Seemingly accepting his departure, she fully turns back to him, but Book is already walking away from Rachel, his back toward her. Eli's admonition to Book—"You be careful out among them, English"—indicates by the use of the word "them" that Book is no longer a part of the world that he left behind when he came to the farm; both he and Rachel have been changed forever by their encounter, neither no longer capable of being completely part of either of their cultures, trapped by indecision and love in some nether region between them. United in spirit but separate in body, they return to their respective worlds, both of them now strangers in familiar territory.[16]

8

MYOPIC VISIONARY

The Mosquito Coast is an interesting and challenging film, not the least of whose difficulties is the personality of its central character, Allie Fox, who is both an attractive figure—a dreamer who attempts to make his dreams come true—as well as a reprehensible individual who takes his family on a terrible journey into a living hell. To an extent, one's response to Allie is determined by the viewer's feelings about progress and industrialization, which are a product of historical perspectives arising out of the myth of the virgin land, especially as such a myth applies to people in the United States.

The reaction to progress in America has shifted radically since the late eighteenth century. Industrialization, now viewed with a certain degree of skepticism and trepidation, was initially regarded as a boon, a technological aid to make life simpler and easier and relieve human beings of the burden of work that, in the mythological view, was foisted upon them as a result of expulsion from the Garden of Eden. It is only one of the many small ironies realized in tracing attitudes toward industrialization that the loss of Eden should eventually result in the creation of machines, Blakean "dark satanic mills" that would at first be looked upon as a blessing and subsequently as a curse, in that their use would result in many people losing their jobs to so-called progress.

Displeasure with mechanization, which occurred simultaneously with the onward push of civilization, the disappearance of the American frontier, and the attendant exploitation of the wilderness caused many people to become alienated from technology even if they had been intimately involved in its creation and employment, precisely the psychology that Allie Fox personifies. At once adventurer and inventor, Allie at first appears in the guise of a pioneer in search of unsullied territory to begin a new life. In this respect, he resembles an individual in the nineteenth-century America described by Frederick Jackson

Turner in his essay "The Significance of the Frontier in American History."[1] Turner's thesis is that Americans regard the frontier as an undeveloped region that promises a new life; thus, the frontier exists as both reality and idea. (Applying this notion to *The Mosquito Coast*, we can see that Allie's idea of Mosquitia—a semi-ficticious Central American country—is at variance with its reality.) As Turner recognized, the frontier's attraction was involved with an essentially subconscious realm in which redemption was a prime factor. Going to a new land meant starting life over.

Turner defined the frontier as "the outer edge of the wave—the meeting point between savagery and civilization."[2] Unlike European frontiers, which Turner referred to as "fortified boundary line[s] running through dense populations"[3] (a distinction that may have had significance for Weir, who is heir to a European intellectual tradition),[4] the American frontier, in Turner's words, lay "at the hither edge of free land,"[5] a notion that seems to capture the essence of Allie's attitude toward Mosquitia.

According to Turner, the attraction of the frontier lay in its promise of a personal renascence.

> American development has exhibited not merely advance along a single line, but a return to primitive conditions on a continually advancing frontier line, and a new development for that area. American social development has been continually beginning over again on the frontier. This perennial rebirth, this fluidity of American life, this expansion westward with its new opportunities, its continuous touch with the simplicity of primitive society, furnish [sic] the forces dominating American character.[6]

Apparently, Allie sees himself as a man who wants to return to the spirit of freedom and adventure that he feels is now lacking in the United States; he also seeks to escape from the oppressiveness of the contemporary American political system. In these respects, too, Turner's description of the frontier's attractiveness is relevant to Allie's frame of mind. "As has been indicated, the frontier is productive of individualism. Complex society is precipitated by the wilderness into a kind of primitive organization based on the family. The tendency is anti-social. It produces antipathy to control, and particularly to any direct control."[7]

Sick of the debilitating influences of foreign-made goods and disposable commodities that he feels are ruining the country, Allie decides, in the spirit of a major American primitivist, Huck Finn, to "light out for the territory." However, it's unlikely that Allie will find the contentment that he desires precisely because he has a built-in dissatisfaction, not only with the external world but with himself. Yet this dissatisfaction is also functional: it's the source of the nervous energy that drives him forward.

Allie claims that he wants to leave America because, as with his ailing mother, he doesn't want to see someone whom he loves suffer and die. He claims to love America, yet we see none of this affection in the film, just disgust and complaints. Moreover, unlike some of the pioneers, Allie is compelled not by a sense of adventure so much as by a desire to make a grand act of protest. As his neighbor says to Allie's son Charlie when he reads Allie's goodbye note, "your father is the worst kind of pain in the neck: a know-it-all who's sometimes right." Especially in light of what happens later in the film, the significant word here is "sometimes"—for indeed, although Allie at first creates many technological wonders in Jeronimo (the Mosquitian "town" that he buys), all of his planning eventually comes to naught.

Allie is also attempting to escape responsibility and change: he's not only unwilling but, to a significant extent, unable to adapt himself to the conditions around him. Rather than fight against what he views as the erosion of the pioneer spirit of independence and ingenuity, he abandons America and moves his family to the coast of Mosquitia with virtually no preparation and no warning, so that when they leave their house one morning with nothing more than what they can fit in his pickup truck, Allie enjoins his wife to even quit doing the morning breakfast dishes, which are left standing in a sink still steaming with the hot water that she's just drawn.

In *The Machine in the Garden,* critic Leo Marx refers to a type of pastoralism that he calls popular and sentimental, which he describes as

> an expression less of thought than of feeling. It is widely diffused in our culture, insinuating itself into many kinds of behavior. An obvious example is the "flight from the city." An inchoate longing for a more "natural" environment enters into the contemptuous attitude that many Americans adopt toward urban life. . . . [W]herever people turn away from the hard social and technological realities this obscure sentiment is likely to be at work.[8]

Even Turner, although he tended to focus most of his analysis on economic matters, recognized the problems inherent in this kind of thinking.

> The democracy born of free land, strong in selfishness and individualism, intolerant of administrative experience and education, and pressing individual liberty beyond its proper bounds, has its dangers as well as benefits. Individualism in America has allowed a laxity in regard to governmental affairs which has rendered possible the spoils system and all the manifest evils that follow from the lack of a highly developed civic spirit. . . . [T]he colonial and revolutionary frontier was the region whence emanated many of the worst forms of an evil currency.[9]

Unlike the individuals alluded to by Marx and Turner, Allie doesn't even want to exist on the fringe of civilization; and when, while still in America, he goes into town, his bad temper flares up. This quality, which initially appears as a relatively harmless eccentricity in Weir's film, seems much more ominous and malevolent in the film's source, Paul Theroux's book, in which Allie is disagreeable a great deal of the time, not only shamelessly manipulating his family but abusing many of the people with whom he comes in contact.[10] Yet even in Weir's film, despite Harrison Ford's giving Allie some attractive quirks, we early on become impatient with Allie's corrosive remarks. Allie's calling the man on the neighboring farm "Doc" seems as much an insult to the man's supposed lack of education as it does a friendly endearment, while his verbal abuse of a clerk in a hardware store in which he refuses to buy Japanese-made rubber sealing seems unnecessary. As Weir makes plain, Allie has been in the store before and, apparently, similarly mistreated the clerk, as is clear from the man's pained expression when he sees Allie approaching. One wonders if the only reason that Allie frequents the store is the pathological pleasure that he derives from getting into arguments.

It's possible that Weir could have tempered our response to Allie by having the film develop his humorous side, or by allowing him to demonstrate a bit of warmth when he's with his family. Weir also could have stylized the film a bit more, exaggerating certain mise-en-scäne elements such as camera placement and movement, which to a degree would have shifted the emphasis away from an almost exclusive focus on Allie. However, true to his current code, Weir wanted to make his directorial presence in the film as unobtrusive as possible.[11] Fortunately, as we will see, Weir was only partially successful in this respect.

Leo Marx is certainly correct when he refers to the romanticization of the wilderness as threatening "clarity of thought."[12] Marx observes that "the soft veil of nostalgia that hangs over our urbanized landscape is largely a vestige of the once dominant image of an undefiled, green republic, a quiet land of forests, villages, and farms dedicated to the pursuit of happiness."[13] He further notes that writers such as Richard Hofstadter, Marvin Meyers, and Henry Nash Smith have remarked that

> this tendency to idealize rural ways has [also] been an impediment . . . to social progress. . . . In public discourse at least, this ideal has appeared with increasing frequency in the service of a reactionary and false ideology, thereby helping to mask the real problems of an industrial civilization.[14]

Marx's observation not only serves as an apt characterization of Allie, who prefers to abandon industrialized civilization rather than deal with it, but also highlights the contradiction in Allie's attitude toward progress, which he conceives of not in social but in technological terms: he's an inventor who despises a civilization made possible by inventions. Sigmund Freud notes that it isn't only those who leave it who are dissatisfied with society. In Freud's view, everyone, even if they don't know it, is discontented, since discontent is built into the nature of civilization, which is based on the repression of instinct. Yet as Freud points out, the repudiation of civilization would involve a return to a condition of lawlessness in which freedom from anxiety and fear would be lost. "The liberty of the individual is no gift of civilization. It was greatest before there was any civilization, though then, it is true, it had for the most part no value, since the individual was scarcely in a position to defend it."[15]

When Allie goes to Mosquitia, which he conceives of as paradisal, he creates so many technological wonders that he clearly hasn't abandoned technology but merely relocated it, away from other people. Paramount among his obsessions is his desire to introduce the inhabitants of the region to ice. As Allie says to his sons Charlie and Jerry after Doc's indifferent response to Allie's prototype ice house, "Imagine the problems they have down there in the jungle without refrigeration. If they saw an ice cube they'd probably think it was a diamond or a jewel of some kind."

This presumptuous attitude, which demonstrates that Allie regards the jungle's inhabitants as little more than fools, resurfaces when travels to a native village deep in the jungle bearing some ice. "Ice is civilization," Allie tells his sons, by which he means not civilization as it has evolved but civilization as it should be, at least as he obsessively conceives of it. One thing manifestly apparent in *The Mosquito Coast* is that the film is a study of one man's mania and the consequences of that mania for himself and those around him; it's a cautionary tale against scientific demagoguery, with a pronounced political element. Surely Allie's calling the gigantic cooling plant that he builds "Fat Boy" (a combination of the names used for the bombs dropped on Hiroshima, Fat Man and Little Boy), along with the fact that the tanks of ammonia that fuel it look like atomic bombs, suggests the use of atomic weapons by a madman. Yet this awesome power source can be viewed either as destroyer (the recognition of the energy's potential for devastation was characterized by Robert Oppenheimer who, when, watching an atom bomb test, quoted from a Hindu text, "Now I am become Death, destroyer of worlds") or creator (e.g., the idealized conception of atomic energy as a wonderful genie that will deliver people from drudgery, a view that was promoted in the early 1950s).[16] Alternatively, atomic energy can be viewed as both destroyer and creator, as in the dropping of bombs on Hiroshima and Nagasaki in hopes of delivering the United States from the Japanese, who during the Second World War were conceived of as barbaric marauders.

The threat of apocalypse, atomic or otherwise, is only one of *The Mosquito Coast's* major themes. Allie's obsession with bringing ice to the natives is more than just a man's desire to share the "benefits" of advanced technology; it's also an indication of his overwhelming ambition and presumptuousness, which are born of an obsession with a science that takes no heed of its discoveries' application. Allie's desire to be worshipped for his science (a trait in evidence from the film's beginning, when Allie is more interested in showing off his ice house prototype than doing the work for which his neighbor hired him) reveals how neurotic he is—and neurosis is a dangerous trait when it's part of a scientist's psychology, especially a scientist on whom many people depend for their well-being.

Allie's science-oriented urge to "educate" the residents of Mosquitia brings him into contact with three men who seize control of the town that he's built, with the result that in order to save himself, his wife, and their children, he must kill the men by locking them inside Fat Boy and freezing them to death. Here, the deadly capability of ice is the only quality that can rescue Allie's new, supposedly improved version of civilization. However, the men fire their guns while trapped inside the cooling plant, setting in motion a series of chemical reactions that cause the structure to explode, decimating the new village of Jeronimo and polluting the adjacent river, thus bringing down some of "corrupt" civilization's worst aspects onto the town. As the cooling plant explodes, Allie and his family take refuge behind a tree. During the scene, which is charged with Maurice Jarre's music (here electronically synthesized), Allie is, for once, unable to talk. The cooling plant's near-human groans seem to be coming out of Allie's open, speechless mouth as though creator and created have become one. In a classic example of the consequences of stealing the gods' fire, divine judgment is brought down upon Jeronimo and its Promethean ruler. Apocalypse is unleashed; Allie has become the destroyer of worlds.

Earlier in the film, dark clouds passed over Jeronimo while the Foxes and their friends were laughing in the jungle. Weir's camera pulls back to give us a panoramic view of the surrounding forest's lushness. The wide shot goes beyond reducing the humans to dwarfs; it eventually obliterates them in a reminder of their contextual insignificance in the midst of the jungle and the inappropriately mechanistic structures that have been constructed in the region to subdue it. The clouds, and the shot's perspective, prefigure the views we get of the thunderstorm that arises after Allie throws the fundamentalist Reverend Spellgood off the property. The thunderstorm follows Spellgood's likening Allie to Pharaoh, at the time an apparently ridiculous comparison but one that subsequently makes sense in that Allie is acting in a godless fashion by not only refusing to heed the consequences of his actions but also by implicitly refusing (despite his statement to the contrary) to "let his people go" to church, with the result that a plague descends on Jeronimo, destroying it.

Like Allie, Spellgood is manipulative, and is careful to maintain distance between himself and other people. When Spellgood visits, Allie is protective of the Jeronimo property line; similarly, Spellgood has barbed wire strung around his encampment. Both Spellgood and Allie are proselytizers, a fact that would explain the antagonism that Allie feels toward the reverend from the very moment that he meets him. It isn't only Spellgood's religious presumptuousness that annoys Allie; what also bothers him is that Spellgood is promoting what Allie regards as a regressive conception of the world, a religious as opposed to scientific one. Yet Allie can't recognize the Jeronimo residents' desire for religion. When he faces off with Spellgood, Allie doesn't notice that some of the people look worried, and rightly so: they believe Spellgood when he implies that by staying with Allie, they're abjuring God, which for them is a very serious act.

What we see waged in the war between Allie and Spellgood is an example of the recurrent battle in Weir's films between a materialist and spiritual philosophy, with the distinction that in *Mosquito Coast,* neither view seems acceptable. The materialist is a paranoid obsessive, while the spiritual character is as hellbent on conversion, without regard to the individual desires of his "congregation," as is his counterpart.

Both Allie and Spellgood feel that the unknown—the workings of nature in Allie's case, the mysteries of existence in Spellgood's—somehow need to be explained to quell people's innate anxiety. Allie uses technology to accomplish this purpose; Spellgood invokes Jesus and the Bible as sources of comfort. Yet it's clear that the natives with whom Allie and Spellgood deal have no anxiety about nature or God; it's these two crazed white men who are projecting their own anxiety onto what are, apparently, well-adjusted people. To bolster their own low self-esteem, both Allie and Spellgood act in the role of spiritual "father" and allow the local residents to call them by this name. The ideological (and, eventually, physical) battle between them ultimately comes down to what kind of a father is prayed to: a material, technological one, or an otherworldly one that is religiously conceived. That the film's action demonstrates that Allie's vision leads to chaos, and Spellgood's to a preservation of order, doesn't solve the dilemma so much as complicate it, since we obviously cannot do without some form of technological aid if we are to survive; nor can we, in Weir's view, live without a sense of the spiritual if we are to progress and prosper. In the end, the issue appears irresolvable.

The Mosquito Coast invites comparison with Theroux and Weir's most apparent source: Joseph Conrad's *Heart of Darkness*.[17] Both works are narrated in retrospect by a character who to a degree stands outside the story's central action; both investigate the nature and effects of colonialism. Prominent characters in both stories start out with what appear to be idealistic values but eventually become bitter; and both feature as a central characteristic a lie: the one possibly told by Allie, the one told by Marlow.

Conrad's book is a meditation on the meanings of the word "darkness." In one sense the word represents that which is unknown, either the land of the Congo (which was, for the most part, unexplored by whites at the time that *Heart of Darkness* takes place) or the innermost regions of the human heart. In the latter sense, Conrad means to inquire into the part of Kurtz (and, by extension, Marlow and the reader) that is disposed toward evil. Yet darkness also refers to the Congo's inhabitants, people who, when they appear in the story at all, do so either as ghostly or abstracted figures (e.g., the "black shadows" that sicken under the grove of trees)[18] or as individuals whose presence is strongly physical (e.g., the priestess who holds out her hands over the water when Marlow departs with Kurtz).[19] Nothing resides between these extremes. *Heart of Darkness's* blacks are either invisible or too visible, suggesting that they are more types than anything else. The story's blacks are certainly not humanized, as are its whites, who are given dramatic touches that make them seem more real; predominantly, *The Mosquito Coast* shares this characteristic, alerting us early on to its inherent bias. What we apparently have in both works are examples of what Toni Morrison refers to as "economy of stereotype."[20]

Just as *The Mosquito Coast* is Allie's story told (as we will see, problematically) by his son Charlie, is Kurtz's story told by Marlow.[21] It's Charlie (to an extent) and Marlow (most pronouncedly) who shape what we see and hear: in these works, especially the latter, the teller is at least as significant as the tale. And though both stories are in one sense about the loss of an esteemed figure, their narrators differ significantly. Unlike Charlie, Marlow at his story's beginning is an experienced man. He is able to comment on the actions of colonization that he witnesses. Marlow refers to conquest (which he contrasts with colonialism only to make an ironic point) as

> just robbery with violence, aggravated murder on a great scale, and men going at it blind—as is very proper for those who tackle a darkness. The conquest of the earth, which mostly means the taking it away from those who have a different complexion or slightly flatter noses than ourselves, is not a pretty thing when you look into it too much.[22]

This passage is reminiscent of the manner in which Allie Fox buys Jeronimo: he does so in a noisy, crowded bar, negotiating with a drunken white man. Marlow, again ironically, states that "what redeems [conquest] is the idea only. An idea at the back of it; not a sentimental pretence but an idea; and an unselfish belief in the idea—something you can set up, and bow down before, and offer a sacrifice to."[23]

Originally, Kurtz meant to enlighten the natives; Allie intends to bring civilization to the residents of Mosquitia. Although Allie equates civilization with ice, what he is really bringing to the territory is subservience for the residents, a colonialist attribute whose symbolically cold aspect is the frozen nature of its morality. Moreover, what Allie intends to do in Mosquitia sounds quite similar to the stated aims of King Leopold II of Belgium, the Congo's original colonizer, who stated,

> The mission which the agents of the State have to accomplish on the Congo is a noble one. They have to continue the development of civilisation in the centre of Equatorial Africa, receiving their inspiration directly from Berlin and Brussels. Placed face to face with primitive barbarism, grappling with sanguinary customs that date back thousands of years, they are obliged to reduce these gradually. They must accustom the population to general laws, of which the most needful and the most salutary is assuredly that of work.[24]

The king's sentiments were echoed by one of the Congo's most notable explorers, Henry M. Stanley, who referred to Leopold's mission as an attempt to "let light on chaos . . . to redeem this vast slave park . . . to relieve it of its horrors, rescue it from its oppressors, and save it from perdition."[25] Leopold and Stanley's statements not only bring into relief the actions of *Mosquito Coast's* dual proselytizers, Allie and Spellgood, but also highlight Allie's attitude toward Mosquitia's natives, whom he treats as though they are ignorant children. Before he begins to plant seeds (of colonial attitudes?), Allie asks the people of Jeronimo what he should do first. When they don't reply (how could they? They haven't the slightest idea who Allie is or what plans he has in mind), Allie answers for them, supplying responses in a manner that invites comparison with the way that Spellgood provides answers to the people's unasked questions about religion.

Leopold and Stanley's smug pronouncements highlight Allie's implicit patronization of Jeronimo's residents from whom (to appropriate historian W. E. H. Stanner's term about the seizing of the Australian continent from its Aboriginal population) Allie has "filched" the territory.[26] In this sense, the film can be read as a thinly veiled representation of Australia's treatment of blacks, which no "idea" (to use Marlow's term) can possibly redeem.[27] Allie's notions about what he wants to accomplish in Jeronimo have less to do with "progress" than with a desire to dominate, a trait that he exhibited in his handling of his family and neighbor before he left the United States.

Perhaps part of the problem with our unpleasant feelings about Allie is the film's conception of his character. Weir intended that Allie initially be seen as a great, admirable man, not just in Charlie's eyes but in the audience's as well. Weir has said,

> The challenge of the story was, for me, that it was a tragedy and very particularly an American tragedy. . . . [I]t reminded me of . . . Shakespeare certainly—of Macbeth. . . . I've always enjoyed watching this great soldier, Macbeth, watching this ambition awaken in him and consume him. . . .
>
> I saw Allie Fox like that and wanted to present a story where you understood what happened to the man and *felt* something, not necessarily for him, but felt something at the end other than anger toward him, which people who read the book felt.[28]

Despite Weir's intentions, the film has a disagreeable tone that is a function of Allie's manipulative behavior and patronizing attitudes. The comparison with *Macbeth* seems unfortunate: we never see Allie's greatness unalloyed with hubris, so it is difficult to feel pity and terror when he fails (although we do sympathize with Allie's family).

Richard Combs's comments on the film are especially pertinent. Combs observes that,

> [Weir] is not the director to find a theme or a structure which would anchor the character of Allie Fox—who in the novel is also quite anchorless, an embodiment of the restless pioneering spirit, of a compulsive American need to tinker and improve which, in export, can become a benignly heedless colonialism. . . . [A]lthough the film has preserved Allie's adventures intact, it does not seem as involved with them as the novelist. . . . Weir is, at best, a cool lyricist, and he has made an unobsessive film about an obsessive character. . . . [T]his *Mosquito Coast* gets away with neither endorsing Allie's fervor nor condemning his tyranny.[29]

The failure in the conception of Allie's character was a fault in the book as well. Combs states that Theroux "originally meant [the novel] to be the story of the eldest son, Charlie, and his struggle to deal with his overweening father, but . . . Allie's voice and opinions, his ambitions and delusions, proved too seductive to the author."[30] The result is that like the book, this faithful film adaptation confuses our reactions.[31] Not surprisingly, the film was a financial and critical failure. As Weir noted, "[The response to the film] was very disappointing for all involved. It was not a success anywhere, and it had vicious reviews in New York."[32] Weir says that the negative reactions to the film were due to its telling "a story people didn't want to see. From early market tests we realized that they didn't like the concept. They did not like the very thing that had moved me to make it."[33] Does Weir mean that Allie's character was unsavory, or was it the film's message about the ugly effects of monomania and colonialism that audiences disliked? There is no way to tell. What is certain is that the director feels "no regret" over the film's failure: "I loved making it," Weir says.[34] Apparently, he doesn't realize that the film is badly flawed; that, unlike the book, it should have focused on the Fox family's disappointment with Allie, thereby bringing some sympathetic characters to the forefront.

Weir recognizes the role that the film's narration takes; he feels that the (supposed) depiction of Allie from Charlie's point of view adds to what he regards as the poignancy of Allie's decline. "It should be as if you are imagining your own father somehow, whom you believed in, and whose weaknesses you begin to see; this giant of a man only gets smaller and smaller as you grow."[35] Unfortunately, the film isn't stylized in such a way so as to suggest that what we're seeing is represented from a relatively innocent point of view. We can't ascribe any part of our negative reaction to Allie to a young man's idiosyncratic responses. Moreover, breaking through Allie's initially amusing diatribes are indications of his racial bias, as in his aforementioned jeremiad against imported consumer goods. And though this aspect is leavened somewhat by Allie's apparent sensitivity to the plight of the migrant workers who are harvesting some of his neighbor's asparagus, as well as his insistence that his children refrain from referring to the workers' living quarters as "the monkey house," it's not enough to temper what we perceive as Allie's inherent bigotry.[36] The result is audience displeasure with Allie, a displeasure that extends to our reaction to the film as a whole.[37]

Like Marlow, Charlie has characteristics that are similar to those of Joseph Campbell's hero, who returns from a journey into the underworld ready to bear witness to an extraordinary experience.[38] As with many Weir films, *The Mosquito Coast* traces a voyage of the conscious mind into the unconscious; the self goes in search of itself. Moreover, much of the film—the initial approach to Mosquitia, the halcyon early days in Jeronimo—seems like a dream. This sense of unreality (partially a result of the unusual nature of the story and the fact that it is being told in retrospect; in this sense only, Charlie's narration has a successful effect) is also present in *Heart of Darkness*. As Marlow says, "It seems to me I am trying to tell you a dream—making a vain attempt, because no relation of a dream can convey the dream-sensation, that commingling of absurdity, surprise, and bewilderment in a tremor of struggling revolt."[39]

After the ice house explosion, *Mosquito Coast* begins to trace a descent into hell. As Lillian Feder points out in her commentary on *Heart of Darkness,* in the *Aeneid,* "Aeneas's descent [into Hades] is part of his initiation for the role of leader of the Roman people."[40] Similarly, after Allie's death, Charlie must assume the role of male head of the family. Moreover, during their experiences in a foreign land, both Charlie and Marlow discover things about themselves. Substitute the names Charlie for Marlow, and Allie for Kurtz, and Feder could be discussing Weir's film.

> Aeneas' voyage to Hades is one means by which he learns of the tragedy implicit in the affairs of men. . . . [L]ike Aeneas, Marlow comes to understand himself, his obligations, and the tragic limitations involved in any choice. . . . Kurtz, like Aeneas, starts out as an "emissary of light," but, unlike Vergil's hero, he cannot conquer himself. Through Kurtz's experience, Marlow learns that a man is defined by his work; Kurtz's work has created a hell in the jungle, which destroys him.[41]

Initially, Kurtz and Allie purport to have good intentions: Kurtz to advance himself in terms of position and wealth as well as to "improve" the populace (he writes a report for the "International Society for the Suppression of Savage Customs"),[42] Allie to start life anew and bring what he considers the best aspects of contemporary culture to the jungle. However, both men's desires are revealed as examples of colonialist hubris, and each descends into madness and racial bigotry. Kurtz appends the words "exterminate all the brutes" to his tract on the benefits of colonialism;[43] Allie, in the throes of a dementia and despair that rival Kurtz's, calls his friend Mr. Haddy a "savage."

In Weir's film, as in *Heart of Darkness,* the jungle functions as a figure for the undiscovered self. Additionally, *Mosquito Coast* posits a classic opposition between materialism and religion, a characteristic split for Weir that here takes an unusual form. Unlike *The Last Wave,* in which Chris and David respectively represent spirituality and materialism, in *Mosquito Coast* the opposition between these forces is mediated by Mr. Haddy, a sympathetic man of color who, apparently, is neither as religiously oriented as many of the other residents of Mosquitia nor as awed by machinery as they are. (When we first meet him, Mr. Haddy, like Marlow, is piloting a steamboat.) Haddy looks beyond Allie's obsessions, accepting them, and treats Allie as a friend; he offers to take Allie to his home when he sees the reduced conditions in which the Fox family is eventually forced to live. Although Allie insults Haddy, it is Haddy who nonetheless brings Charlie the spark plugs that are needed to start the outboard motor that saves Allie and his family when a storm finally arrives. Mr. Haddy is far more than a stereotype; aside from Allie and Charlie, he is the only well-developed character in the film, easily qualifying as Charlie's substitute father. Indeed, Haddy represents wisdom and tolerance, qualities with which Charlie would undoubtedly wish his father's personality could be tempered.

The lies told in *Heart of Darkness* and *The Mosquito Coast* are essential to the narrator's journey toward new knowledge. Despite the significant difference in age between Marlow and Charlie, the contact with falsehood represents an important dilemma for the boy. Marlow knew that Kurtz was corrupt, yet he remains silent when Kurtz's fiancée extols his virtuous nature; Marlow then goes on to lie about Kurtz's last words. Allie, in an statement that Charlie believes is a lie, states that the United States has been destroyed by a nuclear war. In both Marlow and Charlie's cases, the "lies" completely reshape the narrator's world.

Marlow has already made clear his view on lying.

> You know I hate, detest, and can't bear a lie, not because I am straighter than the rest of us, but simply because it appals me. There is a taint of death, a flavour of mortality in lies—which is exactly what I hate and detest in the world—what I want to forget. It makes me miserable and sick, like biting something rotten would do.[44]

After Marlow tells Kurtz's fiancée that the last word Kurtz spoke was her name, he comments that, "It seemed to me that the house would collapse before I could escape, that the heavens would fall upon my head."[45] Despite this anxious premonition, nothing happens. "The heavens do not fall for such a trifle," Marlow comments,[46] the word "trifle" an ironically offered usage that does not mask the fact that Marlow does, indeed, consider the misrepresentation ominous. Marlow has come to realize a bitter but important truth, one that has a major impact on him: the universe is apparently indifferent to the action of human beings. Charlie comments that his father's "lie" had a comparably strong effect on him. "I knew father had lied to us about America being blown up. That lie made me feel lonelier than I had ever felt before." At the end of *Mosquito Coast*, Charlie comments, "Once I had believed in father, and the world had seemed small and old. Now he was gone and I wasn't afraid to love him any more. And the world seemed limitless." Although we must grant that Marlow's passage is into ironic disappointment while Charlie's is into a form of guarded optimism (attitudes appropriate for each character's age), the results are comparable: a liberation out of delusion and into worlds, respectively dark and light, that, at the very least, are now faced more forthrightly.

Mosquito Coast is not only the story of an experiment that was wrong from the start (its failure only partially a result of Allie's presumptuousness); as suggested in an earlier-cited Weir quote, it's also a story about the loss of a family's protective father figure, who functions as a source of compassion, understanding, and support. In keeping with the film's Edenic aspect, the relationship between Charlie and Allie becomes an example of the one between God and Man; the Father/Creator sets down rules for the offspring, but in *The Mosquito Coast*, God needs not only worship (present here as adulation) but approval (hence Allie's repeatedly asking Charlie, "how'm I doing, son?"). Although Jeronimo functions as a new Eden, the same old faults, which are inherently human, are brought into it as well: pride, disobedience, jealousy. Allie's new Paradise may have power tools but, as in the original Garden, the same obedience to God's rules is necessary: the integrity of nature must be respected. In this sense, Weir is correct when he states that the film to some degree is a parable:[47] it re-creates and updates the Eden story, reminding us that its lessons still apply today.

The comedy in the film is kept to a minimum, emerging only faintly as when Spellgood appears at the Jeronimo dock and Allie goes to meet him with his hammer swinging from his belt as though it were a gun, the encounter becoming a Western-style showdown. As one might expect, the two characters do have a face-off at the film's end: after setting fire to Spellgood's church, Allie is shot by the reverend. All of the early humor in the film turns grim just as Allie's hopes turn to ruination and despair and he propels his family toward chaos. What was so baldly stated in *The Last Wave* is more subtly communicated in *The Mosquito Coast*: the forces of the unconscious and nature are not to be treated lightly. Like Victor Frankenstein and his successors in countless horror films, Allie inquires into things that were "better left alone." All that Allie manages to do in his mad dash toward a new, improved Eden is to unwittingly forge a new Hell, bringing down devastation on both the guilty and the innocent alike; in the process he inadvertently creates an ecological and ethical warning about tampering with nature that, again, is like the one in *The Last Wave*, with the difference that here, the warning is more inventively conveyed.

In *Mosquito Coast*, as in *Witness*, culture clash has grim consequences. The difference between the films is that in *Witness*, the displacement into another culture is involuntary, the result of a violent act; in *Mosquito Coast*, although the move to Mosquitia occurs voluntarily (at least, on Allie Fox's part), it eventually results in annihilation. In *Witness* and *Mosquito*, the new world into which the protagonist moves at first appears lush, green, and apparently peaceful, although in both films, the protagonist inadvertently brings with him the potential for violence. The important distinction between the films, though, is that as opposed to John Book, Allie Fox lacks an ethical sensibility. The conclusion we're therefore led to is that without a supporting moral structure on the part of the characters involved, a clash of cultures inevitably leads to some form of brutality that, unlike the confrontation at *Witness*'s end, does not lead to purgation.

At significant points in *The Mosquito Coast,* the camera declares its presence, sometimes in playful ways, as in the previously mentioned showdown with Reverend Spellgood, during which the camera is placed low and shoots with a slightly wide-angle lens. Sometimes the camerawork has an ominous connotation, as in the slow backward track away from the hut in which Allie and family are celebrating their first Thanksgiving, a shot that links up with the god's-eye aerial shots of Jeronimo that, seemingly objective at first, come to serve as a judgment against the village, since the wide view emphasizes the intrusive nature of the buildings that Allie has erected. The camera pull-backs function as preludes to the judgment of an equitable but dispassionate god against Allie, and ironically serve as manifestations of the wrath that Spellgood (who has littered the Jeromino dock with warnings of the fury to come) invokes against the community.

Appropriately, this judgment assumes the form of an explosion that Allie, his discriminatory powers deteriorating, takes to be the nuclear holocaust that he first mentions as a ruse to keep his family in Mosquitia, but which he later apparently truly believes has destroyed America.[48] Allie's ostensible loss of perspective is predominantly the result of a previous loss of discernment: the incorrect assessment of the men who are trapped at the native village, whom he takes to be innocents but who are really mercenaries. The mistake in judgment that he makes regarding these men is partially caused by Allie's attitude toward the village's residents. Apparently, Allie feels that the residents have captured the men because they are ignorant (ironically, it's Allie who turns out to be the dupe, not the natives).

Later, in another example of bad reasoning, Allie places his hut too close to the water of his last-stand camp, something that only Mr. Haddy, who is properly oriented to the surroundings, appreciates. Unlike Allie's wife (who is only referred to as Mother), who late in the film views herself in a pocket mirror that reveals her disheveled state, Allie isn't self-reflective. There's a misalignment between Allie's inward vision of mechanical correctness and the manner in which the world actually works. Allie only partially achieves an awareness of this misalignment at the film's end when he says, "nature is crooked; I wanted right angles, straight lines," the use of the word "crooked" suggesting that in one sense, Allie believes that he's dying because the world has cheated him. Nevertheless, the lack of synchronization between Allie and the "new" country in which he finds himself allies him with David in *The Last Wave* and the investigating characters in *Picnic at Hanging Rock;* all of these people try to make an ineffable realm conform to the material world, with disastrous results, not realizing that the two realms are not meant to blend but are instead coextensive, each accessible through the other and, when left alone, acting in perfectly calibrated harmony.[49]

Although at one point, when he berates Charlie on the way to the native village, one can for a brief moment see the beginning of a sense of regret pass over Allie's face,[50] predominantly, like Spellgood, Allie is so taken with what he perceives to be the moral correctness of his vision that he's blind to any other viewpoint. Twice, cataclysms nearly destroy him: first the explosion of Fat Boy, then the storm that washes him and his family out to sea. In the end, as Allie drifts downstream toward death, he is also pointed back to the America whose major corruption was primarily a function of his own corrupted vision, and toward a deliverance from tribulation that only his family will survive to enjoy.

SCHOOL DAYS

If any film reflects Weir's disappointing university experience and his hope that the negative effects of traditional education can be avoided it is *Dead Poets Society.* Where *Picnic at Hanging Rock* seems to despair of most of its students escaping from the abuses of their predominantly conservative, abusive instructors, *Dead Poets*—although it ends equivocally—at least holds out the promise of a willful escape from oppression.

One of *Dead Poets'* major themes is announced almost immediately. The shot of the mural of young boys that accompanies the film's opening titles yields during a downward pan to an image of a young student who is very much like those depicted in the frieze. What Weir is doing, then, is much like what he attempted in *Gallipoli:* he's taking a series of past events and for a brief time bringing them to life, only to allow us after the film is over to realize that his film's major players have already faded into the past and had their lives frozen in images. Like the photos of former students whom the English teacher John Keating has his students look at in the coffin-like showcase in the building's lobby, the students in *Dead Poets,* which is set in the 1950s, are by now already significantly past their youth, a fact that encourages us to wonder just how they responded to Keating's injunction to make something extraordinary of their lives. There's thus an elegiac, melancholy tone to the film that is communicated in its first few minutes, a feeling complemented by the mist-enshrouded images of the college that Weir periodically inserts, which affirm the sense of romantic idealization that pervades the entire production.

It's also clear early on in the film that *Dead Poets* is an American version of *Picnic at Hanging Rock.* There's the same obsession with mythic journeys, the same desire on the part of the students for sexual release from an atavistic, repressive educational institution. Just as Appleyard College is poised on the brink of change, so too is the Welton School, whose values are soon to be challenged by social trends that will bring in the revolutionary 1960s. In *Picnic*, the students are pubescent girls, ruled over by women, who journey during the day to a phallic rock; in *Dead Poets*, the students are pubescent boys, ruled over by men, who go on night journeys to a vaginal cave. In both films, sexual awakening and discovery are figuratively represented at the forbidden site during what Joseph Campbell would refer to as initiatory "rite[s] of passage."[1] But where *Picnic* at least held out hope for sexual satisfaction in the form of an adult, heterosexual couple with a productive sexual relationship, the only adults of any note in *Dead Poets* who are in a sexual relationship are Keating, who doesn't even live in the same country as his lover, and Neil's parents, whose marriage seems sexually stillborn.

Each film's central student figures are removed from the action either by disappearances, suicides (*Picnic*'s Sara and *Dead Poets*' Neil), or expulsion (the rebel students in *Dead Poets*), or are in heterosexual relationships that come to naught (Michael and Irma in *Picnic*, the essentially unreal relationship between Knox and Chris in *Dead Poets*). Indeed, in each film, physical maturation for the students does not lead to sexual behavior. Although the films are charged with sexual tension, they dramatize a lack of passionate fulfillment that is not completely compensated for by their emphasis on the spiritual and ideal.

Additionally, each film focuses on a canon of approved writings, a sign of authoritarian paternalism at work. *Picnic*'s Mrs. Appleyard insists that Sara commit to memory a poem by Mrs. Felicia Heymans, whom she refers to as "one of our most famous English poets"; Welton School's headmaster, Mr. Nolan, reinvokes canonical attitudes toward poetry when, after dismissing Mr. Keating, he insists that the students in Keating's class return to the staid approach to literature recommended in their poetry book's introductory material, which Keating had characterized as "excrement." The only major thematic distinction between the films is that by alluding to McCarthyism via the "inquisition" that follows Neil's suicide, *Dead Poets Society* has a political subtext, which is absent from *Picnic*.

Keating obviously represents a wish-fulfillment, the type of teacher Weir doubtless would like to have had when he went to school: at once authority figure and emotionally accessible human being. Weir once told this story about his father.

> When I was a kid my father used to tell me serials. He'd make them up. It was a great treat for about three or four years. . . . If I really had to single out an influence, I'd choose that experience—the *pleasure* of telling the tale. . . .

> During the war, when he was very short of money . . .[my father] wrote for the
> radio. . . . I found one of his [scripts] once in a cupboard with a whole batch of
> radio plays. . . . It was a tremendous discovery. In my whole family background, I
> couldn't find anybody with an interest in culture.[2]

Here's the germ of *Dead Poets*' story: a boy from a family that seems devoid of
artistic sensibility whose father entrances him with the exhilaration of literature. Read "father figure" for "father" and you have the character of John
Keating. Yet Weir also draws attention to a somewhat depressing aspect of such
a wonderful situation: one day, the "great treat" of "three or four years" ends.
The "real" world is entered; the world of fiction's harmonies dissolves. What
we see here, then, is not only another example of Weir's familiar oppositions,
but also the implication that if only one could hold onto the joy of directly experienced pleasure, childhood would continue forever. As a spinner of tales
who spends a great deal of time crafting them, Weir is also something of a man/
child, at once storyteller and audience. In Keating, then, Weir has not only
fictionalized his father but projected himself into the character as well.

For Keating, what counts isn't learning but life, and if life can be found in
literature, so much the better. Thus, whether or not Keating's students put into
practice what he taught them is, ultimately, unimportant; what matters is the
fact that for one brief period, these young men were exposed to the possibility
of a life different from the kind that their parents offer them. Of course, to a
certain degree some of the students must have realized that there were other
ways to live, if only as a result of the negative experiences they've had with their
parents. Todd is a prime example: the fact that on his birthday his parents send
him the identical desk set that he had received the year before should tell him
that there's something terribly wrong with the way that his family treats him.
(Their attitude is the obverse of the behavior of Neil's father, whose cruelty derives not from indifference but overzealous, manipulative involvement in his
son's life.) Yet even without the incident of the desk set, we know that there's
something seriously wrong with Todd: he's extremely quiet and very repressed,
embarrassed about participating in class, and unwilling to read aloud at the
meetings of the Dead Poets Society. Sitting in his room with Neil, he constantly
checks his watch against the clock on his desk, as though keeping the two time
pieces in synchronization might afford him a modicum of stability.

The conflict between the repression that seems an integral part of the schooling at Welton and what goes on in the natural world is made manifest in Weir's
shots of the landscape. While the school bells are ringing, Weir gives us images
of birds flying that seem derived from the blended shots of Miranda and birds
that appeared in *Picnic at Hanging Rock*. As in the earlier film, a contrast is be-

ing drawn in the image juxtaposition; here, the fact that the birds are startled by the school chimes sets up an opposition between the repressive education at Welton and nature. There is clearly a strong autobiographical element in this aspect of the film. As I mentioned in the introduction, Weir was appalled by the lifeless, academic approach to literature to which he was exposed when he was in college, contending that the lack of a spiritual dimension in traditional Western education so strongly affected him that even decades later, he can't read Shakespeare, for example, without smelling chalk dust and feeling repulsed. When he characterizes his education as a process that was involved with "training spontaneity out of me and dulling the edge of emotion," Weir might just as well be talking about what seems to happen routinely at the Welton School.[3]

The opposition that Weir posits in *Dead Poets* between nature and education, though, is only between natural forces and the school; as for the students, many of them (like those in *Picnic*) still have the potential to realize in themselves the sensual and sexual forces represented by nature. Indeed, when Weir blends the sounds of screeching birds with the undisciplined cries of the students clamoring between classes, after which he cuts to a shot of the students coming down a staircase, he affirms the connection between nature and the students. Yet the latter image, achieved by shooting straight up the stairwell, not only recalls a similar shot in *Picnic* but also, as in the earlier film, sets up an important contrast between the unnatural discipline and regimentation of a school and the free spirits of many of its students. However, *Dead Poets'* contrast between freedom and coercion represents an exaggeration of the situation in which, we may presume, at least some of the students find themselves: surely some of them must be at the school voluntarily. But then, perhaps it's unrealistic to expect the film to chronicle credible situations and events. It might be far more profitable to view *Dead Poets* as a mythological representation of the conflict between liberal and conservative attitudes, between youth and their elders; or, given Weir's perennial concern with repression, a conflict between unrestrained impulses as opposed to the supposed benefits accruing from the restraints of civilization.

Seen in this way, the film not only takes on more significance but also begins to make Keating more believable; perhaps we should view him not as a "real" teacher so much as a sprite risen from the subconscious and sent to Welton as a benevolent force meant to reveal to the students, at this critical juncture in their lives, that a choice between the ways of their parents and those indicated by their instincts is possible. Keating shows his students that not all adults have to become as priggish as the headmaster and his toadies. In essence, then,

Keating functions as a symbol of possibility. The fact that Keating is unsuccessful in his efforts to remain at the school doesn't represent a failure of the values for which he stands so much as indicate that the school is unwilling to support them. Keating's physical separation from his wife or girlfriend suggests that he has made a difficult but, for him, necessary choice: choosing teaching over sexual satisfaction and gratification, idealization over the practical realities with which he would have to deal as a member of an adult heterosexual relationship. By refusing to ever "leave school," Keating, like Peter Pan, opts to never grow up, to always be one of the boys, even if he must be an adult/boy who looks out at life from the safe confines of academia, observing his students in romantic entanglements without ever actively participating in one himself. Somewhat unfairly, then, Keating recommends to his students an involvement in life that he himself does not exhibit. Moreover, except when advising Charlie about the foolishness of the phone call stunt, Keating advocates courses of action without adequately considering their consequences.

Keating emerges out of nowhere like an archetypal spirit world figure, popping through the classroom door toward the film's beginning and, banished from the material realm at its end, disappearing back through this door at *Dead Poets'* conclusion. Yet though his presence at the school seems somewhat incredible, Keating does make some very essential points that are appreciated by the students. When he takes the students out into the hallway during their first class and makes them stare at the photos of former students and contemplate their own mortality—which should, he reasons, inspire them to seize the day—we see that some of the students are intrigued, while others are merely bemused. At one point, Weir cuts from a shot of Todd to a picture of a boy in one of the photos; the two seem strikingly similar. The graphic juxtaposition makes Keating's point about mortality more tellingly than words might, even if the message achieved through this effect may be appreciable only by the audience. Keating's students are in many ways the same as those of the past: they need to strive to become more than just a dim memory in a long line of essentially identical persons whose lives appear to have been little more than the living out of a sense of desperation. "Show me the man without illusions and I'll show you a happy man," says the Latin teacher, a sentiment doubtless shared by Neil's father, who has repressed all of his feelings so that he can live comfortably. Obsessed, like Todd, with order (Weir's camera dwells on the way that his slippers are carefully lined up and placed near his bed), Neil's father cannot understand or accept the impetuous side of his son's life. "You're going to Harvard and then to medical school," he tells his son, and when Neil objects, saying, "what about how I feel?" his father's heated response makes it plain that he isn't interested in this aspect of his son's life.

Through the love of the spirit of poetry (which is centered on Whitman), forces are unleashed that allow the students to frankly express themselves. True, there may be a degree to which the students take their expressiveness too far, as Keating observes after Charlie's parody of Mr. Nolan. However, Charlie, Neil, and Knox's actions—the only truly rebellious acts shown to us—do seem to make sense, even if one of these acts is a suicide. The outcome of Knox's pursuit of Chris may seem highly improbable, but then perhaps we're meant to view its denouement as an example of romanticism fulfilled. Certainly Knox's reference to Chris as "the most beautiful girl [he's] ever seen" appears to be the result of an infatuation that defies reason. Neil's behavior, too, seems somewhat exaggerated; for this bright, self-conscious boy to commit suicide seems an excessive (but all too common) response to his feeling trapped (in this case, by his father's manipulative attitude), when simply leaving home would surely have been sufficient. The suicide seems to result from the kind of exaggerated romanticism that Mr. Keating has prompted in the boys, a contention that to a degree justifies the school's blaming Keating for the boy's death.

Neil's death has a profound impact on the school. In order to protect itself from negative publicity and accusations that the suicide was a result of lax supervision, the administration decides to find a scapegoat. Not surprisingly, Keating—the only outrageous figure among the faculty—is chosen to take the blame for Neil's death. Keating doubtless would have counseled Neil to take a more reasoned response to his father's oppressiveness. Yet the hunt for a scapegoat is dramatically necessary to the film, since it makes possible its implicit allusion to the anticommunist McCarthyite witch-hunts of the 1950s. As Scott Murray observes about the part of *Dead Poets* that shows the members of the poetry society signing confessions accusing Mr. Keating of responsibility for creating the conditions that led to Neil's death,

> Under a minimal amount of authoritarian pressure (a wrinkled brow, a proffered pen), Weir's schoolboys weaken and sign a false declaration which destroys an innocent man's career. Weir fails to make one believe the boys have gone through a real moral dilemma and their capitulations are staggeringly quick. In short, they are weak, confused and conservative boys who put their own well-being above principle.[4]

Although I think that Murray is being a bit harsh here (resolutely standing up to authority when one is in high school is very difficult to do), his assessment of the symbolic import of the boys' capitulation seems well founded. What is dramatized here is the kind of informing that was rampant during the McCarthy period, when friends accused ex-friends of being communists just to protect themselves from similar accusations. However, Murray's contention that this part of *Dead Poets* functions as "an apology for McCarthyism"[5] is something of an exaggeration. More likely, what Weir is really saying is that those who sold out to McCarthyism were conforming to then-current attitudes.

Charlie's response to Keating's promptings, his playing saxophone and bongos and wearing a beret, provides another important clue to the source for the film's inspiration. The beret and the music, along with the boys' poetry recitations in the cave, make it clear that the main source for the spirit behind Mr. Keating's teachings and the subsequent attitude of the students comes from the Beat movement, which, like the boys' secret society, represented an alternative culture that denigrated conventional responses, linked jazz and free verse, and, in its search for a source of inspiration, cited the spirit of Whitman (as in Allen Ginsburg's poem "In a Supermarket in California"). Also instructive is the manner in which the Beats regarded the structural rebellion inherent in Whitman's verse, which repudiated devotion to traditional poetic metrics in favor of a free verse form that, it was presumed, would allow more open expression of sentiments, precisely the attitude that Keating encourages in his students.

The real lesson that Keating teaches his students is that all things connect, that the ideas and feelings they discover in, and through, poetry and prose come as a result of seeing deeply enough into the underlying fabric of existence that one comes to realize that there is no significant difference between literature and life—that literature is, rather, distilled life, and that, in making one's life extraordinary, one turns it into literature. With this view in mind, one realizes that the distinction between the overly practical, conscious realm (represented by the school) and that of the subconscious (present in the free expression of feelings and ideas that takes place during the society meetings) is somewhat specious. Love, commitment, passion, and self-realization aren't merely literary concepts; they're the issues with which any conscientious person should deal. Moreover, seeing things in a uniformly poetic way yields visions of splendor even in the midst of grief, as Todd realizes after Neil's death when, staring at a snow-covered landscape, he remarks on its beauty. It's in the manner in which the film poetically represents apparently objective scenes, which are nonetheless colored by romanticism that Keating represents, that it reaches high points, as in the golden glow that suffuses the school buildings in the autumn; the shot of the hooded figures moving through the mist toward the cave; the outdoor shot as the boys hoist Keating onto their shoulders (which is nonetheless rendered somewhat bittersweet by the sun setting in the distance).

Where in other Weir films we see explosive actions with political overtones (e.g., *The Plumber, The Mosquito Coast,* and, most obviously, *The Year of Living Dangerously*), *Dead Poets* highlights the emotional source of revolutionary attitudes: a dissatisfaction with life measured not by traditional politics but by the politics of how things feel—in other words, the discovery and invocation of a moral imperative derived from sentiments, with the implication that such sentiments may, possibly, be put into political action. (At least, politics is what we see as a potential response when the emotional curve of the film is on the upswing.) Unfortunately, the film somewhat unwisely places the burden of carrying the spirit of revolution on the shoulders of Robin Williams's Keating. Williams is an capable player, and Weir has managed to have him tone down his more frantic qualities, doubtless something that his character would have had to do to continue working in academe. Nonetheless, Williams is an insufficient presence to bear the burden of representing the spirit of poetry, which he is called upon to do as when Nolan, after taking over Keating's class, asks, "What is poetry?" and, as if in answer, Keating knocks at the classroom door and then enters. His entrance sets up the film's equivocal conclusion. As Keating, having gathered his belongings, is leaving, some of the boys, apparently responding to Keating's earlier behest to get up on his desk and see things from a new vantage point, stand up on their desks, led by the most repressed student among them, Todd. As they do so, and the music swells,[6] what we're seeing acted out is the passing on of a tradition that none of the efforts of Nolan or the rest of his repressed cronies could ever hope to successfully subdue. The film's last shot, of Todd standing on the top of his desk, is viewed through the arch of another student's legs. The effect of framing the shot in this way is twofold. The boy is focused on, and thereby empowered, as a result of the framing; yet at the same time, despite his defiant stance, he is also hemmed in, as though even protest might be some form of conformity. Weir represents as more complex what might otherwise have seemed an act of unalloyed rebellion, thus introducing into the film a degree of satisfying contrariety.

Following the previous image there is a virtual freeze-frame shot. Some of the students are standing defiantly; the other students, who remain at their desks, are all seated in exactly the same posture, slightly bent forward, their heads in their hands. What are we seeing, then, if not Keating's heavily personal vision of the boys' tribute frozen into an image as memorable as the pictures of the students from the Welton classes long gone? For Keating, and his loyal students, this image will also "speak" long after all of the participants are dead; indeed, perhaps the film itself has become something of an icon that will continue to speak beyond the lives of its creators. In this sense, *Dead Poets* ends on an additional note of contradiction that blends melancholy and optimism.

Despite its occasionally rousing tone, there are problems with *Dead Poets Society* that need to be dealt with. For one thing, why is Keating teaching at the school at all? Granted, he is an honors graduate of the institution, but surely the kind of anti-authoritarian behavior that he exhibits at Welton must also have been evident in his previous job, and even in his actions when he was a student. And once Welton's administrators saw how Keating was conducting his classes, why didn't he receive a stern reprimand and dismissal? Moreover, while it's clear that Keating is meant to represent independence and self-determination, qualities antithetical to those promulgated at the school, his antics often seem clichéd and unconvincing. Moreover, the students under his tutelage transform far too easily and quickly, from being repressed to being daring, for the change in them to be real. The annoyingly repetitive cries of "carpe diem" make it seem as though the students have not been liberated from their formerly reserved lifestyles so much as they have unthinkingly adopted one mode of behavior in place of another, with the nagging suspicion that they have done so merely to be rebellious. The only time that the behavior of one of Keating's students seems plausible is when Charlie plays the joke with the phony telephone call during the headmaster's speech, an act whose daring is consistent with the character's already-established sense of bizarre and unruly humor.

In her book *Feminism Without Women,* Tania Modleski has made much of the film's homophilic aspects.[7] Modleski's point is well taken; the bonding among the students is of a special variety. It's with Modleski's view that the film's homophilia is really a repressed homosexuality that I have the most difficulty. This approach is also quite evident in Gary Hentzi's *Film Quarterly* article.[8] I'm going to deal with both criticisms at length since they seem characteristic of a wrongheaded approach to Weir's films.

I have already dealt with the most of Hentzi's assertions in this book's introduction. It bears repeating that Hentzi is hostile to Weir and what he refers to as the director's "pop culture" attitude toward mysticism and the unconscious. Perhaps part of this hostility accounts for his apparent misreading of *Dead Poets.* Hentzi claims that homosexuality, repressed or otherwise, is necessarily suggested via single-sex boarding situations such as occur in *Picnic at Hanging Rock* and *Dead Poets.*[9] If this were true, we'd also have to assert that the armed services is a hotbed of gay longings and activities, an obvious absurdity. Hentzi draws attention to the fact that *Poets'* boys are "strikingly attractive young men,"[10] which seems an idiosyncratic response, since the students represent all sorts of physical types. A few are intentionally made to seem unattractive, as is the case with Cameron, whose somewhat unpleasant physical features give us a clue to the character's potential for being a hypocrite and informer. Moreover, Hentzi seems to be overlooking the film's use of physically attractive actors to sell itself as a product, as *The Year of Living Dangerously* does in its use of Mel Gibson and Sigourney Weaver, whose good looks appeal to audiences.

Hentzi implies that the boys' retreat to the cave "inevitably suggests less elevated adolescent rituals,"[11] by which I must assume that he is referring to group masturbation, an activity that doesn't seem possible given the way that the characters are conceived. As for Neil's playing Puck in the school play, which Hentzi claims is an obvious sign of repressed homosexual yearnings,[12] true, Puck is a fairy, but he's hardly gay; rather, doesn't Neil's assumption of the part signal his desire to escape from the crudities of the material world represented by his father? Along with Hentzi, Modleski contends that there is a pronounced homoeroticism in *Picnic at Hanging Rock, Gallipoli,* and *Dead Poets Society.*[13] Certainly one sees a strong affinity among same-sex characters in these films, but is it justifiable to equate affinity with sexual predilection?

What is additionally troubling about Hentzi and Modleski's writing is that their arguments are often supported either through faulty citations or reductionist assertions. With regard to *Picnic at Hanging Rock*, Hentzi states that "homosexuality . . . becomes a key part of [the film's] mystery . . . when one of the school girls who are shortly to disappear without a trace raises eyebrows by calling her companion 'a Botticellian Venus.'"[14] However, the remark is not made by one of the schoolgirls but by Mademoiselle de Portiers; Miranda is not called a "Venus" but an "angel"; and when Miss McCraw raises her eyebrows in response to this remark, she does so not out of shock or outrage but with the bemused irony that characterizes much of her behavior.[15] Similarly, Modleski maintains that during the investigation into Neil's suicide in *Dead Poets*, "the boys are called individually up to the principal, who orders them to 'assume the position,' and then paddles them,"[16] when in fact the only paddling that takes place in the film occurs much earlier, when Charlie is disciplined after his stunt involving the phony phone call. Modleski thus overlooks the important distinction between an act of rebellion meant to be taken as a sarcastic joke and serious acts of betrayal about which most of the students who "testify" against Keating feel ashamed.[17]

More problematic is the manner of argumentation that Hentzi and Modleski use. Each writer uses as support for their contention that Weir's cinema is rife with evidence of homoeroticism the premise that at least as significant as what is seen in the films is what is not. Writing about what he regards as Weir's "persistent interest in homosexuality,"[18] Hentzi notes,

> The motif of hidden sexuality in [Weir's] films is itself a figure for a larger and considerably more ambiguous set of issues to which he has returned again and again, though with less ponderous obtusiveness in recent years. For it is not gay-

ness as a way of life that interests him, nor is it the discrimination that homosexuals have traditionally suffered. Rather, it is the fact that "the love that dare not speak its name" is a taboo subject in a genteel society, and, as such, exists in near kinship with ideas of the sacred—another invisible and irrational force that cannot be accommodated within polite discourse. This is the theme that remains closest to Weir's heart.[19]

What Hentzi is saying, then, is that the real subject of Weir's films is what they do not say—that not characterizing homosexuality is to draw attention to it by its absence. This type of specious argument, which also makes possible attacks against books such as *Heart of Darkness* for not dealing with issues with which they are not concerned[20] (David Denby refers to this technique as "blaming writers for what they *fail to write about*," which he considers "an extraordinarily wrongheaded way of reading them"),[21] can to a certain extent also be seen in Toni Morrison's analysis of American literature. Morrison contends that "even, and especially, when American texts are not 'about' Africanist presences or characters or narrative or idiom, the shadow hovers in implication, in sign, in line of demarcation."[22] However, Morrison's attitude is more well-founded than Hentzi's, since she provides valid textual evidence for it.[23]

The problems with Hentzi's approach are mirrored in Modleski's criticism, the weight of whose argument rests on what she considers *Dead Poets'* pronounced emphasis on homosexuality. Modleski asserts

> the insistence on boyhood sexual innocence is so extreme that the film may be said to mark the return of the "hysterical" text, in which the weight of the not-said, that which is again rapidly becoming "unspeakable," threatens to capsize the work's literal meaning. According to Geoffrey Nowell-Smith, who uses the term in discussing the family melodramas of the 1950s, the "hysterical text" is one in which the repressed sexual content of a film, banished from the film's narrative, returns to manifest itself in various ways in the *mise-en-scene* and through textual incoherences. In *Dead Poets,* the repressed content is related to homoeroticism and gay sexuality.[24]

The only film to which Nowell-Smith applies his analysis in detail is *The Cobweb,* yet in his (extremely brief) discussion of one scene in that film, he provides verifiable empirical grounding for his argument.[25] The same cannot be said for Modleski's critique of Weir. A critical technique's usefulness is determined by the validity of the evidence that it uses and the applicability of the conclusions that it yields; on this basis, Modleski's assertions are somewhat suspect.

Nowhere in her article, for example, does Modleski provide any evidence that *Dead Poets* "insisten[tly]" and in an "extreme" fashion characterizes boyhood sexuality as innocent; indeed, the displaying of a Playboy centerfold during one of the cave meetings, and the strong sexual anxiety that the boys obviously feel when two young women join them in the midst of a later meeting, point to precisely the opposite conclusion. Modleski goes on to contend that although "Weir['s] . . . previous work (e.g. *Gallipoli, Picnic at Hanging Rock*) is suffused with a lyrical homoeroticism, *Dead Poets* denies this dimension of boarding school life so resolutely that its repression can be systematically traced."[26] She states that the film's failure to mention Whitman's gayness is evidence of its attitude of denial (another example of justifying what supposedly is by what is not),[27] a view that discounts the fact that Whitman is being used in the film as a symbol of free expression and exuberance, qualities that even Modleski would probably admit are separable from his gayness. Modleski goes on to characterize the film's quiet student, Todd, as a young man in the throes of "a sexual identity crisis,"[28] as though virtually all young men of this age didn't pass through this stage. Modleski states, "a more honest version of the film might have . . . shown [Todd] struggling to come to terms with being gay in a heterosexual, homosocial environment,"[29] thereby again judging the film by what it never purports to do and asking us to accept a conditional argument as a workable premise.

Modleski refers to the film's references to heterosexual relationships (the picture of his woman that Keating has in his room; what she refers to as the "banal subplot" involving Knox and Chris) as "'disclaimers'" meant to distract attention from the film's real meanings, and once again backs off from actually asserting her thesis by stating that "such 'disclaimers' . . . and narrative incoherences [which she never identifies] *might be taken* as indicators of the film's repressed homoerotic content" (my emphasis).[30]

Modleski draws attention to the film's final image of Todd enclosed within what she refers to as "the inverted V" of another student's legs as an example of "the sexualized body which has been so systematically denied throughout the narrative."[31] Apparently, Modleski feels that this image confirms her reading of Todd as a repressed homosexual, yet she overlooks the fact that previous to this shot, two shots of Mr. Nolan are identically framed. Would she want to accuse Nolan of repressed homosexuality as well, or would this shot rather compel her to treat all of these images as signs of the repression (or, in Todd's case, the renewed threat of repression) of the adventurous instinct in characters who are heterosexual, precisely the attitude espoused by the school's Latin teacher, who tells Keating that he is proud to be "unfettered by foolish dreams."

Somewhat intriguingly, both Hentzi and Modleski point to the scene in which Keating compels the reticent Todd to spew forth freeform poetry as an example of repression being unleashed.[32] Hentzi never makes the connection between repressed homoeroticism and this scene explicit, but he would doubtless agree with Modleski's statement that the scene demonstrates the presence of a "*possible* 'latent' homosexual theme [that is] overdetermined" (my emphasis),[33] a tentative contention for which no supporting proof is offered. Granted, Todd's outburst is rife with imagery concerning a "sweaty-toothed madman" and "truth," but none of this imagery, which hardly seems to point to homosexuality, is even mentioned by Hentzi and Modleski.

It's clear that Hentzi and Modleski are drawing upon Weir's fascination with the uncanny to posit an equivalence between repressed elements and homoeroticism. The structure certainly fits into Weir's ideas about psychology; the problem is that while there are narrative and structural elements in Weir's films that justify our reading their uncanny elements as relating to certain crises of identity, neither Hentzi nor Modleski provide evidence that these crises embrace homosexuality. Moreover, to satisfy a desire for a purely sexual reading of Weir's same-sex films, Hentzi and Modleski insist on confusing homophilia with homoeroticism.

It's not *Dead Poets*' homophilia (the self-enclosure of which is affirmed in the film's last shot) that is its most striking characteristic but its implausibility. Chris, the young blonde with whom Knox falls in love, would never have so quickly abandoned her boyfriend in favor of Knox; nor does Neil's response to the threat of being pulled out of the school seem anything other than dramatically excessive, this despite its romantic aspects. Indeed, since Neil's character, like virtually everyone else in the film, resembles more of a type than an individual, the suicide, at best, seems more histrionic than tragic. What rescues the film from this depressing conclusion is its fabulous tone. The improbable events and impossible characterizations (has there ever been a parent as sternly unyielding as Neil's father?) are qualities of a fiction in which players represent humors, and action is exaggerated. Seen in this way, *Dead Poets Society* functions as a cautionary tale, reminding us that we must constantly be on guard against our lives descending into unemotional materialism, especially when the potential for joyful, rebellious change is waiting for us at any moment.

Kissing America goodbye: The departure of the Fox family (Harrison Ford, Helen Mirren, River Phoenix, Hilary Gordon, Jadrien Steele, and Rebecca Gordon) in *The Mosquito Coast*

Hiding from technologically induced destruction: *The Mosquito Coast*'s Allie Fox (Harrison Ford)

Aftermath: The Foxes and Mr. Haddy (Conrad Roberts) in *The Mosquito Coast*

"And gladly would he learn, and gladly teach": Robin Williams as *Dead Poets Society*'s John Keating

Liberating repressed impulses: Todd (Ethan Hawke) and Keating in *Dead Poets Society*

Creating the illusion of marriage: Brontë (Andie MacDowell) and Georges (Gérard Depardieu) in *Green Card*

A classic Weir moment of leavetaking: *Green Card*'s Brontë and Georges

Salvation and destruction: Jeff Bridges as *Fearless*'s Max Klein

Resurrecting "the moment of [one's] death": Max in *Fearless*

Carla (Rosie Perez) and Max in *Fearless*

Max's dream recollection of leading survivors "into the light"

Hieronymus Bosch's "Ascent to the Empyrean." (Courtesy Palazzo Ducale, Venice)

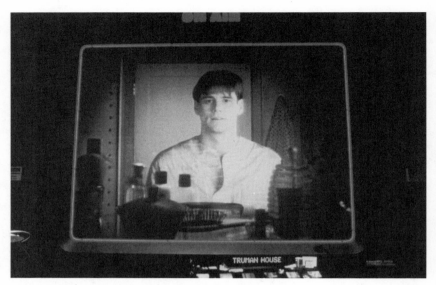

Jim Carrey as Truman Burbank in *The Truman Show*

The plot begins to unravel: *The Truman Show*'s Marlon (Noah Emmerich) and Truman

Domesticity has never seemed more terrifying: Truman and his wife, Meryl (Laura Linney), in *The Truman Show*

Truman at the travel agency

The dark father/puppeteer and (*at his left*) his assistant: Christof (Ed Harris) and the Control Room Director (Paul Giamatti) in *The Truman Show*

The ever-pensive sadist:
The Truman Show's Christof

JUNGLE UNDER GLASS

Many of Weir's thematic concerns are apparent in *Green Card*: the clash of different cultures; the emergence, through confrontation, of repressed feelings and memories; the opposition between the city and sparsely inhabited, fecund regions that represent nature in its unchecked form. Georges, a French immigrant who wants to become a U.S. citizen, is Weir's "primal" character, untamed by many of society's niceties. Brontë, the woman who agrees to marry Georges so that he can become a citizen and she can get an apartment with a conservatory in a marrieds-only co-op, represents the repressed urbanite, a sophisticate with little knowledge of her needs and desires who is contrasted with Georges, a character (whom Brontë at one point refers to as "a beast") associated with the subconscious. Yet Weir modifies this schema somewhat by linking Brontë with a lush world, one that is isolated from the concrete and metal materialism of the city. Brontë's work with the environmental group the Green Guerrillas, who plant shrubs and trees on open city lots, involves attempting to inject a bit of greenery into small pockets of space that are threateningly surrounded with large buildings. Brontë's real respite from urban anxiety, though, is her conservatory. This hermetically sealed jungle acts as a symbol for a protected world within which she feels comfortable. Like Hawthorne's Beatrice Rappacini in the story "Rappacini's Daughter," Brontë only seems to flourish when she is within her "garden": when she first enters it she breathes a sigh of pleasure and release. Otherwise, Brontë is quite similar to her boyfriend, Phil: morally and politically correct, overly intellectual, dull.

In previous Weir films such as *The Last Wave* and *The Year of Living Dangerously*, dark-skinned characters represented the idea of the "other," the subconscious, or notions associated with nature and mystery. In *Green Card*, although there are African-American actors at the film's fringes, there are no central characters of color. Ideas that Weir associates with people of color—the unconscious, unrepressed feelings, the natural world, mystery—remain but are for the most part represented either through a white character, Georges, or through things: plants, the Afrika Café, or Brontë's conservatory. Apparently, Weir has transplanted his usual concerns into an essentially white city environment.

Yet despite the presence of familiar Weir themes, the film is in some respects quite unsatisfactory. For one thing, there's no spark and magnetism between its two main players. As she demonstrated in films such as *sex, lies, and videotape* (1989) and *Four Weddings and a Funeral* (1994), Andie MacDowell (Brontë) is an actress who has an extremely limited emotional range; and though the character that she plays is meant to seem repressed, one needs to intuit in her the possibility of greater responsiveness in order to make her repression seem regrettable. Gérard Depardieu (Georges) is a bit more likable, yet he's hampered by an awkwardness at playing comedy, possibly a result of his being unfamiliar with American acting styles (this quality was also evident in his later film *My Father, The Hero* (1994), which, like *Green Card*, was obviously intended to introduce Depardieu to American audiences and transform him into some sort of international comedy star).[1] Moreover, in *Green Card* Depardieu is essentially used as a buffoon, with Weir going for crude jokes, some based on a lack of understanding of another language, as when Georges, pretending to be a handyman, announces in front of Brontë's parents that he needs "a screw."

Some of the film's elements might have been of interest if they had been given full play, such as Brontë's conservatory (a rather blatant metaphor for her insularity), which mists plants in such a way that it appears as though it is raining indoors, an otherworldly element that seems a carryover from two scenes in *The Last Wave*. In the earlier film, though, the images, being unexpected, had some force. In *Green Card*, the idea behind the image is there, but it isn't presented in a way that makes it seem unusual, thereby denying it any potential power.

It is clear that Weir tried to base his film's structure and approach on American screwball comedies. We have a couple somewhat like the one in *His Girl Friday* (1940), who are really attracted to one another but whose relationship is thwarted by the woman's being involved with a second man who is a crashing bore. But where in screwball films the central couple, by virtue of their wisecracking personalities, seem right for each other, *Green Card*'s Georges and Brontë seem suited only in a conceptual way; they're more an idea of a couple than two people who, deep down, seem compatible. The film's attempts at comedy, such as the rush to accommodate the visiting parents, or the general awkwardness at the society dinner during which Georges seems a bit like Michel Simon's impolite tramp character in Jean Renoir's *Boudu Saved from Drowning* (1932), are for the most part ineffective and embarrassing.

One way to partially rescue *Green Card* from condemnation is to view it as a somewhat naive immigrant's view of America, an approach that would ally Depardieu's character with the sensibility of someone like Weir himself. What often happens in American filmmaking is that a foreign director can bring a fresh perspective to what threatens to become a shopworn genre, such as the gangster film; the work in gangster movies of Michael Curtiz and Fritz Lang is a case in point. We already know that Weir's Australian background predisposes him to themes such as loneliness, alienation, and fundamental symbols, while his interest in melding the past and the present (presumably an outgrowth of his country's continuing awareness of its origins) and his interest in religion (which may derive from the Australian contact with its Aboriginal population) characterize all of his filmmaking. In *Green Card,* many of these elements are brought together. Georges is quite obviously a cultural outsider in America, and it is perhaps not only ironic but, from a fictive point of view, satisfying to see him allied with a woman who only seems to be well-integrated into her culture. In fact, Brontë's insistence on saving trees and working with plants signals not only an alienation from humans and the deleterious effect that they can have on the natural world (a concern that parallels Georges' alienation from people) but also works against her ever feeling comfortable within her own society, which is heavily skewed in favor of industrialization and the concomitant destruction of fertile areas. In this sense, both Brontë and Georges have a built-in affinity, which they only begin to recognize late in the film. Both characters are, in essence, working on their own form of green card, the green color suggesting not only an entrance into a new, restored, Edenic world but also a natural orientation that is almost doomed to failure unless it is played out in an environment sealed off from the inroads of material considerations involving cultural identity, alien status, and the day-to-day demands of living in the material world. In essence, both the plants in Brontë's conservatory and the relationship between Georges and Brontë can only thrive within an artificially controlled and limited milieu.

Through her relationship with Georges, though, Brontë manages to increase the significance of the effect that she has on the world outside of her sealed universe. As a result of Georges' efforts, she obtains a group of trees that she wants to plant so that urban children can get a strong sense of nature. By obtaining the trees, Brontë narrows the gap between her otherwise hermetic world and the material world, with positive effects in both realms.

What we see in the film is another version of the mystical, wish-fulfilling movement into the fantastic Shakespearean green world to which Northrop Frye repeatedly draws attention, a world that offers respite from the demands of what has become a spiritually impoverished material existence.[2] Also invoked in the film is the opposition between the garden and the city (here present as gardens within the city) and the clash between culture and wildness, with Georges representing Rousseau's primal man, with whom Brontë enters into a social contract, ironically in order to allow him to remain within a culture in which he doesn't really fit. Taken in this way, as more of an intellectual exercise than as a representation of convincing emotions, the film seems less an attempt at creating humor than depicting differing humors (Georges as the beast, Brontë as the urban beauty), comedy here being understood not as something amusing but in the classic sense, as a representation of human attitudes.

As the film's resolution makes plain, though, cultural melding is not possible given the restrictive demands of American society, this despite the country's view of itself as a great melting pot of different people. Despite its "welcoming the masses" image, Green Card's America is characterized as an essentially closed society that demands that a foreigner either adapt or be expelled. In this regard, the film functions as a meditation on cultural exclusion and the nature of the United States, with Georges assuming the same misfit role that Sara in Picnic at Hanging Rock, the Aborigines in The Last Wave, John Book in Witness, and John Keating in Dead Poets Society play. In all of these films, characters are thrown into contact with a society that scorns or cannot accept the outsider. Like Book and Rachel in Witness, Georges and Brontë are from two distinct worlds that can meet but not be joined. What Weir seems to be saying in Green Card is that as in Witness, whose conclusion is decidedly melancholy, romance between people from different milieus and with such different cultural attitudes may be destined to fail.

Perhaps the most successful portion of Green Card comes two-thirds of the way through the film, when Georges and Brontë prepare for their upcoming immigration interview. The couple not only study each other's personal habits but also create a fictional past out of words and pictures, spinning a fantasy to convince a dubious audience. Georges and Brontë's emotional and intellectual distance starts to vanish in the process of creating this fiction. Brontë begins to realize that she is attracted to Georges; in a letter meant for the immigration people to read, Georges writes, "it is hot here in Africa and very green," inadvertently referring to his passion for Brontë and the color of her plants. After the study session, Georges and Brontë prepare for bed, each in complementary fashion undressing. When Brontë is in her bedroom, her point of view takes over and she focuses on her bedroom door, wondering, as does the audience, if Georges is going to enter the room. Frustrating the desires of both Brontë and the audience, he doesn't, although in distance there is still closeness, as can be seen when Georges, talking to Brontë through the wall, asks her which side of the bed she sleeps on and, finding out, takes the opposite side on the couch. Their sleeping together, albeit in suggestive fashion, has become complete.

At the interview, when Georges and Brontë are once more separated, the cross-cutting between the two interviews again unites them until Georges inadvertently reveals their collusion. Yet it's precisely through their lies that the couple come to the truth about each other, realizing just when their enforced separation is imminent how devoted to each other they have become. At the end of the film, before they once again exchange symbolic rings and separate, Weir makes it plain in a poignant way that the greatest distance between people isn't physical but psychological.

At *Green Card*'s conclusion, as in *Witness*, the apparently ill-suited couple comes together one last time. As she had at the film's beginning, Brontë sees Georges through the greenhouse-like barrier of the Afrika Café's window. She runs outside and they embrace, after which the law (in the person of immigration officer Gorsky) acts to separate them (another *Witness* borrowing). Yet unlike *Witness*, *Green Card*'s farewell may be only temporary.[3] The hope that the film holds out is that like its metaphoric Africa, love is lush and green, and may someday flourish even in the midst of New York's noisy concrete jungle.

A POSTHUMOUS LIFE

Fearless does more than present the story of an airline crash survivor. The film also chronicles a series of extraordinary physical and psychological experiences in the life of its central character, architect Max Klein, at the same time as it comments on the manner in which language and imagery can divert attention from the ways in which people deal with stressful circumstances, the most paramount being the threat of impending death.

Unfortunately, contemporary moviegoers have been repeatedly exposed to films involving the theme of death that use clichéd, safe representations. There is usually very little in these films that deals forthrightly with the pain and suffering that often accompany dying. What we get instead is the American way of cinematic death: death that is sterile, clean, sanitized. This isn't a surprising situation. Films are now so heavily market-driven that it's difficult to sell one about death to a studio unless it romanticizes the dying process. Somehow, though, Weir managed to convince Paramount Pictures to finance *Fearless*. Along with screenwriter Rafael Yglesias, he also cut through another kind of resistance: people's denial concerning death, which makes possible productive living but also prevents us from realizing the valuable lessons that can be gleaned from confronting our own mortality.

Max doesn't undergo the period of grief and mourning that sometimes occurs with the survivors of violent events who find it difficult to rationalize the fact that they lived through an event that killed other people. And though he tells the airline-appointed psychologist, Perlman, that like Carla, another crash survivor, he's also full of guilt and shame, he never exhibits these qualities. We must assume that Max is telling the truth. Max is probably unaware of his guilt and shame because they have mutated into a virtually pathological opposite form: instead of being fearful and inactive, Max feels indestructible.

158

Fearless starts placidly, with a shot of a cornfield in virtual silence, and then gradually introduces grey smoke drifting through the field, a sign that some unnatural event is taking place. We see Max carrying a baby and leading a young boy through the field; only after some extended, anxious moments, whose submerged anxiety is at odds with the smooth manner in which the camera tracks, does Weir cut away to a shot of a man kneeling on the ground and crossing himself, the first indication that something extraordinary has occurred.[1] To affirm this reaction, Weir cuts back to a shot of Max and then has him move from the cornfield onto a highway. In the shot's background, we see the wreckage of part of a jet plane.

Weir doesn't want us to dwell on the individual human aspects of this event at this point in the film, so he disengages our close response by cutting to an overhead shot taken from a helicopter passing over the scene, which shows us black smoke rising from the plane wreckage in a slow announcement of destruction. The god's-eye shot distances us from the event in an emotional and physical sense, the precise response that Max exhibits throughout the film's early sections, and then increases the image's complexity by having the helicopter's shadow (shadows traditionally being images of death and the spirit) pass across the landscape, reflect off the billowing smoke from the crash, and then again pass back across the landscape, all in such a fluid manner that the helicopter's shadow might be that of some great bird passing over this event. The image foreshadows one that Max later paints, in which a dark bird is flying over a fiery conflagration. Both the early and later images simultaneously represent the viewpoint of a dispassionate god as well as the attitude of someone who watches a disaster but is not directly involved in it; the latter is precisely Max's response. Thus, when he is asked by an airline employee who is assisting some survivors if he had been in the crash, Max replies "no." In a sense Max is, perhaps involuntarily, telling the truth here. As we will see later in the film, during the latter part of the crisis in the plane (after the pilots lose control of it), Max underwent a dissociation from his sense of self and experienced peace of mind in the face of death, a fearless response to a fearful situation.

As Max walks across the highway, Weir imperceptibly (as he will periodically throughout the film) shifts to a slight slow motion, an effect that reflects how, in extraordinary situations, events often seem to be taking place very slowly, another distancing effect that places us at a remove from what we perceive. This distancing is, doubtless, a typical human protective reaction. Although in *Fearless* this distancing takes the form of Max's delusion of invulnerability, it nonetheless has religious implications, since such a reaction could also result from a serene faith in God. The fact that *Fearless* posits a dual view, both secular and religious, and, further, promotes the idea that love, even the secular and sexual kind, has a redemptive and religious aspect,[2] testifies to the film's belief that God may be apprehended in multitudinous ways, and that sometimes, it takes a life-threatening event to make one realize just how precious life is. This dual approach, which emanates from the teleological ambiguity on which the best of Weir's films relies, not only affirms the existence of the divine in the commonplace but melds the dream and non-dream realms, suggesting that everything and everyone (even if they don't realize it) are part of a universal, purposeful existence.

In a representation of Max's point of view, we are shown various objects that are strewn on the highway: a baby's shoe and an adult boot, a burned corpse that is being covered, a rolling champagne bottle. Weir immediately shifts to an objective shot that for a time releases us from a close involvement with Max but which encourages in us a complex response of its own. Again depicted in slow motion, Max is seen walking toward the camera; as he does so, a young girl, in front of him and at screen left, starts running toward the camera, crying for her mother. The image calls to mind the famous photograph of a young Vietnamese girl running down the road away from the site of a napalm attack. Implicitly cited here, then, are those Vietnam veterans who experienced a sense of fearlessness as a result of post-traumatic stress syndrome. Present as well in the shot is the notion of a traumatized victim seeking a parent or nurturing figure for solace, a situation duplicated not only in the reaction of Byron, a young crash survivor whose hand Max is holding, but also in Max's attitude toward his wife at the film's end, when he asks her to save him and, through an obvious affirmation of the redemptive power of love, she does so.

One of the ways in which Weir tells us that, despite Max's supposed inner calm, the effects of the crash are never far from him is to place Max in a location in which visual or sensory aspects of the inside of a jet plane are present as reminders of the source of his present, unusual psychology. Immediately after leaving the crash site, Max checks into a hotel. Weir gives us a shot of Max walking down the hotel's corridor. The evenly spaced lights along the corridor's walls combine with a slight ventilation noise to duplicate two of the most prevalent aspects of an airborne plane's cabin: the lights along the aisle and the engines' background hum. It's only the audience that makes this connection, though, not Max, who throughout most of the film is, as one might expect of a disaster survivor, incognizant of the precise significance of what has happened to him. All that Max realizes at this point in the film is that, as he says to himself while in the hotel bathroom, "You didn't die."

Before Max finally arrives in Los Angeles (he has not telephoned his wife to let her know that he is alive, another indication that Max's emotional responses are skewed), he visits an old friend, a woman whom he hasn't seen in twenty years. The woman's husband's current situation, we later realize, parallels Max's, not so much with regard to his unfulfilled life but primarily in the fact that, as the woman explains, her husband is "screwing" one of his students, a situation roughly comparable to that between Max and Carla, who for a time functions as Max's disciple, and to whom he is sexually attracted.[3]

The woman refers to her life as "a disaster," one that is pathetic and tragic. Max contradicts her, telling her that her life is not a disaster, just as he doubtless feels that the plane crash wasn't a disaster either. The most significant point, though, is that the woman doesn't mean "disaster" literally; for her, it's a catch-all term whose use here (although she doesn't know it) represents a distancing between word and literal meaning. This situation not only mirrors Max's displacement of his feelings, but is a classic example of linguistic alienation, a separation between what is felt and what is expressed that we can most productively view (in Max's case) as a protective response. It's notable that not once in *Fearless* do we see Max *consciously* reliving (or even talking about) the trauma that he underwent during the moments before the crash (Max recalls the events during dreams that, atypically for Weir, are usually depicted without overt stylization). Instead, when he does panic—first during a negotiating session in the office of Brillstein (a lawyer working on damage suits related to the crash), and later, when Carla becomes terribly upset about the death of her son—he does so because of the compromising of his ideals in the first instance, and his powerlessness to help Carla in the second, both of them situations that replay, albeit on a small scale, his helplessness after the plane lost control. In each case, Max violently rebels against circumstances that bring back to him the worst aspects of the plane experience, although he attempts to detach himself from them when they occur by recreating the giddy feeling of invulnerability that he felt on the plane, either by going up to the roof of Brillstein's office building and dancing wildly on the ledge or hazarding his and Carla's lives. In each case, Max's conviction that he is not susceptible to death is reinvoked through extraordinary circumstances.[4]

Like *The Year of Living Dangerously,* in which Guy's loss of vision signaled a lack of critical insight, *Fearless* uses figurative representation to comment on a character's existence. The loss of the plane's ability to steer acts as an analogue for one of Max's attributes, in this case a life lived without direction, one in which one's architecture projects are often no more significant than the design of discount stores for a ridiculously named chain, Nutty Nick's. The spiritual bankruptcy of Max's firm's designs yields to the richness of the symbolic representations to which he is exposed first via Carla (who is associated with the fecundity of Christian iconography), then via her husband Manny (who creates sensitive, ornate wood carvings). Later, during a tour of what Max refers to as "beautiful downtown Oakland," he and Carla gaze at the architectural splendor of churches and ornate buildings that eventually give way to the painful destitution of an inner-city neighborhood that for Max seems to represent the spiritually impoverished life that he is afraid of falling back into.

Yet the work of Max's that we see after the crash, his drawings and washes, is significant, reflecting an obsession with death that, if properly channeled and integrated into an existence in which the compromises and realities of life are dealt with instead of avoided, promises a fulfilling existence that wouldn't have been possible before the crash. The crash, then, can have significant value, depending upon how Max responds to it.

For now, though, Max is experiencing a displacement between event and response that has converted him into something of an automaton. In a pancake house with his old friend, Max eats some strawberries, to which he knows he is allergic. After eating the strawberries, though, Max does not have any kind of allergic response. "I thought you nearly died once eating one of those," the woman states, to which Max replies, "I'm past all that. See, no reaction, no reaction at all," an (unintentional) indication of how divorced Max's responses have become from his real feelings.

One of the ways that Max is able to deflect the unpleasantness of the crash—this despite the fact that he consciously contends that it was the best thing that ever happened to him—is to speak about surviving it in terms that deflect his underlying feelings or that refer to him in an impersonal way. In essence, this displacement is characteristic of Max's behavior throughout the film up until its final sequence, when the most significant aspect of the pre-crash experience, that of impending death, is repeated after Max, intentionally placing himself in jeopardy, eats a strawberry and, the logic of his bodily reactions restored as a sign of his return to emotional health, has a near-fatal anaphylactic shock reaction during which his role as savior (which is heralded by the media throughout the film) is transferred to his wife.

The experience and psychological effects of the crash are invoked in the film in four different ways: in the already-mentioned linguistic displacement (e.g., before the crash, Max calmly says to himself, "This is it; this is the moment of your death"); through slow motion (itself a displacement between real time and film time); through the use of hands, which take on secular and religious significance; and through images of light, which become symbols for the religious experience that Max had on the plane.

During the scene in which Max and Carla are shopping at a mall for "presents for the dead," Carla notices a woman with a small child about her son's age and moves closer to smell the child and touch his hair. At this point,

Weir—as in *Witness* and at other points in *Fearless*—virtually imperceptibly shifts to a slight slow motion effect, creating the impression that Carla's actions have an otherworldly sense to them, as though they are taking place in a dream. (Noting the mother and child's lack of reaction to either herself or Max, Carla says to Max, "maybe we *are* ghosts.") Like *The Last Wave*'s David, Carla and Max are in the dreamtime without realizing it, and they remain there until another event as violent and life-threatening as the crash occurs to deliver them back into the material world.

Given the stress that the film places on images of hands and light, we are encouraged to view *Fearless*'s entire action not only as an investigation into the relation between the secular and religious realms, but also as a spiritual metaphor for life and death, with the plane crash acting as one of the many disasters that occur in life, and the survival of it as a sign, not of human effort, but of divine intercession. In the film's view, all people are acting out a part in some great cosmic plan. In this sense, the iconic painting on Carla's apartment's wall makes perfect sense: a hand, below the clouds, holds up divine figures. We see many hands throughout the film: Max's partner's, which is braced against the plane's interior; Max's hand, which is seen against the window of the bus that takes his son to school; the hand belonging to Byron, the boy whom Max comforts on the plane, who doesn't want to let go of Max's hand; Carla's hand, which Max grasps; Max's own hand, with which he grasps his partner's hand, which he places on the heads of various people before the crash, and which he uses to lead people out of the wreckage, beckoning to them to follow him out of the darkness of the crash and into a deliverance from disaster that is conceived of in terms of light. Finally and most importantly, there is the hand that Max's wife extends to him when she literally brings him back from the dead during his allergic reaction toward the film's end. All of these hand gestures symbolize reaching out for comfort and assurance. Ultimately, then, the film acts as a parable of salvation.

The emphasis on hands resurfaces prominently when Max talks about the death of his father. "It looked like somebody with a big hand just reached out and squeezed the life out of him," he says. Carla replies, "That was God." Even though in Carla's more traditionally oriented view it is God's hands that touch people, she nevertheless regards Max as an angel sent from God, a notion that Max's wife contradicts when she says, "Max is a man." It's on the tension between these notions of the source of comfort that the action of the film is based. Are acts of mercy divine or secular in origin? Ultimately, *Fearless* renders the question moot by collapsing the realms; in the film's view, *all* acts of kindness have a religious aspect.

It is through manifestations in the material world that signs of an otherworldly presence come. Most of the time, such signs take the form of light, a traditional symbol for god and inspiration. Thus, just before Max has his idea about what needs to be done to deliver Carla from her fit of guilt over her child's death, a gust of wind and a flash of light (probably from a passing car) brush over Max, while at the same time, Maurice Jarre's musical accompaniment begins to sound like an organ, hinting at the religious nature of what has just occurred.

Throughout his work, Weir has been searching for new, more effective ways of communicating the divine or otherworldly, the dream world, through images and objects from the material world. The uncommon nature of the rain and water images in *The Last Wave,* the light around Rachel's head in *Witness*—examples like these testify to this tendency on Weir's part. In each of these cases, we see the otherworldly realm announcing itself, with the attendant, strong suggestion that the religious element of the dream world, of the subconscious realm, surrounds us at all times and resurfaces despite our materialist bent.

Fearless depicts the search and need for some form of deliverance—thus the newspaper headline word "savior" (from an article about Max) that Max's son has pasted onto the cover of his scrapbook. The transcendent light that breaks through in all of Max's dreams of the crash show him that all he really needs to be delivered from the burden of being a savior is to have someone save him. The implication of this round of salvation is that a good deed done by one encourages a good deed to be done by others: after saving the people on the plane, and redeeming Carla from her guilt, Max is saved from a deadly anaphylactic shock reaction by his wife, who literally breathes life into him. In so doing, she brings him back into the world of the living, a world, as Weir depicts it, permeated with the religious in even the most common places.

Given the manner in which otherworldliness, either as a representation of Max's dispassionate status or as an indication of the presence of some god-like power in this life, becomes an informing principle throughout *Fearless,* it is not surprising that there are so many barely noticeable mirror shots in the film, which suggest an alternate realm.[5] When Max is standing in the hotel bathroom after the crash and says to himself, "You're not dead," the effect of the scene's previous, straightforward shots (along with a subsequent shot's framing, which places Max at the frame's far left) tend to divert us from realizing that the Max whom we see speaking these lines is a mirror image of the real Max who, in psychological terms, is already (in his own words) a "ghost." (The scene's effect is repeated later when Max and his wife stand in front of a mirror; his wife's paleness at this point reflects the currently enervated state of their marriage.) Later, when Max and Carla leave her apartment to go to church,

Max again passes in front of a mirror. This time, as he does so, Carla's off-screen opening of the apartment door casts a beam of light onto Max's face, at once (as in the later examples of this trope, which include the reflection off a vagrant's tin can before Max decides to cross a busy highway) emphasizing inspiration, divine light, and underscoring Max's status as a savior.

Each of these light-and-mirror events reinvokes the film's original moment of divine intercession when Max, on the plane, looked out of a window, saw a light, and entered into a soundless, otherworldly region in which he was delivered from his fear. At points like these (as when he walks past a sign reading "Danger—Keep Out" and onto an abandoned highway ramp), Max has passed into a realm in which the usual cautions have given way. Yet it's only through the repeated hazarding of his life that Max discovers its true significance. In this sense, Perlman (who, like Brillstein, takes a materialist reading of events and situations) is only partially correct when he says that what Max (whom Perlman diagnoses as having post-traumatic stress syndrome) is doing by repeatedly endangering himself is trying to relive the fearless feeling that occurred during his near-death experience. Unknowingly, what Max is also trying to do is to reestablish contact with that power which at the moment of his near-death interceded for him and made him lose his fear. At this point in the film, only Carla, the only other central "religious" character in *Fearless*, perceives that in his own way, Max is trying to reach God.

When Max's wife looks through his artist's folder, she realizes (as Carla has) that the crisis Max is going through isn't psychological but spiritual, which she comes to understand when she discovers in the folder the reproduction of a painting showing a group of spirits approaching God. Although the painter's name is not identified in the film, the painting is clearly Hieronymus Bosch's "Ascent to the Empyrean" or "Ascent of the Blessed,"[6] one of four of what have come to be referred to as the Venetian "Paradise and Hell" panels. In these four panels are depicted redemption and damnation, concepts that have a strong relevance to *Fearless*'s action. "Reading" the panels from left to right,[7] there is, first, in the words of commentator Walter S. Gibson, "the Terrestrial Paradise, a sort of intermediate stage where the saved were cleansed of the last stain of sin before being admitted into the presence of God,"[8] a phase that seems equivalent to the time in the plane when Max saw the light coming through the window and felt delivered from his fear. The second panel, the "Ascent of the Blessed," is the one in Max's folder. Gibson describes this panel in the following way.

> Shedding the last vestiges of their corporeality, the blessed souls float upwards through the night, scarcely supported by their angel guides. They gaze with ecstatic yearning towards the great light which bursts through the darkness overhead. This funnel-shaped radiance, with its distinct segments . . . has become a

shining corridor through which the blessed approach that final and perpetual union of the soul with God which is experienced on earth only in rare moments of spiritual exaltation. "Here the heart opens itself in joy and desire," [the fourteenth-century mystic] Ruysbroek tells us, "and all the veins gape, and all the powers of the soul are in readiness." Suso describes how the tremulous, enraptured soul is conducted above the ninth heaven in the *coelum empyreum*, the flaming heaven, there to gaze at the "immeasurable, all-pervading, immovable, incorruptible brightness."[9]

All of the essential elements of *Fearless* are contained here: the release from fear of death; the ecstatic yearning for union with the godhead (as art critic Lynda Harris describes the panel, the route depicted leads to a world "far beyond the illusions of the material universe");[10] the "funnel-shaped . . . shining corridor" (after the crash, this aspect is present in the film in the form of the plane's cabin); the "flaming heaven" and "incorruptible brightness" into which Max leads the crash's survivors as he urges them to pass through the plane's burning destruction (which, though it is represented as a vague darkness, is figuratively construed in a positive sense) and "follow [him] into the light." Moreover, the Bosch painting of which this panel is only a part even contains a panel depicting the fall into Hell, a descent figuratively and potentially present in the film each time Max feels his fearlessness slipping away from him, threatening to send him into emotional depths. The "Ascent of the Blessed" panel, then, sums up all of the joys and sorrows that Max experiences in the film; and it must be, not coincidence, but spiritual insight that has compelled Max to keep this image in his folder.

Realizing, albeit unconsciously, that he has been touched by something religious during the plane experience, Max struggles after the accident with the feeling that he is being impelled toward a divine explanation for his sense of fearlessness. At the same time, though, having rejected God after his father's death ("I didn't know why God killed my daddy. There was no reason to, so I decided there was no God," Max says),[11] Max resists what he apparently considers a reductionist, religious explanation for his symptomatic unease. Instead, visually trained as an architect (even in the church with Carla, while he scoffs at her devotion to Christian belief, he still looks around, somewhat appreciatively, at the building), he finds an outlet for his feelings through drawing; and what he draws expresses his desire for a return to the sense of wholeness that he felt on the plane, and which he reinvokes at the film's end.[12]

With only one exception (the previously mentioned "dark bird" image), there is an additional, recurring pattern in the art in Max's folder that he has created himself: a set of circular shapes that become increasingly more geometric as the pictures are flipped through. Most of Max's images are mandalas, images that draw upon collective unconscious representations of desires also expressed in the Bosch work. The significance of the mandala is explained by Jung.

> The analysis of [the patient's] situation will therefore lead sooner or later to a clarification of his general spiritual background going far beyond his personal determinants. . . . [T]his phase of the process is marked by the production of symbols of unity, the so-called mandalas, which occur either in dreams or in the form of concrete visual impressions, often as the most obvious compensation for the contradictions and conflicts of the conscious situation.[13]

Thus, rejecting Perlman's offered assistance, Max tries on his own to resolve his personal dilemma: the conflict between his view of himself as a materialistic atheist and the spiritual feeling he experienced on the plane. He does so in two ways: by helping Carla, and by creating art.[14] Moreover, virtually all of Max's drawings prominently feature a circular area at their center (the Bosch reproduction also contains such an area, which is placed somewhat off-center). In an early part of his study of psychology and alchemy, Jung notes,

> The first of the following two studies . . . deals with a series of dreams which contain numerous symbols of the center or goal. The development of these symbols is almost the equivalent of a healing process. The center or goal thus signifies *salvation* in the proper sense of the word. The justification for such a terminology comes from the dreams themselves, for these contain so many references to religious phenomena that I was able to use some of them as the subject of my book *Psychology* and *Religion*. It seems to me beyond all doubt that these processes are concerned with the religion-creating archetypes. Whatever else religion may be, those psychic ingredients of it which are empirically verifiable undoubtedly consist of unconscious manifestations of this kind.[15]

Innately, then, Max is aware of this aspect of his work as well, another reason why the Bosch reproduction is in his folder. Thus, when Max asks his wife toward the film's end to save him, he finally verbalizes his need for an essentially religious salvation, thus admitting it not only to his wife but to himself.

The fact that in the movie Weir has Yglesias make far more explicit than in the novel the story's underlying religious aspect (the book does not contain references to Carla's husband's beautiful wood carvings nor the stress on Christian imagery) makes it clear that Weir has resolved the conflict in his earlier films between the empirical and spiritual realms by appealing to a religious reconciliation of contraries. Weir has made his themes less arcane and more accessible at the same time as he has deepened their focus by transforming a concern with intellectual and psychological matters into one that is more emotional and personal.

In order to show Carla that she couldn't have prevented her son's death, Max, in a replay of the plane wreck, drives his car into a brick wall. Later, in the scene in which Max's wife comes to pick him up at the hospital, there is a row of street lights balanced on either side of her as she approaches the building. Two qualities prominent in the scene—the enclosure created by lights, and a character who leads another character out of a critical area—invoke the scene in which Max leads the plane crash survivors "into the light."[16] Paralleling this linkage of an event in the material world with Max's spiritual experience is the image on the cover of his son's scrapbook: the black bird from Max's drawing of the crash has been literalized as the dark body of the plane, which flies over a cornfield that the boy has drawn, and into which he has inserted a burst of reddish color. As in Max's drawing of the same event, two time periods, that of the plane's flight and the subsequent fiery crash, are collapsed in a notable demonstration of psychological correspondence between Max and his son.

Max's attempt to console Byron did more than soothe the boy: it also saved Max and, by extension, those whom he saved, since if he had remained sitting next to his partner and not gone forward to be with Byron, Max, like his partner, would very likely have been decapitated. The compassionate gesture, then, which represents Max's move from passivity to action, from being merely a nondescript architect who accepts work without considering its importance to an individual performing a spiritual act of redemption, is divinely fortuitous, initiating a chain of salvation that ultimately ends in an essential replay of the post-crash events, but this time with Max as the helpless victim and his wife as the savior who leads someone back to life. In both cases, the physical act of rescue becomes a spiritual act of salvation. What Weir himself has all along been moving toward in his films with his insistent depictions of confrontations between the material and spiritual realms, between idea and feeling, is this kind of satisfying synthesis, in which contradictions become meaningless in the light of grace. In *Fearless,* Weir has dared to assert a simple but profound truth: deliverance from metaphysical ambivalence is possible if one has faith and accepts that real significance comes from without, from the sacred presence that is all around us, even in the most quotidian of places. As the film demonstrates, with love—all of which is, ultimately, divine—anyone can truly be fearless.

12

A NIGHTMARE

The critical response to *The Truman Show* is characteristic of the range of reactions to Peter Weir's films. Some of the press coverage on the film was laudatory.[1] Alternatively, critic Michael Sragow said that "*The Truman Show* isn't 'about' nothing. It is nothing,"[2] thereby implying that not only was the acclaim over the film the result of people mistaking poorly formed notions for well-developed ideas, but that the film was inconsequential.

Throughout this book, I have worked from the premise that Weir is a filmmaker of ideas. To communicate his concepts, though, Weir often has to embed them in the films. At the same time, Weir is also aware of the fact that since he works in a popular art form, he has to provide entertainment. Certain critics feel that this type of approach is unnecessary. As Alain Robbe-Grillet said with regard to the supposed distinction between form and content,

> art is not a more or less brilliantly covered envelope intended to embellish the author's "message," a gilt paper around a package of cookies, a whitewash on a wall, a sauce that makes the fish go down easier. Art endures no servitude of this kind, nor any other pre-established function . . . it expresses nothing but itself.[3]

Weir is not quite like the artist to whom Robbe-Grillet implicitly alludes. He feels that he has to provide a certain amount of "sauce" to make "the fish" go down easier. At least for American filmmaking, Weir's approach seems warranted, since this country's films often place a greater stress on entertainment than edification, even if the two effects are not exclusive. However, Weir avoids using many of the techniques that other filmmakers employ. This is particularly true with regard to his insistence on allusiveness instead of concreteness, and his refusal to conventionally end his films.

However, *The Truman Show* does play some very interesting games. For one thing, it teases the viewer into thinking that they're in on the plot against

Truman Burbank (Jim Carrey), not a victim of it. Moreover, its sunny world is so diverting that we at first take no notice of the many signs Weir places into it which tell us that something in its unique world-within-a-world is woefully wrong. (How often do the film's twins, for example, shove Truman against the same wall on successive days just so that some more product placement can be achieved?)

Keeping the distinction between *The Truman Show* and "The Truman Show" (the television show within the film) in mind does more than allow us to distance ourselves from what happens in Seahaven; it also makes it possible to see that Weir has placed a dream world within a larger dream context. If the Seahaven dome proscribes Seahaven, then the film itself proscribes "The Truman Show." We measure the verisimilitude of "The Truman Show" against the reality of the film, and we measure both against the view of reality that we bring with us into the theater. Weir plays upon all three of these realms. In his role as the creator of the film, he is, at least in terms of function, somewhat like Christof, the creator of "the show." Outside of the film (e.g., when he talks about it in interviews), Weir functions as a somewhat distant observer of his own work. In this last regard, he resembles the audience, who both watch the film and reflect upon the way that their own lives are slowly unreeling.

Given the first two of these forms of awareness, it becomes difficult at times to determine which realm we're in at various points in the film. The iris shots and sound effects of lenses zooming in and out tell us that it's "the show" we're watching. When Truman and Sylvia (a young woman to whom Truman is attracted while in high school) escape from the school library and, out of Omnicom camera range, run off to the beach, it's purely the film in operation (a fact not without ramifications, since it implies that those moments not seen by the Omnicom eyes are the "truth" within this great fiction).[4] But what of the shots of the Ford logo, seen on the grill and front radio panel of Truman's car? Whose film, or "show," are we in then? Is this *Truman Show* product placement, and if so, how does it differ from the objectionable kind that occurs in "the show"?

Despite the fact that "the show" is a contrivance, it is at times quite moving for both audiences, "the show"'s and the film's. When, at night, Truman sits staring out at the sea while stray flashes of lightning appear in the sky and a lighthouse beam periodically washes over him, a wonderful sense of bittersweetness pervades. But moments such as this one are at variance with those "emotional" moments that Christof creates for the show's audience, as in the reunion between Truman and his "father." At these points, Weir is heavily emphasizing the distinction between what he and Christof do. All of the elements used by both "the show" and the film are, essentially, identical: actors, props, sets, technicians, special effects, music. What, for example, is the difference between the beach scene with Truman and Sylvia (which is accompanied by a lovely selection from a Chopin piano concerto)[5] and the one in which Truman and his long-lost father meet (behind which Christof lays in some evocative piano music played by Philip Glass)? The only difference (given that we accept the "reality" of the film) is that in the first instance, the emotions are prompted by a genuine moment, while in the second they're a response to a contrivance. At the time, Truman may feel that each scene is comparably real (although it is strongly suggested that by the time of the second scene, Truman has already decided that everything in Seahaven, even this highly emotional moment, is fake). But for those of us who (to appropriate the words of Truman's friend Marlon) are "in on it," the second scene is not only fake, it's offensive.

One has to wonder how Weir can maintain the distinction for himself between moments that seem real and those that may be perceived by the audience as contrived. To a great extent, he must rely on his intuition for guidance, and must guard against falling into the kind of ethical and emotional dishonesty, born of megalomania and self-delusion, to which Christof is prone. One additional way to avoid being duped is to refrain from surrounding one's self with sycophants or toadies, as Christof does.

Early on in the film, things begin to come undone when a klieg light falls from "the sky." Labeled with the name Sirius, the light seems to be part of a gallery of artificial stars that twinkle above this self-enclosed town in which the emphasis is on cleanliness and order. (In this respect, Seahaven is not unlike *The Cars That Ate Paris*'s community.) The fallen light marks a typical Weir beginning: a self-enclosed, apparently placid little community's serenity begins to unravel until, at the film's end, the protagonist—through a near-death cataclysm—steps completely outside of the realm of what has formerly passed for reality, having been led to this juncture as a result of an inquiry into his or her identity. *The Truman Show* is literally a quest film: in his quest for himself, Truman begins to question his world and his sense of self.

In many ways, Truman is encouraged to sublimate his most profound feelings. Freud's *Civilization and Its Discontents* is of great value in considering this type of behavior. Freud writes, "it is impossible to overlook the extent to which civilization is built upon a renunciation of instinct, how much it presupposes precisely the non-satisfaction (by suppression, repression or some other means?) of powerful instincts."[6]

Although the ambience of freedom that Seahaven weaves around Truman is illusory, the town in this respect is quite similar to the society in which many people live. The only difference is that since *The Truman Show* is a fable, Seahaven's manipulations are exaggerated, and therefore visible to us. Yet the film doesn't just make us root for Truman: it also encourages us to be like him, to be skeptical (in the literal sense of the word) with regard to our own worlds as well, to examine them more closely for signs of manipulation, deceit, techno-trickery. Weir wants us to be a bit more discerning so that even the minor impurities in our perceptions start to stand out as spots that seem to be very dark indeed. The film relies on our sensing that there is a stark opposition between the freedom that we, as audience, often take for granted and the controlled aspect of Truman's world. Perhaps one of the film's greatest achievements is that we do not at first see ourselves in Truman's shoes. The machinery behind Seahaven's placid exterior is so intricate that surely, it couldn't be similar to the forces that govern the world in which we live. Yet the more that we come to identify with Truman's plight and project ourselves into the Seahaven bubble, the more we begin to consider whether our own world is really as full of possibilities as it seems, or whether it may be as manipulated as Seahaven.

As Truman is told, every day in the town is beautiful—and why shouldn't it be, since the weather is technologically managed? As a domed city, Seahaven is an environment without discretion. It seals out vagaries in the weather, but seals in a vacuous existence. (In this respect, Seahaven is the antithesis of *Green Card*'s conservatory, which connotes fertility.) There's no unpredictability in this world, a fact that Truman turns to his advantage during his second attempt at escape. Spontaneity is not only the way that he defeats the system, but a means of preserving his sanity. For as Freud points out, in a severely repressed environment, there is a great danger of pathology. "If the loss [of instinct] is not compensated for economically, one can be certain that serious disorders will ensue."[7]

Truman dupes Christof into believing that he will stay in Seahaven even after he's discovered that there's a plot against him. (In Laingian terms, the paranoid view here is the only sane one.) Christof obviously thinks that Truman has accepted Marlon's explanation that what he views as a plot against him is just the projection of his own anxieties. Apparently assured, Christof arranges for another woman to take the place of Truman's departed wife, Meryl. But Truman is planning his escape. Eventually, he tunnels out of his basement like a desperate nocturnal creature and heads for the place of freedom, the sea. What he leaves behind is a host of nightmarish creatures for whom we can only feel the most intense disdain.

In Alfred Hitchcock's *Shadow of a Doubt* (1943), Uncle Charlie says, "Do you know that if you rip the fronts off houses you'd find swine?" Seahaven collapses like that. When Truman can't be found, the town's mask of goodwill falls off (a similar reaction occurs in *Cars* when Arthur tries to leave Paris). The friendly dog snarls and bares its fangs; taking part in the search party, one of the mirror-image twins (each with hair parted on the opposite side) vows to find "the son of a bitch."

Although it is clear from a bare outline of the story that the film fits in with Weir's other work, and that *The Truman Show* brings up many ideas about media manipulation and fame, it also has a more frothy, superficial feel to it than Weir's other films. Is this a fault of the film? Perhaps. Yet it seems more likely that this frothiness is a function of the pop culture nature of the world in which Truman resides. Consider: how appropriate would it have been for Weir to have woven into *The Truman Show* notions too weighty for the film to bear? Would it have been productive to have had Jim Carrey's Truman declaiming on the meaning of life or man's relation to the universe? And if not Truman, what other character within the glitzy media world of Seahaven could have acted as the chorus to comment on such notions while Truman went about his daily business?

More than anything else, *The Truman Show* seems a representation of elemental, yet not simplistic, manichean conceits. One of the basic notions with which *The Truman Show* deals is appearance versus reality, with the qualification that the precise nature of reality is unknown. All that Weir chose to show us of what exists outside of the dome is people watching "The Truman Show," a limited (and decidedly media-oriented) view of existence. Thus, for the most part, reality in *The Truman Show* is that which is not shown. If we define reality as a constant scanning pattern, then Seahaven is a great success: for thirty years, it has tricked Truman into believing its lies. Obviously, the manner in which Truman is treated is quite cruel. Yet Truman isn't just the dupe of a technology-mad director; his good-natured behavior is used by the audience of "The Truman Show" as a way of avoiding the emptiness and frustration in their lives. Indeed, the audience that watches "The Truman Show" seems vampiric in its desire to drink in not only Truman's (occasional) pleasures but also his pain. Like people who are obsessed with tabloid scandal sheets, the viewers of "The Truman Show" are fascinated with a person's misfortunes. In this respect, Truman is less a model of behavior for the show's audience than a figure to whom they can feel superior. In more than one respect, Truman is looking for a sense of genuineness, which he will only be able to find, not in the world of Seahaven, but in his subconscious, which takes the symbolic form of his basement. Truman has to go down there to plumb the depths of his personality because it's where he (figuratively) keeps it hidden, locked inside a box. The basement scenes' secretive tone suggests that Truman has to hide his true self from the unrelentingly invasive, mock affability of the town and his wife. This fact goes a long way toward helping us appreciate the truth in Weir's observation that on some profound level, Truman is aware that he is a performer, a notion that suggests that for Truman there is a fictive quality to his life that is even greater than the one experienced by people who regard their lives as somewhat unreal. In *The Truman Show*, this sense of unreality is implied through the pathological focus of "the show" on everything that Truman does. Truman is never given more than a few fleeting minutes to feel that he is alone (which, until he escapes from his basement, he never really is, since he's always on camera). For the crew and the audience, Truman can't be left alone; were the cameras to veer away from him, the audience might very well feel that there would be nothing to occupy their time.

Although *The Truman Show* tells us that people have become dependent upon "the show" to escape the dissatisfactions in their own lives, the film also demonstrates that people are more than willing to forego their fixation on "The Truman Show" when it ends. Perhaps this lack of fidelity is a function of the diminished attention span of an audience that has been pounded by ten-second promos and twenty-second commercials, and emotionally drained by overexposure to thrill-a-minute shows with little substantive content. The audience's superficiality is mirrored in the nature of the people running the shows, who are drunk on their power, who disdain their audience, who routinely lower their shows' standards because doing so doesn't seem to adversely affect the shows' popularity.

All of these tendencies indicate that many people are losing sight of the values and concerns that elevate life above the mundane. In *Network* (1976), newsman Howard Beale tells a television audience, "television is not real, none of it is real. So turn off your television sets, turn them off and keep them off." I don't think that Weir would be averse to having audiences walk out of *The Truman Show* resolving, if not to never see a movie again, at least to be more selective the next time that they choose to do so. If this film can turn people away from superficial media and back toward what is meaningful in life (and, aside from love, precisely what that is Weir refuses to say) then, as with Weir's other films, which encourage us to distrust appearances and look for greater meanings, it has accomplished one of its purposes.

Any piece of media can escape the paradox of telling us that media is a hoax; *A Face in the Crowd* (1957) did it, as did *Network*. The situation becomes problematic, though, when the piece of entertainment warning us of media's flimsiness itself becomes a media event that threatens to become the monstrous thing that it criticizes. A great deal of the coverage that *The Truman Show* received was hyperbolic. While this was surely not entirely Weir's doing, it does tend to potentially compromise the manner in which we perceive the film. Indeed, at times, *The Truman Show* seemed almost as popular as "The Truman Show." Periodically, we may find ourselves as fixated on the movie screen as are the people in the film watching Truman on TV.

At one point during an interview, Christof says of Truman, "while the world he inhabits is somewhat counterfeit, there's nothing fake about Truman himself."[8]. The implication is that there is a part of the personality that is independent of the effect that culture and media has on people. Through his films, Weir has been telling us this all along. But in *The Truman Show* he has raised the intensity of cultural influence so dramatically that it's difficult to believe that this is true. Where does Truman get the integrity to keep his "true" personality intact? On what source of self-affirmation does he draw to keep his inner self alive? It certainly doesn't come from his society, his wife, or his friends. Christof's assertion overlooks how difficult it must be for Truman to be genuine when his whole world is contrived. Christof also claims that people "accept the reality of the world with which [they're] presented." Some people may be this naive, but it's presumptuous of Christof to think that this is so for everyone. And when we consider that Christof is a prime creator of reality (at least for one person), the remark begins to smack of self-righteousness. Christof elevates himself to the status of a god, one who isn't above using turning the potential for duplicity in certain well-turned phrases to his own account.

Does "The Truman Show" really, as Christof claims, give "hope, joy, and inspiration to millions" of people? If so, what does this tell us not only about the impoverished emotional and spiritual lives of the show's audience but also the hubristic attitude of Christof, who asserts in all seriousness that "Truman prefers his cell"? How can he contend this when all he has to do is watch the manner in which Truman reveals his innermost longings when he's in his basement? Surely Christof realizes how miserable Truman really is. Christof also knows that Truman is lying when he tells a newsdealer that he's buying a woman's magazine for Meryl. He's aware that Truman is trying to piece together a real life from scraps, attempting to create a collage that approximates what a meaningful existence might have been. How, then, can he—and "The Truman Show's" audience—continue to take pleasure in Truman's pain?

It's hard to believe that Christof isn't more than a little desperate to keep Truman in the dome. After all, he's built his thirty-year reputation on the show's success. As portrayed by Ed Harris, Christof is pretentious, egotistical, and weary. We repeatedly see him hunched over, walking slowly, apparently bent down under the weight of the (presumably) great aesthetic responsibility he is under to keep this show going. Christof says at the film's beginning that people are "bored with watching actors give us phony emotions." The statement sounds like an echo of Weir's repeated references to film's ability to create in us a sense of wonder. Yet what *this* creator offers us is a mock world. Complete control doesn't yield freedom but bondage. Christof's attitude echoes one of the slogans from 1984: slavery is freedom. Yet the only person enslaved in Seahaven is Truman; everyone else is there by choice. The town's slogan is "Omni Pro Uno": all for one. The "all" is the city of actors and technicians that is needed to maintain "the show." These people's livelihood depends on one man: Truman. In some respect, Christof, the actors, and the show's crew must resent Truman's importance. Perhaps that's why the town turns vicious when Truman escapes. Perhaps that's why Christof periodically feels compelled to smite Truman with some new loss: in order to reassure himself of his own power and worth. As psychiatrist Karen Horney writes, "it is contrary to human nature to sustain appreciation without resentment toward capabilities that one does not possess."[9] Christof is clearly not averse to being vindictive during Truman's sea voyage escape. When Truman gets close to the edge of "the sea," Christof tries to kill him. "He's going to drown and he [Christof] doesn't care," one of Christof's technicians says.[10]

Freedom from uncertainty and pain is what Christof says he offers Truman. Yet this promise is, of course, impossible to keep. As Sigmund Freud suggests, one cannot eliminate suffering from life.[11] Discussing the antagonism between the desire for pleasure and what most people accept as the necessity of living in society (which, as Freud emphasizes, thwarts the pleasure principle), Freud considers various forms of adaptation.[12] Among these possibilities, he mentions the type of person who keeps the world at a distance by creating a separate reality that is completely responsive to his needs.

> [O]ne can do more than [become a hermit]. One can try to re-create the world, to build up in its stead another world in which its most unbearable features are eliminated and replaced by others that are in conformity with one's own wishes. But whoever, in desperate defiance, sets out upon this path to happiness will as a rule attain nothing. Reality is too strong for him. He becomes a madman, who for the most part finds no one to help him in carrying through his delusion.[13]

We could view Seahaven as an example of this kind of separate reality, but it's more likely that this separate reality is the ecosphere, in which Christof seems to live. Far more than Truman (a Galatea who at the film's end walks out on his creator), Christof is a prisoner of technology. Indeed, it would seem that Christof is (inadvertently) characterizing not Truman but himself when he tells Sylvia that Seahaven's world is better than the "jaded" one outside the Seahaven dome (the use of the word "jaded" tells us a great deal about what Christof's experiences in life must have been). What is the result of all this monomania? Freud writes, "A special importance attaches to the case in which this attempt to procure a certainty of happiness and a protection against suffering through *a delusional remoudling of reality* is made by a considerable number of people in common" (my emphasis).[14]

Freud's equation of mass delusion with religion[15] seems apposite to the film: for Christof and its audience, "The Truman Show" has become a devotion. Yet the pathological nature of this fixation on what is, after all, just a piece of media escapes them all. As Freud notes, "no one, needless to say, who shares a delusion ever recognizes it as such."[16]

Repeatedly in the film, via television programs and newspaper headlines ("Who Needs Europe!"), Truman is told to cherish his claustrophobic life. Yet there are indications that on a conscious level, Truman understands how empty and predictable his life really is. At one point, he says that he's not in a hurry to get to work; and he certainly never seems to exhibit any affection when it comes to Meryl. When in high school, Truman's wife-to-be was literally dropped into his lap, forced on him via the scenarist of "The Truman Show." It's therefore understandable that he can't feel any passion toward Meryl: he never chose to be in a relationship with her. Opposing this sense of determinism are the many scenes that take place near bridges or overpasses, all potential pathways to escape. Christof and "The Truman Show's" audience know that Truman wants to leave, yet they hope that he'll stay put to keep entertaining them. Talking about Fiji (which is where he thinks that Sylvia lives), Truman tells Marlon, "you can't get any farther away before you start coming back." He doesn't want to be where he is; he wants to be in a diametrically opposite world, one which (we know) is (at least in some respects) genuine as opposed to contrived. "Was nothing real?" Truman asks Christof. Nothing was real, except that part of Truman to which he remained faithful: that genuine moment of irrational affection to which he gave expression while on the beach with Sylvia, a brief juncture during which emotion overpowers the reasonable script that Christof has fashioned.

Two characters, one genuine, one duplicitous, are associated with points of revelation for Truman. In each case, part of what he increasingly comes to feel is his fragmentary life begins to fit into the puzzle he's putting together. First,

Truman spends a few brief moments at the beach with Sylvia. The fact that this scene takes place at the water's edge is significant, since water for Truman represents both escape and imprisonment. The aquaphobia that Christof has created for Truman is a function of Truman's father's drowning, which, like everything else in Truman's life, was staged. To learn the truth about his father's death, though, would also grant Truman knowledge of the evil father behind the scenes, pulling all of the strings. In a way, Truman comes to resemble the speaker in *The Waste Land*: he fears death by water, and runs the risk of becoming the Hanged Man, which in many ways he already is if we see him as Christof's marionette. Not surprisingly, the scene with Sylvia is counterbalanced by the cruel ironies of the scenes with Marlon, many of which also take place on bridges or by the water's edge, and in which Truman gives voice to longings that he feels he can't possibly fulfill—partially because he's in despair, partially because he's been traumatized into staying on the island.

Like *Cars'* Paris, Seahaven is no haven. The sea for Truman is a threat, not a comfort. His fear of drowning is an extension of the fear of symbolic, ritualistic immersion. In many respects, he's a character who has yet to be baptized into the truth. It's therefore cruel of Christof, responding to Truman's question about Seahaven's unreality, to tell Truman that "you were real," since the only "you" that Truman has ever known has been the one that he had to keep hidden in his basement, where he longs for reunion with a woman whom he only knew for a few minutes, but who has come to represent the only "real" moment in his life.

What's also being suggested in the film via its theme of a search for the truth is the nature of the reality of the player who plays Truman (Truman himself is a great player of roles). What, one wonders, is at work behind the many masks that Jim Carrey has worn in his screen roles, as well as the mask that he wears in his personal appearances? We know that he had a difficult childhood, that he has had romantic problems. As Weir points out, there's often a great melancholy in the laughter of clowns, and this is certainly true of Carrey. When watching Carrey in earlier films, one often hoped for, yet never received, a genuine moment of joy or pathos. Histrionic gestures were all that we'd come to expect from him. Yet it's not unlikely that, as with Truman, there's a genuineness to Carrey hidden away in some symbolic basement of the unconscious. The affinities between Carrey and Truman function as one more subtle way in which *The Truman Show* breaks down the line between screen reality and empirical reality.

The Truman Show is quite unlike Patrick McGoohan's television show "The Prisoner" (1967–1968), which in terms of setting it otherwise resembles. As is made clear in the last two episodes of "The Prisoner," the whole plot against McGoohan's character Number 6 is a function of his own egoistic delusions. Unlike Number 6, Truman is guilty of no psychological infractions. In many ways, he's a pristine figure, born and nurtured inside a sealed environment that is ruled over by a capricious and, at times, ill-tempered god. If Christof is a sadistic deity, in the manner of the one in the Book of Job, he is also a god who is highly cognizant of psychology. Christof creates scenarios that speak directly to some of the most primal fears in human beings: loss of love, of family, of identity. Christof experiments on Truman, trying out different scenarios on him to see how they'll play; predominantly, he does this to entertain himself and the audience, who act as his surrogate. Truman is given a "father" only to have him taken away, and is left with a "mother" who isn't above lying to her "son" about his "father's" death. When, by virtue of an actor's desire to break back into the show, Truman's supposedly dead father reappears on the street one day (how is it that the careful Christof didn't foresee this eventuality; is security at the dome this bad?), it becomes another unraveling of the seemingly perfect plot that Christof has fashioned for Truman.

If the melancholy scenes involving Truman's confiding in Marlon often take place at the beach, thereby suggesting a fisher king brooding over a great personal loss (a sensibility that infuses the entirety of the waste land that is Seahaven), the father's resurrection functions as a tawdry rebirth. Yet even though both Sylvia and the death of Truman's "father" are associated with grail legend questions about existence that might revitalize the land (Sylvia wears a button that reads "how will it end?"; Truman asks his mother if his father is really dead), the events associated with neither character lead to an immediate change in Truman's day-to-day behavior, nor move the film's action toward a swift restoration of the Seahaven waste land to some form of fertility.[17] If anything, the paramount force that rules in the community is sterility. Truman and Meryl's marriage is loveless and childless. Nobody's emotions, aside from Truman's, are genuine, and even Truman often has to put on a false front to buoy up people's spirits. It's as though, having been inside the dome his whole life, Truman has either lost the ability to react directly or has practiced deception for so long that his responses are slowed down. However, when there is no one left to whom he can turn for comfort, Truman realizes that the only way to escape his world is not to retreat inward, into the unconscious, but to act outwardly, by leaving Seahaven. In a fascinating piece of business that testifies to the power of media to engage and deceive us, toward the end of Truman's sea escape we so fully enter into the dramatic reality of his flight that when the prow of Truman's boat hits a scrim that has been painted to look like the sky, we're shocked. For a time, we've come to believe that this phony backdrop was real.

As one might have expected, some critics have expressed intense dissatisfaction with the film's ending, saying that, as in other Weir films, the director stops the action just at the point when it might have gotten interesting, that the film is obliged to show us what happens after Truman leaves the dome. Weir prefers to leave the story's final resolution up to the viewer. For him to have extended the film's action, as he did in the shooting stage (the material was edited out), would have literalized the endless possibilities inherent in Truman walking out on a fiction and into so-called reality. Besides, we already know what's on the other side of the door through which Truman walks: it's the region in which (one hopes) fakery does not rule existence. It may be the harshest region of all. It's not planned, not perfect. It's a world of sorrow and joy, pleasure and pain, all mixed together in unpredictable proportions. It's a world worth living in, worth escaping to.

By leaving the film hanging, Weir not only makes it possible for us to continue to have Truman function as an everyman, but also leaves us free to fantasize about all sorts of different endings to Truman's adventure. The present conclusion also allows the viewer to refuse to sketch in any ending at all, to just linger on that final insouciant goodbye which Truman, with great irony, flings in Christof's (unseen) face. Weir's refusal to resolve the film's end focuses our attention on that sublime moment (one not compromised by actuality) when, anticipating the thrill of discovering what is outside the claustrophobic womb in which he's been imprisoned, Truman ventures into the unknown.

At the film's end, Truman says to Christof, "If I don't see ya, good afternoon, good evening, and good night," a statement followed by a barely perceptible look of disgust on Truman's face. With this parting line, Truman brings down the curtain on a fake play only to ring one up on the rest of a genuine life. It's an exit line worth cherishing, and Weir knows it, since it's rich with potentiality. In that respect, *The Truman Show* is one of the most optimistic films that Weir has yet given us.

APPENDIX

FILMOGRAPHY

NOTES

BIBLIOGRAPHY

INDEX

APPENDIX

Keeping Your Sense of Wonder: An Interview with Peter Weir

As one might expect, it isn't only Peter Weir's films that are enigmatic. Weir himself is the same way. During our three-hour talk a week after *The Truman Show* opened in the summer of 1998, I found Weir to be a sensitive, intelligent, and insightful person with a wonderful sense of humor and an extremely open personality. Yet as I subsequently discovered, Weir is also very protective of his personal opinions and beliefs. Much of this response may have to do with being a high-profile director whose words can often be misinterpreted; part of it may be a desire to be as private as possible. Weir has often expressed anxiety about doing interviews; when he does so, he is very careful to measure his responses. I am grateful that I was able to talk to him on as personal a level as I did, and thankful that at least some of that openness—which confirmed for me that he is, indeed, as fascinating a man as I had intuited he might be—came through in the version of the interview to which he gave his approval.

Bliss: You came to prominence during the time of what was referred to as the New Australian Cinema. What's your sense of the current state of the Australian filmmaking industry?

Weir: National film industries tend to move in cycles. In Australia right now, 1998, we're on a high, a feeling of potential, which as yet shows no sign of flagging. But the word "industry" is misleading. A small national cinema has no industry in the Hollywood sense. It depends for its reputation on a highly talented group of individuals, writer/directors essentially.

Bliss: Do you think of yourself as an Australian director who works in Hollywood or an international director who occasionally uses Hollywood as a temporary base?

A somewhat shorter version of this interview appeared in *Film Quarterly* 53:1 (Fall 1999).

Weir: An Australian director certainly. But I think it was Hitchcock who said, "a film is its own country."

Bliss: Is there any difference between making films in Australia and working within the demands of the Hollywood system?

Weir: There's certainly no difference when that troublesome scene is staring you in the face! You could be standing in the outback or on Sunset Boulevard. The creative struggle remains the same: to get the scene right. As for Hollywood, the system hasn't bothered me, and no one has ever dictated how I should make my films. All of my mistakes are my own.

Bliss: The Year of Living Dangerously's emphasis on feelings instead of ideas seemed to presage your move into Hollywood filmmaking. What prompted you to begin working in the States?

Weir: I was ready for a change after *The Year of Living Dangerously* and looked for an American subject to film. I'd made five features, a tele-movie, and numerous short films over a sixteen-year period and felt in need of fresh stimulation. The first American film was to have been *The Mosquito Coast,* from the Paul Theroux novel, but we couldn't get the financing together, which was very disappointing at the time, 1984. I felt so frustrated that I asked my American agent to only send me scripts that had been "green lit"—in other words, financed and ready to go. He sent me three such scripts, one of which was *Witness. Witness's* success revived *The Mosquito Coast,* and I went ahead and did that. There was no plan on my part to continue working in the United States. Projects just came along in seemingly random ways. But it's true to say I've enjoyed working with the Americans both behind and in front of the camera. Nonetheless, I continue to live in Australia and am always looking for Australian subjects.

Bliss: In a number of interviews you tend to repudiate the influence on your work of your extensive reading in Freud and Jung. Do you really think that these men's work has no bearing on your films?

Weir: It's hard to know what influences are working on you when you make a film, or engage in any creative endeavor for that matter. You may know years later, perhaps when looking at an earlier film, that it seems remarkably under the sway of the work of some director you've admired. I saw *Mon Oncle* recently and was surprised at how influenced by Jacques Tati I'd been in my early short films of the 1960s. As for Freud and Jung, nobody working in a creative field can help but admire their pioneering work in mapping the unconscious, that mysterious landscape that plays such a major part in the creative life. Jung's book *Memories, Dreams, Reflections* had a powerful impact on me. I still find myself going back to it on occasion.

Bliss: There certainly seems to be a consistency of concerns in your films: unusual states of mind, exaggerated actions, dream or near-death experiences that cause radical shifts in consciousness. Yet you often express a resistance to being typed as a certain kind of director. How do you reconcile this apparent contradiction?

Weir: So much of the work is intuitive. The resistance you detect is just that, a kind of evasion, a sense that too much analysis will inhibit creativity. I've become wary of interviews, in which you're forced to go back over the reasons why you made certain decisions. You tend to rationalize what you've done, to intellectually review a process that is often intuitive. I also find interviews uncomfortable because in one sense, you don't want to know why you made certain decisions. There's almost a fear that if you understood too deeply the way you arrived at choices, one could become self-conscious. In any case, many ideas, which are full of personal meaning, seem rather banal when you put words to them. Apart from that I don't want to repeat myself. I'd get bored! I want to be open to new ideas, to new ways of seeing things.

Bliss: Would you at least agree that there's a strong divergence in your work between serious films such as *Fearless* and, to appropriate Graham Greene's term, "entertainments," a class of film into which *Green Card* might fall?

Weir: I'm not working to any pattern that I'm aware of.

Bliss: Do you think that you will ever be able to achieve the "invisible" style of filmmaking, modeled (as you've said in interviews) on the work of journeyman directors from the forties and fifties, who simply, in your words, "took the projects given them and got on with the job?"

Weir: I'd prefer to be like the early Japanese potters who regularly changed their names, presumably to efface themselves and let the work stand on its own. I try to be "invisible" because only the story counts. The idea. I'm the servant of that idea. The film, whatever it is, is not about me.

Bliss: But doesn't your concern for invisibility often get subverted, as it seems to in *Fearless*'s pronounced mythical and religious concerns? In other words, how can you ever escape the influences that have made you who you are, even if one of the effects of these influences has been to abjure them?

Weir: That's why the favorite moments in my own films are those I had the least to do with.

Bliss: Let's talk about your latest film, *The Truman Show.* Did the script appeal to you immediately?

Weir: I admired it, but I didn't know whether it was possible to make it work. The screenplay was much darker and portrayed the central character as more of an everyman. It was also set in Manhattan. It was good science fiction, but the first thing I thought was, you couldn't do it in New York. Why build New York? Why build something that's known instead of having an idealized setting? Nevertheless, the script absolutely intrigued me. It was most untypical of Hollywood. It's just not the province of Hollywood to make a film of ideas, which is what *The Truman Show* is. The film was also on a knife edge. If you removed Jim Carrey from the equation, it probably wouldn't have been made.

Bliss: Was Jim Carrey involved in the film from its inception?

Weir: No. While I was thinking about whether or not to accept the project, the producer, Scott Rudin, called to say that Jim was interested. I'd seen *Ace Ventura* and *The Mask* and had been impressed by Jim's originality, but he never would have occurred to me, given the tone of the script. Naturally, I'd been thinking about the casting of Truman and had come to the conclusion that he had to be a movie star. This would be necessary for the logic of the story—in other words, why did the world watch this man twenty-four hours a day? The answer had to be that he was a natural star. I also felt that having grown up in such a weird, unnatural atmosphere, the character would in some way be a little strange. I don't know but there's something a little "alien" about Jim. He's not the guy-next-door type.

Bliss: What was your collaboration with Carrey like?

Weir: One aspect Jim and I discussed was the expectation of Truman to perform. I told Jim that I think we have to assume that Truman knows in a sense that he's a performer, that he's always been one. I said, let's discuss his reality, because consider: as he grew up, he had all of these faces leaning toward him with great smiles. There was a lot of touching, a lot of false bonhomie, because people around him were actors and they wanted to get in the shot with him. These people knew that if Truman made friends with them, they'd become part of the regular cast. So one, I think he's learned that behavior. Second, he's unconsciously felt that he needed to help other people, to make them feel better. Without realizing it, he's responding to the pressure to perform.

When Christof tells him what it's all about, his being on a TV show, it would have been impractical, and perhaps problematical, for Truman to have said, "what do you mean? How could that be?" especially since the audience was well ahead of him and knew all about it. *We* want him to say, "ah, so that was it." When he nods his head, then, everything falls into place, everything from his childhood onward. I think that what's kept him all along from questioning his world is that he unconsciously sensed that he had a very important job to do—to give love and good cheer through the smiles; to keep people's spirits up. In certain respects, this isn't dissimilar to a lot of Jim's life; there was some borrowing.

Bliss: You feel that behind Truman's smiles there's a great melancholy operating.

Weir: Well, extremes always lie together. There's the cliché that all comics are sad or angry people. The clown is often quite a malevolent figure, as in horror films. Underneath, you sense there's a kind of rage. You certainly see that rage in Truman when he begins to suspect that his wife is in on the conspiracy. It comes out in that cruel, mocking humor as he's driving her around in circles.

Bliss: The notion of cruelty naturally brings up the character of Christof, who to me seemed incredibly manipulative and unfeeling.

Weir: When we were in the shooting script stage, he was the character I knew the least about. In some respects he was a kind of stock villain, dressed up by scriptwriter Andrew Niccol in an interesting, new way, but nonetheless not terribly different from the sort of controlling character you'd see in a James Bond movie. It was just the *idea* of Christof that was smart and original. I thought, well, I'll deal with that down the line. I had enough to think about getting Truman and everything else right.

We shot all of the Truman show material first, and then did the control room, so by the time I came to that I had a very strong idea of what I wanted, which was influenced by all sorts of things, among which were certain politicians I've known on both sides of the political spectrum, people who are not that different from Christof in the sense that they feel that the end justifies the means. Christof also sees himself as an artist, with Truman— "True Man"— as his greatest creation. Terrifying. A kind of Dr. Frankenstein of the airwaves.

I'm also intrigued by the phenomenon of the postwar couturier, especially in the last twenty years or so, people whose persona is that of an artist, yet in actual fact they're producing commercial products. People like this have a vast and powerful empire, yet they have an aura of sensitivity, and they generally wear black, like Christof.

An additional idea is that of the artist *manqué,* a person born with all of the attributes and personality traits of an artist, what you might call an artistic personality, but with no *metier.* That type of person is often very difficult, because they just don't have a way of expressing themselves, of calming themselves through creativity. I folded all of these notions into the Christof character. And then, of course, Ed Harris came along at just the right time and understood all of this on some profound level.

Bliss: Some reviewers have commented that your films often leave the audience hanging, with no satisfactory resolution being achieved. I find your films' refusal to resolve themselves quite satisfying, such as the end of *The Truman Show* for example.

Weir: It took some time for the right ending to become apparent. Andrew and I did something like ten drafts. In the latter stage of this process we dropped all of the scenes exterior to the dome. There were all sorts of scenes that we tried outside, but eventually the ending emerged, with Truman just walking through the studio door. It struck me that ending the film that way would allow the film to keep making itself for the viewer. I do love to walk away from a movie that keeps making itself in your mind, and I thought this one in particular would, because when you leave the enclosed world of the cinema and walk out into the reality of your world, you would, in a way, step into Truman's shoes.

Bliss: Imagine, though, if you had extended Truman's ending, if you had done what you originally planned to do with the end of *Picnic at Hanging Rock*, to literalize things, in *Picnic's* case by showing Mrs. Appleyard's death instead of having it narrated in voiceover.

Weir: It would have been ghastly. That seemed to me to go against the deep power of what film can do: to suggest, to provoke the viewer's imagination.

Bliss: Your reliance on ideas and images associated with the unconscious opens up your work to a lot of criticism. One critic I came across accuses you of a particular kind of intellectual vagueness that he refers to as "New Age" thinking. He says that this attitude might have been fine in the late sixties and early seventies, but we're living in the real world now.

Weir: The "real" world? I'm as impatient with this kind of critic as they are with me. There's not much to say here. I see mysteries, ambiguities, contradictions all around me. Moreover, the term "New Age" is often used as a derogatory expression, often with justification. Yet this shouldn't for a minute stop us from thinking about who we are and what we believe in and what's real and discussions about religion. Yet you do increasingly strike people who agitate against any incursions into the area of what we agree is the material world and what they see as the correct ways of thinking.

Bliss: You never get the feeling from this type of criticism, which tends to disparage the mystical or unconscious, that this is merely a point of view.

Weir: True. There's often a kind of anger in response to this form of expression.

Bliss: What's also involved here is one of the themes in *The Truman Show:* the nature of reality.

Weir: Yes. Interestingly, the idea of what constitutes this agreed-upon reality is often spread via the medium of television.

Bliss: That's rather frightening, don't you think?

Weir: Very much so, because of its stultifying quality, the power to brainwash people into beliefs.

Bliss: Yet in *Truman Show*, there is a part of Truman that the media can't touch. It's hidden in his basement, a very symbolic place which suggests the unconscious.

Weir: Well, I'd always loved that part from *Memories, Dreams, Reflections* when Jung talks at length about the basement, where he had some of his epiphanies and breakthroughs in thinking with regard to the symbolism of the basement, its underground aspect, and that attribute's connection with the archetypal aspect of human experience. Initially, in *The Truman Show* screenplay, what takes place in Truman's basement occurred in his garage. I said, I want to make it his basement where, rather pathetically, he has his secrets, his boxes within boxes, the box inside the trunk. In that basement scene we see his darker side. He's less the friendly guy in his basement; he snaps at his wife when she comes down there, into that somewhat creepy, infantile place.

Bliss: There seems to be a connection between the reality/unreality theme of *The Truman Show* and such films as *Picnic at Hanging Rock* and *The Last Wave*.

Weir: Yes, but *The Truman Show* deals with the concept of reality/unreality from another angle. In the case of the earlier two films there was, at least, an agreement on what "reality" is. In the media age (and remember, *The Truman Show* is set in the near future), this is not necessarily the case. The media, specifically television, has blurred the line between reality and unreality. We've even coined the phrase "virtual reality." So *The Truman Show* is really quite another story.

Bliss: I take a cue from your films and tend to concentrate more on the pattern of thought in and behind them, rather than in attempting to reduce them to details.

Weir: This is, after all, the point: there is this area in some of my films, some more than others, that has to do with the spontaneous, the unconscious. This is a very important aspect to discuss because it's quintessentially a part of my way of thinking, and part of the way that many of my films operate, *Picnic at Hanging Rock* for example. Acknowledging the importance of the unconscious relates to the way I've seen the world through my life; it's how I express myself.

Bliss: *Picnic* was re-released this summer. How did you approach that film?

Weir: I was aware from the start that I would have to do a lot of thinking about how I was going to make the film because it didn't have an ending. The whodunit has always been a rather difficult genre. That's why it was interesting reading that part of Truffaut's interview with Hitchcock in which Hitchcock talked about his impatience with a whodunit. I think that generally, the ending is a bit of a letdown in mysteries—you know, the butler did it or whatever. This genre has waned; people require much more of a visceral reaction to what they see in films. In *Picnic*, which involves a mystery without a solution, I knew that I had to, in a sense, mesmerize the audience, to induce in them a kind of dream state in order that they wouldn't have the expectation of a conventional ending.

Bliss: Isn't a dream-like effect present from the film's very beginning, in those irresolvable dissolves that begin the film?

Weir: I also did it with sound.

Bliss: Are you referring to the earthquake sounds you used in *Picnic*, which you slowed down and transferred to the track?

Weir: That's right. I wanted through this method to access the audience's unconscious, since this sound is supposedly part of those collective memories that we all have with respect to sounds or vibrations. I used this sound in both *Picnic* and *The Last Wave*. We did experiments to make sure that we got it onto the optical track, even though you'd have to be in a theatre with a good sound system to hear it. Under optimum conditions there is at times a slight vibration in the theatre itself, as well as in the viewer's breastbone! I think I was more successful with this effect in *The Last Wave*. But in both films, this attempt was really part of experimenting with how far cinema can go in the sense of getting past the guardians of logic and freeing up and gaining access to unconscious areas and bringing the viewer into the film, having them join in its making. That's what I wanted to have happen right from *Picnic*'s opening credits.

Bliss: I was disappointed that even when *Picnic* was re-released, many reviewers didn't seem to enter into the film's spirit or talk about the ideas in it. How do you deal with criticism that doesn't at all touch what you feel is going on in the films?

Weir: I think when you start off in your career, that's when criticism is really important to you. You need encouragement, because at that stage you don't really know what you're doing; you're learning on the job. After a few films, you start to look at things differently. Within that reassessment, criticism falls into its rightful place because you have so many ways of understanding it.

Bliss: Are you familiar with the theory that a work of art is just a vehicle, an intermediate object between artist and viewer that facilitates unconscious transmission of thought? In this view, artists don't create information so much as channel it.

Weir: That reminds me of a Japanese potter I knew at one time. He explained to me how pottery to the Japanese is as highly regarded as painting in our western tradition. The potter serves a long apprenticeship, working under a master, turning out plates, cups, bowls, that kind of thing. Every now and then the gods will touch the potter's hands, and that object will be a work of art. That's another way of expressing the theory you mention.

Bliss: Don't you use music a great deal in your creative process?

Weir: Music will block thinking for me; it stops the voices in my head, opens the way to another kind of approach to the job at hand. A kind of musically-induced meditation. Certain pieces of music will gather around a film. Someone will give me a CD or I'll hear something on the radio. Quite often, a piece of music becomes so important to me that it even finds its way into the soundtrack.

Bliss: As a director, is music useful to you in other ways as well?

Weir: Yes; I'll give you an example. Shooting the end scene of *Dead Poets Society* over several days presented problems. At 7 A.M. in the morning, the young actors were hardly in the mood for an emotional scene. But at the first rehearsal, I'd played a powerful piece of music to them, and they'd been very moved and gave the scene everything it needed. I found that if I played the music again on subsequent days, even at 7:30 A.M., the experience of that first rehearsal was preserved, as it were, in the music.

Bliss: Talking about *Dead Poets* reminds me of what I've read about your educational background. You said in your 1983 interview for the Australian Film and Television School that during your time at university you felt that traditional education was trying to train the spontaneity out of you.

Weir: Yes, and I touched on that in *Dead Poets* when Williams is putting that figure up on the board that proposes to show you how to graph the success of a poem, and many of the students are copying it down verbatim.

Bliss: Is that the kind of thing you saw happening in your poetry class?

Weir: Absolutely. The type of analysis we were taught destroyed the enjoyment of the poetry.

Bliss: I understand that, as with the new cut of *Picnic at Hanging Rock,* there are certain changes you'd like to make to some of your previous films.

Weir: Let me answer that parenthetically. I find my own films hard to look at again. You'll often hear filmmakers say this. You move on, your viewpoint changes, you don't like to be reminded of a younger self—whatever it is.

Of late, I've been affected by a quote of Matisse's, from a collection of his interviews. (It was Matisse who said that painters should have their tongues cut out, and he was right. The same could be said of directors!) Anyway, as you can imagine, it's a slim volume, and I find what he has to say very interesting. He felt that his early paintings had too much emotion in them. He found them agitating and had to take them down off the wall of his studio. He said that what he'd learned over the years is that once you've found the emotion, experienced it, and begun painting it, the feeling will never go away. You don't have to make a great deal of it; it's better to simplify it and put it in its fundamental form. The emotion may be a little less charming, in the sense of being immediately accessible, but it will never go away. In fact, it will have more power as a result of the simplicity because as a result of that restraint, the viewer will join in with the painter in creating the emotion. In other words, the viewer brings more to the work when the work is less emphatic.

Matisse used the example of a particular nude that he'd painted in his youth; he contrasted it with one of his dancing shapes from his later period, during which he was using cutouts, which didn't have the literal lines of a female nude but still possessed the suggestive lines of one. Yet in viewing the cutout and staring at it, looking at it longer and living with it, you find a great richness of emotion in the latter work.

Bliss: Speaking of suggestiveness in art, I've always been intrigued by the recurrence or tripartite shapes in *The Last Wave.*

Weir: Those shapes probably harken back to my discovery of a stone sculpture in the Tunisian city of Duga. We stopped to stretch our legs and there was rubble by the roadside in a field. We were walking, picking up bits of marble. I was about 100 yards from the car when an electrifying feeling went through me and I thought, I'm going to find something. It was then that I saw three parallel lines on a stone.

Bliss: Three lines?

Weir: Yes. Take your hand now, make a fist—you see the lines between your fingers? That's what I saw sticking up out of the ground: a clenched fist. It was attached to the side of a head, broken off at the neck, about the size of a doll's head. When I told people the story their reaction was, "That *would* happen to you." So I wrote out a storyline which had a lawyer, someone used to dealing with facts and precedents, with the rational, having this kind of premonition. The story went through many changes, but I did put the head on the set. Gulpilil picks it up at one point.

Bliss: One of the issues I deal with in the book is that *Gallipoli* makes it seem as though it was a British officer who ordered the final, fateful attack on The Nek. Yet Bill Gammage's book, and subsequent histories, make it plain that the man who ordered the attack was Australian. Were you aware of this fact during the production of the film, which you stated in an interview was not intended to be "anti-British"?

Weir: The order for the third wave to attack, after the disaster of the first two waves, was given by an Australian officer, Colonel Antill. I made two changes in the dramatization of this account. First, I changed Antill's name. I couldn't be absolutely certain, so long after the event, that there weren't some mitigating circumstances that might be called to his defense. Despite his uniform being that of an Australian officer, some audience members assumed, wrongly, that he was British. Perhaps it was his English-sounding accent, or simply the desire to blame someone else for the needless deaths that followed. It's true that the troops in the main attack at Suvla were British, and untested in battle. It's also true that after coming ashore they were ordered to have breakfast, before pushing the advantage of their successful landing. This was disastrous leadership, and British leadership at that. Secondly, for dramatic reasons, I had Frank carry the message from the front line back to headquarters, rather than the Colonel Brazier mentioned in the official history.

The British, despite widely acknowledged poor leadership, fought bravely at Gallipoli, and laid their lives down in the thousands. The bitterness in the film was directed at this leadership, not at the character of the British soldiers and sailors.

Bliss: I think my favorite film of yours is *Fearless,* which didn't do well here in the States. Did its poor financial showing upset you?

Weir: I was disappointed, but I knew that the film involved a roll of the dice. I had to make *Fearless.* I became infatuated with it. I knew that it was highly risky material, because its success would depend exclusively on the audience's desire to go and see a film about a plane crash. I wanted to make that crash incredibly effective without being shocking. But I also knew that the film's main chance, the only way that it was going to work, was if the plane crash became a metaphor. I wanted to widen the story's scope instead of narrowing it down, as do many films about illnesses or accidents in which you may feel pity or sorrow for the victim, but in a distanced way. The best case is the reverse, in which the calamity carries a wider meaning.

When the first review came in, it said, "I loved this film, but I must warn you right off before I go into details that if you're thinking of flying tomorrow, don't go see it." Well, there it was. The majority of the good reviews had little jokes like that and I thought, I'm finished, I'm done—a good review that says, "Don't go see it!"

Bliss: Did those kinds of reviews make you feel that the film should have been altered in some way?

Weir: Well, there's nothing that I'd change, there's nothing that I'd do differently. Afterwards, though, you start to think, well, now, do I take on something commercial after that? But I decided quite the reverse. I was looking for something as interesting and difficult as *Fearless*. I told producer Scott Rudin, I don't want safe material; I'm looking for something challenging because that's what keeps me interested, keeps me alive. He sent me *The Truman Show,* which certainly fulfilled the brief I'd given Scott.

Bliss: Was that script "broken" in the same sense as the one you looked at for *Fearless*?

Weir: "Broken" was really a word I was using to communicate the idea that a script was interesting but didn't quite work. All scripts need work on them. The curse of getting on the "A" list in Hollywood is that you're often not sent that kind of difficult material.

You know, it's really not that hard to direct a movie when you have good components: good script, good cast and crew. That kind of film can look pretty good. That's why a lot of actors who turn to directing make quite reasonable first films. It is hard, though, to add the X factor, to make a film luminous or have a strange power, to have it get a grip on you.

My concern is mostly with finding things that I want to do. To some extent there's a childish aspect to filmmaking. You could lose your enjoyment of it and lose interest. Keeping that interest alive is the important thing, which has a lot to do with the material you choose and the ideas inherently in it. As long as filmmaking is a way of reflecting on your life and your times, it remains very interesting.

Bliss: So you have to work hard to keep that perspective, to keep that childish aspect, not in a pejorative sense, but in the form of an undiluted response to stimuli?

Weir: Yes, to keep your sense of wonder.

FILMOGRAPHY

The Cars That Ate Paris (1974)

Direction: Peter Weir
Script: Peter Weir, from a story by Peter Weir, Keith Gow, Piers Davies
Cinematography: John McLean
Editing: Wayne Le Clos
Music: Bruce Smeaton
Produced by: Jim McElroy, Howard McElroy

Cast: Terry Camilleri (Arthur Waldo), John Meillon (Mayor), Melissa Jaffa (Beth), Kevin Miles (Dr. Midland), Max Gillies (Metcalf), Bruce Spence (Charlie), Max Phipps (Reverend Mulray), Rick Svully (George Waldo), Kevin Golsby (Insurance Man).

Picnic at Hanging Rock (1975)

Direction: Peter Weir
Script: Cliff Green, from the novel by Joan Lindsay
Cinematography: Russell Boyd
Editing: Max Lemon
Music: Gheorghe Zamphir (pan pipe); Ludwig van Beethoven, "Piano Concerto No. 5"; additional music by Bruce Smeaton
Produced by: Hal McElroy, Jim McElroy, Patricia Lovell

Cast: Rachel Roberts (Mrs. Appleyard), Dominic Guard (Michael Fitzhubert), Helen Morse (Dianne de Portiers), Jacki Weaver (Minnie), Vivean Gray (Miss McCraw), Kirsty Child (Dora Lumley), Anne Lambert (Miranda),

Karen Robson (Irma), Jane Vallis (Marion), Christine Schuler (Edith), Margaret Nelson (Sara), John Jarratt (Albert Crundall), Martin Vaughan (Ben Hussey), Wyn Roberts (Sergeant Bumpher), Peter Collingwood (Colonel Fitzhubert), Olga Dickie (Mrs. Fitzhubert).

The Last Wave (1977)

Direction: Peter Weir
Script: Peter Weir, Tony Morphett, Petru Popescu, from an idea by Peter Weir
Cinematography: Russell Boyd
Editing: Max Lemon
Music: Charles Wain
Produced by: Hal McElroy, Jim McElroy

Cast: Richard Chamberlain (David Burton), Olivia Hamnett (Annie Burton), Gulpilil (Chris Lee), Frederick Parslow (Reverend Burton), Vivean Gray (Dr. Whitburn), Nandjiwarra Amagula (Charlie), Walter Amagula (Gerry Lee), Athol Compton (Billy Corman).

The Plumber (1980)

Direction: Peter Weir
Script: Peter Weir
Cinematography: David Sanderson
Editing: G. Turney-Smith
Music: Rory O'Donohue

Cast: Judy Morris (Jill Cowper), Ivar Kants (Max), Robert Coleby (Brian Cowper), Henry Szeps (David Medavoy), Candy Raymond (Meg), Yomi Abioudun (Dr. Matu), Beverly Roberts (Dr. Japari), Meme Thorne (Anna), David Burchell (Professor Cato), Bruce Rosen (Dr. Don Felder), Pam Sanders (Ananas).

Gallipoli (1981)

Direction: Peter Weir
Script: David Williamson, from a story by Peter Weir
Cinematography: Russell Boyd
Editing: William Anderson

Music: "Adagio in G Minor for Strings and Orchestra" by Tomaso Albinoni;
   "Oxygene" by Jean Michael Jarre; "The Pearl Fishers" by Georges Bizet;
   "Tales from the Vienna Woods" and "Roses from the South" by Johann
   Strauss; Centone di Sonata No. 3 by Niccolo Paganini
Additional Music: Brian May
Produced by: Robert Stigwood, Patricia Lovell

Cast: Mark Lee (Archie Hamilton), Mel Gibson (Frank Dunne), Bill Hunter
(Major Barton), Robert Grubb (Billy Lewis), Tim McKenzie (Barney Wilson),
David Argue ("Snowy"), Bill Kerr (Uncle Jack), Ron Graham (Wallace
Hamilton), Charles Yunupingu (Zak), John Morris (Colonel Robinson), with
the men of Port Lincoln and Adelaide; the 16th Air Defense Regiment; cadets
of the No. 1 Recruit Training Unit, Edinburgh, South Australia.

The Year of Living Dangerously (1982)

Direction: Peter Weir
Script: David Williamson, Peter Weir, C. J. Koch, from the novel by C. J. Koch
Cinematography: Russell Boyd
Editing: William Anderson
Music: Maurice Jarre (uncredited: Stathis Vangelis)
Produced by: James McElroy

Cast: Mel Gibson (Guy Hamilton), Sigourney Weaver (Jill Bryant),
Linda Hunt (Billy Kwan), Bembel Roco (Kumar), Domingo Landicho
(Hortono), Michael Murphy (Pete Curtis), Noel Ferrier (Wally O' Sullivan),
Mike Emperio (President Sukarno), Bernardo Nacilla (Dwarf), Bill Kerr
(Colonel Henderson), Kuh Ledesman (Tiger Lily), Norma Uatuhan (Ibu).

Witness (1985)

Direction: Peter Weir
Script: Earl W. Wallace, William Kelley, from a story by William Kelley,
   Pamela Wallace, Earl W. Wallace
Cinematography: John Seale
Editing: Thom Noble
Music: Maurice Jarre
Sound: Barry D. Thomas, Humberto Gatica
Produced by: Edward S. Feldman

Cast: Harrison Ford (John Book), Kelley McGillis (Rachel Lapp), Josef Sommer (Deputy Commissioner Schaeffer), Lukas Haas (Samuel Lapp), Jan Rubes (Eli Lapp), Alexander Godunov (Daniel Hochleitner), Danny Glover (McFee), Brent Jennings (Carter), Patti Lupone (Elaine), Angus MacInnes (Fergie).

The Mosquito Coast (1986)

Direction: Peter Weir
Script: Paul Schrader, based on the novel by Paul Theroux
Cinematography: John Seale
Editing: Thom Noble, Richard Francis-Bruce
Music: Maurice Jarre
Produced by: Saul Zaentz, Jerome Hellman

Cast: Harrison Ford (Allie Fox), Helen Mirren (Mother), River Phoenix (Charlie Fox), Jadrien Steele (Jerry Fox), Hilary Gordon (April Fox), Rebecca Gordon (Clover Fox), Jason Alexander (Clerk), Dick O'Neill (Mr. Polski), Andre Gregory (Reverend Spellgood), Martha Plimpton (Emily Spellgood), Conrad Roberts (Mr. Haddy).

Dead Poets Society (1989)

Direction: Peter Weir
Script: Tom Schulman
Cinematography: John Seale
Editing: William Anderson, Lee Smith, Priscilla Nedd
Music: Maurice Jarre
Produced by: Steven Haft, Paul Junger Witt, Tony Thomas

Cast: Robin Williams (John Keating), Robert Sean Leonard (Neil Perry), Ethan Hawke (Todd Anderson), Josh Charles (Knox Overstreet), Gale Hansen (Charlie Dalton), Dylan Kossman (Richard Cameron), Allelon Ruggiero (Steven Meeks), James Waterson (Gerard Pitts), Norman Lloyd (Mr. Nolan), Kurtwood Smith (Mr. Perry), Carla Belver (Mrs. Perry), Leon Pownall (McAllister).

Green Card (1990)

Direction: Peter Weir
Script: Peter Weir

Cinematography: Geoffrey Simpson
Editing: William Anderson
Music: Hans Zimmer
Produced by: Edward S. Feldman, Peter Weir

Cast: Gérard Depardieu (Georges Faure), Andie MacDowell (Brontë Parrish), Bebe Neuwirth (Lauren Adler), Gregg Edelman (Phil), Robert Prosky (Brontë's lawyer), Jessie Keosian (Mrs. Bird), Ethan Philips (Gorsky), Mary Louise Wilson (Mrs. Sheehan), Lois Smith, Conrad McLaren (Brontë's parents).

Fearless (1993)

Direction: Peter Weir
Script: Rafael Yglesias, based on his novel
Cinematography: Allen Daviau
Editing: William Anderson
Music: Maurice Jarre
Production Design: John Stoddart
Art *Direction:* Chris Burian-Mohr
Produced by: Paula Weinstein, Mark Rosenberg

Cast: Jeff Bridges (Max Klein), Isabella Rossellini (Laura Klein), Rosie Perez (Carla Rodrigo), Tom Hulce (Brillstein), John Turturro (Dr. Bill Perlman), Benicio del Toro (Manny Rodrigo), John de Lancie (Jeff Gordon), Spencer Vrooman (Jonah Klein).

The Truman Show (1998)

Direction: Peter Weir
Script: Andrew Niccol
Cinematography: Peter Biziou
Editing: William M. Anderson, Lee Smith
Music: Philip Glass, Burkard Dallwitz
Produced by: Edward S. Feldman, Andrew Niccol, Lynn Pleshette, Scott
    Rudin, Adam Schroeder, Richard Luke Rothschild

Cast: Jim Carrey (Truman Burbank), Ed Harris (Christof), Laura Linney (Meryl Burbank/Hannah Gill), Noah Emmerich (Marlon/Louis Coltrane), Natascha McElhone (Lauren Garland/Sylvia), Holland Taylor (Truman's

Mother), Brian Delate (Kirk Burbank), Blair Slater (Young Truman),
Ron Taylor (Ron), Don Taylor (Don), Judy Clayton (Travel Agent), Mal Jones
(News Vendor), David Andrew Nash (Bus Driver/Ferry Captain),
John Roselius (Man at Beach), Paul Giamatti (Control Room Director),
Philip Glass (Keyboard Artist), Terry Camilleri (Man in Bathtub).

NOTES

Introduction

1. The term "feature-length" is generally agreed upon as meaning a film running in excess of one hour. Against the contention that *The Story of the Kelly Gang* was a feature-length film, cinema historian Graham Shirley states, "Today there is no certainty in knowing the exact running time of *The Story of the Kelly Gang*, beyond the fact that its length was advertised as 4000 feet and in reviews was mentioned as running between 40 minutes and more than an hour." Graham Shirley, "Australian cinema: 1896 to the renaissance" in *Australian Cinema*, ed. Scott Murray (Australia: Allen and Unwin, 1994), p. 7. (Of course, the film's running time would have been affected by the speed at which the projector motor's rheostat was set.) Historian Eric Reade refers to the film as "Australia's first commercially produced feature film" (Eric Reade, *History and Heartburn: The Saga of Australian Film 1896–1978* [Rutherford, NJ: Fairleigh Dickinson University Press, 1979], p. 5), while critics Andrew Pike and Ross Cooper state that the film is "quite possibly" the world's first feature. Andrew Pike and Ross Cooper, *Australian Film 1900–1977: A Guide to Feature Film Production* (Melbourne: Oxford University Press, 1980), p. 7.

2. Brian McFarlane, *Australian Cinema 1970–1985* (London: Secker and Warburg, 1987), p. 4.

3. Murray, *Australian Cinema*, p. 28.

4. Reade, p. 149.

5. McFarlane, pp. 20–21.

6. Reade, p. 169.

7. McFarlane, p. 25.

8. McFarlane, p. 26.

9. Brian McFarlane and Geoff Mayer, *New Australian Cinema: Sources and Parallels in American and British Film* (Cambridge: Cambridge University Press, 1992), p. 135.

10. Kevin Brownlow, *The Parade's Gone By* (New York: Bonanza, 1968), pp. 260–67.

11. McFarlane and Mayer, p. 31.

12. McFarlane, p. 40.

13. There are two Australian directors named George Miller. The one probably most familiar to American audiences is the director (and co-writer) of the Mad Max films and the director of other productions such as *The Witches of Eastwick* (1987) and *Lorenzo's Oil* (1992). In 1995, Miller produced *Babe*. The George Miller who directed *The Man from Snowy River* has also directed the German film *The Neverending Story II* (1990) and the 1991 U.S. production *Frozen Assets*.

14. McFarlane, p. 54.

15. Ross Gibson, "Formative landscapes," in Murray, *Australian Cinema*, p. 45.

16. Gibson, p. 49. The quote is from Marcus Clarke's preface to the poems of Adam Lindsay Gordon. The First Fleet was the initial "convoy of convicts transported to Australia." Robert Lacour-Gayet, *A Concise History of Australia*, trans. James Grieve (Australia: Penguin Books, 1976), p. 82.

17. As McFarlane points out, Australian films of the 1920s and 1930s saw the bush as "a testing-ground for manhood . . . as a site for struggles between man and nature, where hard-working, decent men might live with a peculiarly Australian dignity in an anti-city, anti-boss, anti-European ethos; as the setting for simple, uncorrupted egalitarian values as compared with the heartless capitalism of the cities. If by the 1930s this was no more than a dream and an ideal, by the 1970s it was not even this." McFarlane, p. 71.

18. In *Picnic* and *Wave*, the desired world is associated with things Aboriginal.

19. For more on the concept of the "green world" as elucidated by Northrop Frye, see Frye's *Anatomy of Criticism* (Princeton: Princeton University Press, 1957), p. 182.

20. Frederick Jackson Turner, "The Significance of the Frontier in American History," in *The Frontier in American History* (New York: Holt, Rinehart and Winston, 1962). Leo Marx, *The Machine in the Garden: Technology and the Pastoral Ideal in America* (New York: Oxford University Press, 1970), p. 65. As Marx points out, the alienating effects of urbanization make the embracing of such illusory romanticizing possible.

21. McFarlane, p. 111.

22. McFarlane, p. 111.

23. A. C. Palfreeman, "The White Australia Policy," in *Racism: The Australian Experience*, vol. 1, ed. F. S. Stevens (New York: Taplinger, 1971), p. 136.

24. Palfreeman, p. 137.

25. S. Encel, "The Nature of Race Prejudice in Australia," in *Racism: The Australian Experience*, vol. 1, ed. F. S. Stevens (New York: Taplinger, 1971), p. 36.

26. Weir comes close to making this point in the *American Film* interview when, talking about the sense of dislocation that Australians feel, he comments, "that's an interesting experiment, to take people and chop off their roots and put them down in

Asia, and, not only that, but in a country that was inhabited, as your country was with Indians, with aborigines." Peter Weir, "Dialogue on Film," *American Film* 11 (March 1986), p. 13.

27. Leslie Fiedler, *Love and Death in the American Novel* (New York: Anchor, 1993).

28. W. E. H. Stanner, "Australia and Racialism," in *Racism: The Australian Experience,* vol. 1, ed. F. S. Stevens (New York: Taplinger, 1971), p. 10.

29. Stanner, pp. 10–11.

30. I will deal with this aspect of Australian history in the chapter on *The Year of Living Dangerously.*

31. There is an Aborigine in *Picnic,* but he is seen only very briefly, during a search party scene.

32. Toni Morrison, *Playing in the Dark: Whiteness and the Literary Imagination* (New York: Vintage, 1992), p. 6.

33. Morrison, p. 9.

34. Morrison, p. 59.

35. Morrison, p. 67. Apparently, Weir also employs what Morrison refers to as "fetishization . . . a strategy often used to assert the categorical absolutism of civilization and savagery" (p. 68). Note, for example, the fears of the civilized Mrs. Appleyard concerning the schoolgirls' trip into a wild, uninhabited region in *Picnic at Hanging Rock.*

36. To some extent, this attitude is what critic Jan Dawson seems to be identifying when he says that Weir is more concerned with atmosphere rather than theme. Jan Dawson, "Picnic under Capricorn," *Sight and Sound* 45:2 (1976), p. 83.

37. In *Green Card,* there are no central black or "dark" characters at all; the film uses the *idea* of Africa as a symbol for passions and yearnings unchecked by civilization.

38. David Denby, "Jungle Fever," *New Yorker,* November 6, 1995, p. 129.

39. Denby, "Jungle Fever," p. 128.

40. Denby, "Jungle Fever," p. 128.

41. Denby, "Jungle Fever," p. 128.

42. H. O. McQueen, "Racism in Australian Literature," in *Racism: The Australian Experience,* vol. 1, ed. F. S. Stevens (New York: Taplinger, 1971), p. 119. Notable Australian films that, at least in part, condemn blacks to death for sexual interest in white women include Fred Schepisi's *The Chant of Jimmie Blacksmith* (1978) and British director Nicolas Roeg's *Walkabout* (1971), which was shot on location in Australia.

43. Denby, "Jungle Fever," p. 128.

44. Pauline Kael, "Doused" (review of *The Last Wave*), *New Yorker* 54:49 (January 22, 1979), pp. 102–3

45. Kael, "Doused," p. 102.

46. I'm taking Morrison's lead here in this neologism, à la her term "Africanist."

47. *Witness's* morally unimpeachable Amish also fit into this pattern.

48. Michael Dempsey, "Inexplicable Feelings: An Interview with Peter Weir," *Film Quarterly* 33:4 (Summer 1980). pp. 10–11.

49. Weir acknowledges these qualities in both the *American Film* and *Film Comment* interviews. See Weir, "Dialogue on Film," p. 13; and Pat McGilligan, "Under Weir . . . and Theroux," *Film Comment* 22 (November/December 1986), p. 32.

50. Denby, "Jungle Fever," p. 128.

51. Neil Rattigan, *Images of Australia: 100 Films of the New Australian Cinema* (Dallas: Southern Methodist University Press, 1991), p. 12.

52. Peter Weir in the 1983 video interview for the Australian Film, Television, and Radio School.

53. Weir video interview.

54. Richard Combs, review of *The Mosquito Coast, Monthly Film Bulletin* 54 (February 1987), p. 53

55. Weir directed a segment titled *Michael* in a three-part film called *Three To Go* (1969). Weir's segment chronicles the activities of a young man torn between his conformist family and his new friends in the 1960s youth rebellion. *Homesdale* (1971) is Weir's feature-length film about a group of people at a lodge that may be a hunting retreat or may be a mental institution. Each film clearly focuses on dualities. Unfortunately, no archive in the United States has a print of either film.

56. The film's depiction of a clash between an outsider and a strange town repeats certain themes present in Weir's first two long films. *Michael* tells a story of a conventional young man attracted to the alternative lifestyle of the Australian youth culture; *Homesdale* is concerned with a hunting lodge, whose institutional repressions anticipate those in evidence in *Picnic at Hanging Rock, The Last Wave,* and *Dead Poets Society.*

57. "When people ask me why I always make films about the occult, I say . . . I think these things *were* natural. Maybe they're not now, but we've only chosen to see the world in a certain way." Peter Weir quoted in "It doesn't take any imagination at all to feel awed," an interview by Judith M. Kass, *Movietone News* 62/63 (December 1979), p. 7.

58. Miranda misquotes lines from Edgar Allan Poe's poem "A Dream Within a Dream," which actually reads, "*All* that we see or seem / Is but a dream within a dream" (emphasis in original). See chapter 2 for the significance of the alteration.

59. Dempsey, p. 9. Also see the extensive references to writings on this subject in the bibliography of Robert Eberwein's *Film and the Dream Screen* (Princeton: Princeton University Press, 1984).

60. Roger Shattuck, *The Banquet Years: The Origins of the Avant Garde in France, 1885 to World War I* (New York: Vintage, 1968), p. 34.

61. Thomas Kuhn, *The Structure of Scientific Revolutions,* 2nd edition (Chicago: University of Chicago Press, 1970), pp. 62–63.

62. The surrealists were fond of using images involving violence as part of their juxtapositions (e.g., Lautreamont's "He was as beautiful in his overalls as the water in which a wound has recently been washed"); shocks were employed to draw attention to the beauty inherent in violence, a quality captured during the ice house explosion in *The Mosquito Coast.* See Maurice Nadeau, *The History of Surrealism* (New York: Macmillan, 1966).

63. Kuhn, p. 64.

64. Stanley Palombo, "Hitchcock's *Vertigo:* The Dream Function in Film," in *Images in Our Souls: Cavell, Psychoanalysis and Cinema,* ed. Joseph H. Smith and William Kerrigan (Baltimore: Johns Hopkins University Press, 1987), p. 44.

65. Palombo, p. 46.

66. Palombo, p. 47.

67. Palombo, p. 48.

68. According to McFarlane and Mayer, Graeme Turner, in *National Fictions: Literature, Film, and the Construction of Australian Narrative* (Sydney: Allen and Unwin, 1986), argues that the "isolation and powerlessness . . . in . . . Australian literary narrative produc[es] . . . characteristic weak climax and closure, or no effective resolution at all." Thus, lack of closure in Australian films may partially derive from a trend in the country's literature. McFarlane and Mayer, pp. 239–40.

69. McFarlane and Mayer, p. 224.

70. McFarlane and Mayer, p. 136.

71. McFarlane and Mayer, p. 136.

72. McFarlane and Mayer, p. 136.

73. In this respect, Weir's statement that "I always thought when I died and went to heaven the first thing I'd ask God would be, 'Whatever happened to those people on the Marie Celeste?'" seems highly uncharacteristic in that Weir seems to be searching for precisely the kind of solution that in his films he repudiates. Peter Weir quoted in David Stratton, *The Last New Wave* (London: Angus and Robertson, 1980), p. 75. I feel that the films which have the most traditional closures, with the possible exception of *Fearless* (1993), are to a degree less satisfying precisely to the extent that they conform to this expectation.

74. Richard Combs, review of *The Mosquito Coast, Monthly Film Bulletin* 54 (February 1987), p. 53.

75. Gary Hentzi, "Peter Weir and the Cinema of New Age Humanism," *Film Quarterly* 44:2 (Winter 1990–1991), pp. 2–12.

76. Hentzi, p. 6.

77. Hentzi, pp. 4–5.

78. Shattuck, pp. 36–37.

79. Dempsey, p. 10.

80. Indeed, as Weir noted in 1986, his attitudes and techniques are always evolving. "One changes, and one's personality changes . . . it's a cliché—but I was never satisfied. I was always changing, and that is what kept me going." Peter Weir quoted in McGilligan, p. 29.

81. McGilligan, p. 32.

82. Richard Combs, review of *Witness, Monthly Film Bulletin* 52 (May 1985), p. 167.

83. Dawson, p. 83.

84. Earlier Weir films, especially *Picnic at Hanging Rock,* were international successes, but Weir was always nonetheless perceived as an Australian filmmaker.

85. Weir video interview.

86. Weir video interview.

87. Despite this apparent trend, critic Scott Murray singles out Weir for what he contends is the complete lack of positive heterosexual relationships in his films. In support of his assertion, Murray cites writer Meaghan Morris, who says that

Australian cinema could scarcely be accused of promoting the virtues of life-long love and marriage. There is little or no glorification of full-blown love, for example, and none of the heightened respect for the eternal drama of the couple that defines the themes of so much European and American cinema. Instead, there is a fascination with group behaviour, and with relationships seen in the context of social institutions.

Yet for the sake of his thesis, Murray misrepresents Weir's work: he overlooks the supportive heterosexual relationship in the Australian production *Picnic at Hanging Rock* between the handyman, Tom, and the school maid, Milly; claims, somewhat oddly, that the casting of Linda Hunt in a male role in *The Year of Living Dangerously* creates "unsettling reverberations" that compromise the resolution of the affair between Guy and Jill; and states that *Witness*'s John Book backs away from a relationship with Rachel "for no convincing reason," although it is quite clear from Book's statement to Rachel that he refrains from making love to her because of his respect for the irreconcilable differences between their cultures. Meaghan Morris quoted by Scott Murray in "Australian cinema in the 1970s and 1980s," in Murray, *Australian Cinema*, p. 121.

88. McFarlane and Mayer divide Weir's cinema along different lines. In their view, what distinguishes Weir's Australian from American films is the American films' reliance upon the classical Hollywood model of melodrama. Commenting on *Witness*, for example, they note that the film's script "encourages the audience to participate in its narrative 'game' through the *regular* supply of compositional and generic cues that allow the successive formation of *hypotheses* with some *confidence*" (p. 58, my emphasis). The value-laden rhetoric makes it clear that we're not receiving a critical assessment here so much as a highly idiosyncratic reaction. When McFarlane and Mayer go on to note that "[The series of responses that we have just elucidated] is not possible in *Picnic at Hanging Rock* and . . . is not encouraged in Weir's earlier films" (p. 58), their bias is clearly revealed. The "earlier films" comprise all of Weir's Australian work. Thus, for McFarlane and Mayer, a film such as *Witness* is capable of "generat[ing] audience involvement" by using the melodramatic device of a "threat to innocence." Although McFarlane and Mayer admit that the potential for such a device exists in *Picnic at Hanging Rock,* they contend that this potential is "subverted by the narrative form used in the film" (p. 115). Yet is the threat in *Picnic* any less real than the one in *Witness* just because it is implied, not concrete? In *Picnic,* the threat is an interior one, burgeoning sexuality, which is reflected by, but does not emanate from, the rock. Thus, the film's action stresses psychological forces, thereby allying *Picnic* with that part of Weir's filmmaking that places a premium on the unconscious (as opposed to empirical) realm. Although Weir does allow the viewer to form "hypotheses" about how *Witness*'s action

will be resolved, the film's success cannot be attributed solely to its empirical focus. Indeed, *Witness* is successful only to the extent that its external action is equal in intensity to its psychological action. In fact, the film's overtly physical actions—the murder, the shootouts—are less effective than its psychological violence (e.g., Schaeffer's talk with Sergeant Carter).

89. Sigmund Freud, "The Uncanny," in *The Complete Psychological Works of Sigmund Freud*, vol. 17, ed. James Strachey, trans. James Strachey, Anna Freud, Alix Strachey, and Alan Tyson (London: Hogarth Press, 1955), p. 241.

90. Freud, "The Uncanny," p. 241. In this regard, Freud anticipates Jung's notion of the collective unconscious, within which what is known has always been known: in the present quote, it is asserted that the unknown is always known. Cf. Palombo's assertion about recognition (Palombo, p. 48).

91. Freud, "The Uncanny," pp. 244–45.

92. Sigmund Freud quoted in Palombo, p. 59. See chapter 2 for the full version of Weir's "refinding" story about the gestation of *The Last Wave*.

93. Palombo, p. 59.

94. Otto Rank, *The Double: A Psychoanalytic Study*, trans. and ed. by Harry Tucker Jr. (Chapel Hill: University of North Carolina Press, 1971), pp. 84–85.

95. Jung recognized the historical basis of Freud's materialist attitudes when, commenting on *The Future of an Illusion*, he stated that the book's approach to religion reflects "the rationalist materialism of the scientific views current in the late nineteenth century." Carl Jung, *Psychology and Religion: West and East*, trans. R. F. C. Hull (New York: Pantheon, 1963), p. 349.

96. Jung, *Psychology and Religion*, p. 19.

97. Sigmund Freud, *The Future of an Illusion*, trans. and ed. by James Strachey (New York: Norton, 1961), p. 30. See also *Civilization and Its Discontents*, trans and ed. by James Strachey (New York: Norton, 1961) pp. 11–19.

98. Sigmund Freud, *On Dreams*, trans. and ed. by James Strachey (New York: Norton, 1952), pp. 35–36.

99. Freud, *On Dreams*, p. 34.

100. Carl Jung, *Seminar on Dream Analysis*, ed. William McGuire (Princeton: Princeton University Press, 1984), p. 3. In the same way that Weir feels that dreams encourage the dreamer to discover the self, Toni Morrison asserts that

As a writer reading, I came to realize the obvious: the subject of the dream is the dreamer. The fabrication of an Africanist persona is reflexive; an extraordinary meditation on the self; a powerful exploration of the fears and desires that reside in the writer's conscious. It is an astonishing revelation of longing, of terror, of perplexity, of shame, of magnanimity. It requires hard work not to see this. (Morrison, p. 17)

101. Jung, *Seminar on Dream Analysis*, p. 4.

102. Jung, *Seminar on Dream Analysis*, p. 93.

103. Jung, *Seminar on Dream Analysis*, p. 93.

104. Jung, *Seminar on Dream Analysis,* p. 441.

105. Jung, *Seminar on Dream Analysis,* p. 93. For further useful distinctions between Freud and Jung's conception of the origin and significance of dreams, see *The Freud/ Jung Letters,* ed. William McGuire, trans. Ralph Manheim and R. F. C. Hull (Princeton: Princeton University Press, 1974). However, Freud did abandon his view that when you dream of someone it *is* that person, and instead began, at Jung's urging, to use the word "image" to refer to the person being represented. Jung, *Seminar on Dream Analysis,* p. 457.

106. Jung, *Psychology and Religion,* pp. 26–27.

107. Carl Jung, *Psychology and Alchemy,* trans. R. F. C. Hull (London: Routledge & Kegan Paul, 1953), p. 12.

108. Jung, *Psychology and Alchemy,* p. 15.

109. Jung, *Psychology and Alchemy,* p. 22.

110. Jung, *Psychology and Alchemy,* p. 17.

111. Jung, *Psychology and Alchemy,* pp. 23–24.

112. Jung, *Psychology and Alchemy,* p. 27.

113. Jung, *Psychology and Alchemy,* pp. 29–31.

114. Jung, *Psychology and Alchemy,* p. 34.

115. Joseph Campbell, *The Hero with a Thousand Faces* (Princeton: Princeton University Press, 1949), p. 30.

116. Robert Winer, "Witnessing and Bearing Witness: The Ontogeny of Encounter in the Films of Peter Weir," in *Images in Our Souls: Cavell, Psychoanalysis and Cinema,* ed. Joseph H. Smith and William Kerrigan (Baltimore: Johns Hopkins University Press, 1987), p. 84.

117. Additionally, entering a movie theater, watching a film's dream images unfold in the dark, and then re-emerging into the light to discuss what one has seen can also be seen as a form of the night journey.

118. Campbell, p. 17.

119. Campbell, pp. 17–18. In an interesting footnote, Campbell notes that the Australian Arandas refer to these archetypes as "the eternal ones of the dream." According to Geza Roheim, to whose book *The Eternal Ones of the Dream* Campbell alludes, this term, which in Aranda is *altjiranga mitjina,* "refers to the mythical ancestors who wandered on the earth in the time called *altjiranga nakala,* 'ancestor was.' The word *altjira* means: (a) dream, (b) ancestor, being who appears in the dream, (c) a story." Thus for these people, as for Weir, stories, the people who appear in these stories, and dreams are equivalent. Campbell, p. 19.

120. Frye, pp. 169–70.

121. Frye, p. 182.

122. Frye, p. 182.

123. Frye, p. 183.

124. Campbell, p. 20.

125. Winer, p. 84.

126. In a reciprocal fashion, Book moves from an active role to a passive one after he is wounded.

127. Søren Kierkegaard, *The Sickness unto Death,* in *Fear and Trembling* and *The Sickness unto Death,* trans. Walter Lowrie (New York: Doubleday, 1954), p. 154.

128. Weir, "Dialogue on Film," p. 14.

129. "I decided it was a good idea not just to make films which obsessed me. I wanted to be like those directors in the '40s who took assignments from their studios and got on with them." Peter Weir, quoted in Robert S. Birchard, "Witness/John Seale, ACS," *American Cinematographer* 67:4 (April 1986), p. 75.

130. Birchard, p. 75.

131. Weir, "Dialogue on Film," p. 14.

132. McGilligan, p. 32.

133. See David Williamson's comments on Weir's "strong-minded[ness]" and the conflicts that this quality caused between Weir and C. J. Koch, who worked on the film's script and on whose novel the film was based. David Williamson in Ray Willibanks, ed., *Australian Voices: Writers and Their Work* (Austin: University of Texas Press, 1991), pp. 177–78.

134. Peter Weir quoted in McGilligan, p. 30.

135. McGilligan, p. 32.

136. Weir, "Dialogue on Film," p. 13.

137. McGilligan, p. 32, and Weir, "Dialogue on Film," p. 15.

138. McGilligan, p. 29. The attitude that Weir admires is commented upon by Eliot Deutsch in an essay on the *Bhagavad Gītā.* One of the preliminary knowledges with which the *Gītā* deals "involves the understanding that all actions of the self are really only the action of Nature acting through one. . . . It is only when one functions harmoniously with the inner causal matrix of some action-be it wrestling, cooking, painting, or anything else-that it achieves its natural-spiritual fulfillment." Eliot Deutsch, "The Nature of Karma Yoga," in *Bhagavad Gītā,* trans. with critical essays by Eliot Deutsch (New York: Holt, Rinehart and Winston, 1968), pp. 164–65. Deutsch further comments that according to the *Gītā,* "the self is not the real doer . . . it is the bringing of the self to the awareness that there is a fundamental distinction between the empirical self and the real Self, that one is not really the self that one ordinarily believes oneself to be . . . a full realization of this is precisely the task of *jnana yoga*" (p. 165). Deutsch defines *jnana yoga* as a "non-dualistic system [of thought which] demands a rigorous intellectual discrimination between the phenomenal world and the real world of Brahma [what Deutsch calls the "unitary, undifferentiated principle of all being, the knowledge of which liberates one from finitude" (p. 12)], and culminates in an intuitive identification which shatters the independent existence of everything but the non-dual One" (p. 15).

139. McGilligan, p. 29. As Weir notes,

I stopped filmmaking in 1978 and put myself through a course I was sorely lacking. For 12 months I watched movies: I was in touch with a library with a very good collection of world film culture. I started with Griffith; then I moved from him to the Russians; then I moved to England and looked at Hitchcock's films; then I shot back to the States for Chaplin; then I went across and dipped into France, then Germany, working my way forward up to the period of the Forties movies, which is where I'd begun, through television, to see the great filmmakers. I was astounded, astonished, and fascinated with the great gift of these films and so glad that I hadn't looked at them earlier. If I had, I don't think I would have made films. Because I was at the bottom of the hill.

140. Peter Weir quoted in Stratton, p. 75.

1. Car Crash Derby

1. In the short version of the film, which is titled *The Cars That Eat People* and which Weir has repudiated, Arthur's car crashes again at the film's end. As Weir has noted of this version, "no, it's not my film . . . when I saw what the American distributor had done to it, I was shattered." Peter Weir quoted in Dempsey, p. 5.

2. Stratton, p. 62.

3. Dempsey, p. 5.

4. In this regard, see Robin Wood's essay "An Introduction to the American Horror Film," in *The American Nightmare* (Toronto: Festival of Festivals, 1979), pp. 7–28.

5. McFarlane, pp. 62–63.

6. For a discussion of how people tend to treat their cars as people, see Andrew Wernick's essay "Vehicles for Myth: The Shifting Image of the Modern Car," in *Cultural Politics in Contemporary America,* ed. Ian Angus and Sut Jhally (New York: Routledge, 1989), pp. 198–216

7. Wood, pp. 7–28.

8. Reade, p. 214.

9. Philip Strick observes that the film's theme, "the erosion of humanity by techno-logical influences," allies it with other films such as *Point Blank* (1967), *Weekend* (1962), and *Duel* (1971). Strick, review of *The Cars That Ate Paris* in *Monthly Film Bulletin* 42 (May 1975), p. 102. It should also be noted that in this respect, the film antici-pates the effect that a near-religious, obsessive devotion to technology has on *The Mosquito Coast*'s Allie Fox.

2. Deadly Déjeuner

1. Peter Weir quoted in McFarlane, p. 73.

2. McFarlane, p. 73.

3. See, for example, *Village Voice,* February 26, 1979; *New York Times,* February 23, 1979; *New Yorker,* April 23, 1979; *Film Quarterly,* November 4, 1979; and *Time,* April 26, 1979.

4. Joan Lindsay, *Picnic at Hanging Rock* (Melbourne: Penguin, 1970), p. 8.

5. Graeme Turner quoted in Murray, *Australian Cinema,* p. 79.

6. Murray, *Australian Cinema,* p. 79.

7. Another version of the St. Valentine story involves a fourteenth-century martyr who helps the son of Cato, a Roman. Cato is so grateful for Valentine's curing his son of a "seemingly incurable paralytic disease" that his household is converted to Christianity. One of Cato's students is the son of the Roman emperor. "When this young man expounds his new-found Christian beliefs before his pagan father . . . three fellow students and Valentine himself are beheaded, but not before news comes that most of the population has been converted to Christianity, as God had promised the saint." Nigel Wilkins, ed., *Two Miracles* (Edinburgh: Scottish Academic Press, 1972), p. 3.

8. *Picnic* was re-released in the summer of 1998 in a newly edited version. Part of the subplot involving Irma's fascination with Michael was removed; Weir told me that he felt that this action detracted from the plot's movement in the film's second half. Interestingly, the new cut inserts a shot that is not in the original print: a view of a man with a camera taking a picture of Appleyard College, which had apparently become something of an attraction after the girls' disappearance.

9. Weir's theory of the disappearances is as follows: "The descriptions of the things that happened on the rock are like those that occur when a comet passes near the Earth's surface. If you had taken a line round the world you might have found that it was super-hot in Chile and that watches stopped. . . . I think that the rock literally opened and swallowed them. The girl who survived saw something that was so beyond description—to see into the earth any distance and to see her friends falling—that the mind could not possibly accept what it saw and retain sanity. Really the film is as good as your own imagination." Peter Weir quoted in David Castell, "Weir, weird, and weirder still," *Films Illustrated* 6 (November 1976), p. 94.

10. Chris Wallace-Crabbe, *Melbourne or the Bush* (Melbourne: Angus and Robertson, 1974, p. 8), quoted in McFarlane, p. 72.

11. McFarlane, p. 74. McFarlane cites Nicholas Roeg's 1971 film *Walkabout* as an example of the perils of the bush, although in Roeg's film, the whites in the bush are rescued from destruction by an Aborigine. Nonetheless, McFarlane's statement seems to imply that any natural phenomenon, if examined closely, may contain an element of threat.

12. When Irma returns to the school, she meets with a violent response from her classmates, whose anxiety about the disappearances, heretofore repressed, bursts forth.

13. In what appears to be a reciprocal response, the clock in Mrs. Appleyard's study stops ticking towards the film's end.

14. This aspect is mirrored in the removal of the girls' gloves after they pass through an adjacent town, an act that anticipates the casting off of shoes and stockings by three of the girls who explore the rock.

15. As Weir notes, "Traditionally, [St. Valentine's Day is] the day of the pairing of birds. And from the moment the day begins, the story is about the failure of birds to pair and of connections to be made." Peter Weir quoted in Dawson, p. 83. Naturally, this

linkage fortifies the implicit connection between Miranda and swans that is intuited by Michael and reinforced by the film's editing, as well as suggests that the failure to establish a sexual link with others also implies an inability to understand the manner in which there are affinities ("connections") among numerous things in the universe that tend to go unrecognized by many people.

16. Weir did not originally plan to conclude the film this way.

We started with an entirely different ending from the one in the final film: we had Mrs. Appleyard returning to the rock, she climbs it, she goes through a series of experiences much like the girls had gone through, and is found dead at the base of the rock. All this was shot, with her carried back in a stretcher with the police in attendance. It was terrible! And then—I think it was Max Lemon, the film's editor's, suggestion—we had the idea of step printing the picnic sequences again. I thought we needed to go back to the girls and divert attention from the reality of events at the school. The great battle was always the second half of the film—once Irma is found, I thought the picture fell apart. So we decided to bring Miranda back through a series of dreams, change the ending, and put in as much as we could to divert the attention of the audience from a thriller-mystery until we almost mesmerised them and in doing this to take them into another film. And Max did a brilliant job.

Peter Weir quoted in Stratton, pp. 70–71. See also McFarlane and Mayer, pp. 54–55.

17. Lindsay's book states at the bottom of its prefatory list of characters that readers will have to decide for themselves whether the book's events are real or fictitious. According to Lindsay's note, since the events took place in 1900, and all of the characters are long since dead, the issue "hardly seems important.". When Weir met with Lindsay, he advised her, "Keep your secret. It's not the point." Peter Weir quoted in Kass, p. 7. However, in the 1976 David Castell interview, Weir stated, "We had to make the decision when it came to the film, so we simply said it was true. Certainly all the characters and the settings were true: every one of those characters lived. And there was a scandal at the school—some dreadful, dreadful thing. Whether it was exactly that, I don't truthfully know." Unfortunately, where Weir got the idea that there is an historical basis for the film's action is unclear. Castell, p. 94.

18. Later, this technique is duplicated when Mrs. Appleyard looks at herself in a mirror in Sara's room.

19. There's a slight blur and jump in the image, which doesn't occur in a later Weir film such as *Fearless* in which a shift in film speed is also used. However, this "glitch" in *Picnic* may also be the result of a poorly executed bit of film editing.

20. According to Weir, other effects that he used in the film (in which he says he "pulled every trick in the book") include "earthquakes on the soundtrack, slowed right down so they'd just register on the optical to create an uncomfortable feeling in the theater," "different camera speeds within ordinary dialogue scenes," and "[asking] the actors not to blink while listening." "Dialogue on Film: Peter Weir," *American Film* 11 (March 1986), p. 14.

21. In a fascinating article on *Picnic,* Karelisa Hartigan derives parallels between the film and a number of Greek myths, noticing that Mrs. Appleyard functions as the jealous authoritarian Artemis, that the rock has Dionysian qualities, that the swan is involved with myths of transformation, and that it is Pan who, at noontime, seems to pipe a drowsiness over the girls. In Hartigan's reading, Mrs. Appleyard's death represents a necessary function of the rock's magnetic power. "Artemis in South Australia: Classical Allusions in *Picnic at Hanging Rock,*" *Classical and Modern Literature* 11:1 (Fall 1990), pp. 93–98.

22. Cinematographer Russell Boyd quoted in "The 'New Vintage' Cinematographers of Australia Speak Out," *American Cinematographer* 57 (September 1976), p. 1038.

23. Later, when he falls into a swoon on the rock (at what appears to be the same location at which the girls had also been overtaken by drowsiness), Michael accurately intuits earlier dialogue from the girls, Miss McCraw, and Mademoiselle de Portiers; envisions Irma, Miranda, and Marion ascending the rock; and is awakened by Edith's scream from the earlier scene.

24. "A Dream Within a Dream," in *The Complete Tales and Poems of Edgar Allan Poe* (New York: Vintage, 1975), p. 967.

25. Perhaps we can also read the remark as a statement from Weir to stop talking so much about his films and just experience them. Indeed, Weir once said, "What I attempted, somewhere towards the middle of the film, was gently to shift emphasis off the mystery element which had been building in the first half and to develop the oppressive atmosphere of something which has no solution: to bring out a tension and claustrophobia in the locations and the relationships. We worked very hard at creating an hallucinatory, mesmerizing rhythm, so that you lost awareness of the facts, you stopped adding things up, and got into this enclosed atmosphere." Peter Weir quoted in Dawson, p. 83.

26. As Weir notes, "I knew I was going against the rules to have a mystery without a solution but, of course, that's what interested me about it. Curiously, the picture was a big hit in Europe, but it was not a success in the U.S. The reaction here was, How can there possibly not be a solution? In a country that puts people on the moon, what are you talking about? I had to take the audience past that point." Peter Weir quoted in *American Film* 11 (March 1986), pp. 13–14. Nonetheless, despite Weir's effort to the contrary, people persisted in trying to rationally account for the film's events. In 1980, Yvonne Rousseau's book *The Murders of Hanging Rock* (Melbourne: Scribe, 1980) included nine different explanations for the film's unusual events. In 1987, even writer Joan Lindsay seemed to join in the frenzy: the "missing" final chapter of her novel was published in *The Secret of Hanging Rock* (Sydney: Angus and Robertson, 1987), which proposed time dimensions as the explanation for the girls' disappearance. See Scott Murray, "Australian cinema in the 1970s and 1980s," in Murray, *Australian Cinema* p. 144, n.24.

27. Peter Weir quoted in Dawson, p. 83.

28. Obviously, this is not the reaction of some critics. As previously noted,

McFarlane and Mayer in *New Australian Cinema* place a great premium on melodrama's emphasis on traditional closure, and therefore find films such as *The Last Wave* and (it is implied) *Picnic* somewhat unsatisfying. McFarlane and Mayer, p. 57.

29. Gary Hentzi posits this view in "Peter Weir and the Cinema of New Age Humanism," pp. 2–12. Hentzi's article, with which I dealt in this book's introduction, is an academically oriented, but nonetheless ad hominem, attack on Weir's use of mythical and anthropological themes and symbols. For a detailed response to Hentzi's contentions with regard to *Dead Poets Society*, as well as a discussion of Tania Modleski's views on the film in her book *Feminism Without Women* (New York: Routledge, 1991), see chapter 10.

3. Notes from Underground

1. Peter Weir quoted in Stratton, p. 75.
2. Carl Jung, *Man and His Symbols* (New York: Doubleday, 1964), pp. 20–21.
3. Jung, *Man and His Symbols,* p. 21.
4. Weir himself has remarked on the symbolic placement of the film's Aboriginal culture cache. "Talking with David [Gulpilil], I realized the Aborigine culture was very much alive, if underground, so to speak." Peter Weir quoted in McGilligan, p. 28.
5. Kael, "Doused," pp. 102–3. Kael also feels that the film uses the Aborigines as racist fonts of stone age wisdom, a view that has validity but which also ignores the fact that everyone in the film, white or Aboriginal, represents a type.
6. Weir comments on his use of Chamberlain, "I thought he'd always been photographed in white light. When I think back to [Dr.] *Kildare* I think of those hot lights and I thought he'd never been photographed at night. I don't mean that literally, but there was something in his face; there was some alien quality, and in my story my character had that quality." Peter Weir quoted in Kass, p. 2.
7. Later, though, the coroner states during the trial that Billy died of drowning; this inconsistency is never explained in the film.
8. Two of David's friends, one a white lawyer, one a man who works with legal aid, say that there are no tribal people in the city.
9. Robert Eberwein asserts that the film uses what he refers to as "proleptic dreams. Virtually all of the dreams experienced by [the film's] hero . . . are identified [as dreams] retroactively." Eberwein, p. 158.
10. Inadvertently complicating this situation, David later tells Chris about this episode, stating that he was in his study and then woke up and saw Chris. David thus forgets that he only dreamed that he woke up, thereby making it clear that he is losing the ability to distinguish between his dreaming and waking states.
11. Historian D. J. Mulvaney estimates that Aborigines settled in Australia approximately 25,000 years ago. Mulvaney quoted in Robert Lacour-Gayet, *A Concise History of Australia,* trans. James Grieve (Australia: Penguin, 1976), p. 56.
12. Weir, "Dialogue on Film," p. 13.

13. Jung, *Psychology and Alchemy*, p. 31.

14. Lacour-Gayet notes in this respect that in the Aboriginal world view, "Men partook of the same essence as all things and were an integral part of a natural system that had been given its shape in the 'dream time.' A human being was doomed if he lost touch with this natural system, for it was both the source of his own life-force and his purpose in living." Lacour-Gayet, p. 68.

15. Peter Weir quoted in McFarlane and Mayer, p. 54.

16. Stratton, p. 77. Yet McFarlane and Mayer quote Weir as saying that "there is no ending and I was painted into a corner . . . You can't end it. You can try to be clever, and I tried a couple of other endings that did stop short of any wave, but they were just too neat," a statement that seems to imply that the film's lack of resolution was forced upon Weir by circumstances resulting from the script. McFarlane and Mayer, p. 57.

17. Weir notes, "We did at one stage consider making another, quite separate, film to come at the end, which would take you into the water—but there was no money to do it." Stratton, p. 77.

18. The reference in *Positif* (no. 204, March 1978, p. 54) is a caption to a photo of Richard Chamberlain, in David's house, holding an electric lantern.

19. In one of the versions of the stone discovery story that he tells, Weir refers to the stone's having "three parallel lines" on it, a description that seems very similar to the three circles of Charlie's painting and those on the stone that David sees Chris holding out to him. See Kass, p. 4, and p. 192 in the present book's Weir interview.

20. To make sure that there was no artificial distinction made in the film between the empirical and visionary scenes, cinematographer Russell Boyd (who also shot *Picnic at Hanging Rock*) photographed the entire film without technically altering the film's images. *American Cinematographer* noted that Boyd "adopted a photographic style of sharp, cold images, filmed entirely without fog, low contrast or diffusion filters. The effect is completely opposite to the soft, poetic, heavily diffused style of his previous effort, the lyrical 'Picnic At Hanging Rock.'" "Photographing *The Last Wave*," *American Cinematographer*, 59:4 (April 1978), p. 353. Even the scene in which David's wife "sees" Charlie standing outside her house was shot in natural moonlight. (Russell Boyd quoted in the same article, p. 354).

21. Kass, p. 7.

22. Jung, *Psychology and Religion*, pp. 39–40.

23. Jung, *Psychology and Alchemy*, p. 24.

24. Weir notes, "It's a very interesting effect in a conversation sometimes, just to shoot the conversation at the 24-frame speed and then shoot one of the characters, as I did with Richard Chamberlain a couple of times, at 120-frames-a-second, just his reactions, and then cut that into the dialogue conversation." Peter Weir quoted in Dempsey, p. 8.

25. David Gulpilil quoted in Stratton, p. 75. During the shooting of *The Last Wave*, Weir was struck with how Gulpilil, an Aborigine, saw nothing unusual about seeing the future in dreams or having visions; this was, Gulpilil explained, the normal way of

looking at things. The essential point here is that one's view of what is real dictates the reality that one perceives, not the other way around. Stratton, pp. 75–76.

4. Water Pressures

1. Quoted in M. Kinder, "The Plumber," *Film Quarterly* 33:4 (Summer 1980), p. 17.

2. Jill's friend Meg tells a story of comparable sexual duplicity about a strange woman who had asked a stranger if she could use her bathroom. After fifteen minutes, when the stranger went into the bathroom, she found a nude man sitting on the edge of the tub, his female clothing strewn on the bathroom floor.

3. Morrison, p. 52.

4. Historian A. Grenfell Price notes, "The Aborigines suffered seriously from opthalmia and yaws in various revolting forms, but, until their contact with Malay visitors, the whites, and various colored peoples introduced by the whites, their external and internal isolation, culture and simple diet appear to have protected them from scurvy, smallpox, measles, diphtheria, tuberculosis, cancer, venereal diseases, leprosy and malaria." *Island Continent: Aspects of the Historical Geography of Australia and Its Territories* (Australia: Angus and Robertson, 1972), pp. 23–24.

5. Peter Weir quoted in Kinder, p. 19. Kinder also perceptively comments on the trip of one of Brian and Jill's guests to their bathroom. "The civilized ritual of the dinner party is suddenly transformed back into the biological process which, as Buñuel reminded us in *Phantom of Liberty,* has two ends" (Kinder, p. 19).

6. Kinder, p. 19.

7. Kinder, p. 18. Kinder's article also contends that our attitude toward Jill at the film's end is divided: "we are not really sure whether we should interpret her deceptive move as a strong decisive victory or as a desperate moral defeat" (p. 18).

8. Kinder, p. 18.

9. Kinder, p. 18.

10. Kinder, p. 18.

5. The Death of a Nation

1. C. E. W. Bean, *The Official History of Australia in the War of 1914–1918, Volumes I and II* (Sydney: Angus and Robertson, 1921, 1924).

2. Bill Gammage, *The Broken Years: Australian Soldiers in the Great War* (Canberra: Australian National University Press, 1974).

3. For an excellent photographic and textual book on the campaign, see Christopher Pugsley, *Gallipoli: The New Zealand Story* (Auckland: Hodder and Staughton, 1984).

4. Kenneth T. Jackson, "Gallipoli," in *Past Imperfect: History According to the Movies,* ed. Ted Mico, John Miller-Monzon, and David Rubel (New York: Henry Holt, 1995), p. 182.

5. Jackson, p. 182

6. Jackson, pp. 182–83.

7. Gammage, p. 74.

8. Bean quoted in John North, *Gallipoli: The Fading Vision* (London: Faber and Faber, n.d.), p. 219.

9. North, p. 219.

10. C. E. W. Bean, *Anzac to Amiens* (Canberra: Australian War Memorial, 1983), p. 155.

11. Gammage, p. 74.

12. Lt. C. C. D. St. Pinnock quoted in Gammage, p. 75.

13. On August 16, Australian Salvation Army Padre McKenzie wrote of the assault, "many . . . never reached the trenches, blown to pieces with shells or riddled with machine-guns and rifles. I was in it and saw it all. Men were killed on every side of me. The 4th Battalion went in with 843 and came out with 283." Peter Liddle, *Men of Gallipoli* (London: Allen Lane, 1976), pp. 199–200. According to R. R. James in *Gallipoli* (London: Pan Books, 1974), p. 256, out of 600 men, 372 died.

14. It appears that Weir may have appropriated the story of two friends, both runners, taking part in the campaign from Bean's history. As T. H. E. Travers notes, "[In his history of the campaign], Bean had written of two brothers . . . perhaps suggesting to Peter Weir the structure of the film . . . but Bean also clearly suggests the idea of two athletes, for he writes: 'Gresley Harper and Wilfred, his younger brother, the latter of whom was last seen running forward like a school-boy in a foot race, with all the speed he could compass. . . .'" T. H. E. Travers, "*Gallipoli*: Film and the Traditions of Australiian [*sic*] History," *Film and History* 14:1 (February 1984), p. 17. (The reference appears in Bean, *Official History*, vol. 2, p. 618.) Apparently, Travers was not aware that two years earlier, in the Fonda-Bonardi interview, Weir, without mentioning it specifically, had credited Bean's book (which is generally regarded as the official account) as the source for *Gallipoli*'s running theme. See Claudia and Peter Fonda-Bonardi, "The Birth of a Nation: An Interview with Peter Weir," *Cineaste* 11:4 (1982), p. 41.

15. Writing about *Gallipoli* and a 1915 Australian film, *The Hero of the Dardanelles* (which Brian McFarlane refers to as a "recruitment-propaganda feature"), both of which feature shots of soldiers silhouetted against Egyptian pyramids at sunset, McFarlane quotes critic Sylvia Lawson, who states, "There are sixty-six years of history between these two intensely mythic shots; there is no ideological space between them at all." McFarlane, p. 48. It's clear, though, that Lawson is somehow overlooking the antiwar tone of Weir's film.

16. Gammage, p. 3.

17. Liddle, p. 202.

18. One of the soldiers whom Archie meets just before the final assault against the Turks is Les, a young man who worked on Archie's parents' ranch, and who belittled

Archie for being friendly with an Aborigine, Zack, to whom Archie referred as his "mate." Seeing Archie and Zack together, Les had remarked, "prefer the company of blacks, eh Archie?"

19. Gammage, pp. 5–6.

20. McFarlane, p. 169.

21. Interview with David Williamson in Willibanks, p. 177.

22. As Weir notes, "we had to tell a personal story, and our interest centered on the type of men who went. It was the human aspect of [the battle] that began to fascinate [scriptwriter] David [Williamson] and me." Fonda-Bonardi, p. 41.

23. Peter Weir quoted in Fonda-Bonardi, p. 42.

24. Weir has remarked that the challenge of *Gallipoli* was "to kill just one man in a war movie." Peter Weir in "Dialogue on Film," p. 13.

25. As Weir notes, "It took us a great deal of research, including many conversations with these old veterans, to realize that we did lose our own flower of a nation." Weir quoted in Fonda-Bonardi, p. 42.

26. Peter Weir quoted in Kathleen Tulich, interview with Peter Weir, *Cinema Papers* 80 (August 1980), p. 9.

27. Peter Weir quoted by McGilligan, p. 30. It bears repeating that *Gallipoli* was the first feature film that Weir made after leaving filmmaking for a while and putting himself through a filmmaking "course" by watching a large number of films by different directors. The result was that Weir felt humbled by the great films that he saw and came to regard his previous work's stylizations far more critically.

28. McGilligan, p. 30.

29. Fonda-Bonardi, p. 42. Weir notes that "we [Australians] celebrate it each year, April 25th, the day the boats first landed in Gallipoli . . . [it's] a national holiday."

30. Critic John Pym refers to the film's "anonymous" quality, going on to note that it "strenuously avoids argument in favour of the creation of mood." John Pym, review of *Gallipoli* in *Monthly Film Bulletin* 48 (December 1981), p. 245.

31. Critic Nick Roddick, who feels that Weir erred on the side of commercialism in the film, wrote, "Expecting an Australian director to make a film about Gallipoli that was both commercial and personal is a little like expecting a British director to do the same about Dunkirk." Roddick also believes that the film's running metaphor is "too slight to bear all the strain" of trying to achieve a balance between "the general—history and landscape—and the personal (an exercise in problematic male bonding)." Review of *The Year of Living Dangerously, Monthly Film Bulletin* 50 (June 1983), p. 147.

32. Weir does allow himself one very apparent stylization: when Archie and Frank are crossing the desert, Weir elides time by dissolving between shots of the two characters walking away from the camera (one shot finds them close to the camera; in the succeeding shot, after the dissolve, they are far away).

33. Fonda-Bonardi, p. 42.

34. Fonda-Bonardi, p. 42.

35. Gammage, p. 75.

36. Jackson, p. 184.

37. North, p. 220; Pugsley, pp. 283–84.

38. Jackson, p. 185.

39. Jackson cites Geoffrey Moorhouse's book *Hell's Foundations* (New York: Henry Holt, 1992) and Alan Moorehead's book *Gallipoli* (New York: Harper Brothers, 1956). Moorhouse's book makes no mention of the August 7 assault at all. Moorehead barely mentions the assault. He cites part of the "you have ten minutes to live" quote without identifying the speaker, and never refers to any of the military command by name. His book seems a pale appropriation of information from other sources. Moorehead, pp. 280–81.

40. Jackson has stated,

The Australians were in command at Anzac Cove, especially General Monash. Local attacks are almost never determined by area commanders. . . . Immediate decisions such as sending forth another wave would have been made by the local commanders, not the British at Suvla Bay or Cape Helles. . . . I was told several times in Australia that a British officer had not ordered the fourth wave over the top.

Kenneth T. Jackson, personal communication, November 24, 1997.

41. Pugsley, p. 284.

42. Cf. this book's Weir interview, p. 193.

43. Jackson, p. 185.

44. David Williamson, screenplay for *Gallipoli* (n.d., n.p.). North and Liddle mention the marker flag report, but it is obvious that they are merely repeating what Bean wrote. North, p. 220; Liddle, p. 202; Bean, *Official History*, vol. 2, pp. 615–16. As a testament to the film's reliance on Bean's book, this part of *Gallipoli* virtually duplicates the following passage from his history:

Major Todd, who commanded the third line [of attackers], reported to the regimental commander, Colonel Brazier, that [a subsequent attack's] success would be impossible. . . . Brazier . . . went to brigade headquarters, which was slightly in rear, and finding there only the brigade-major, Colonel Antill . . . informed him that, in view of the strength of the enemy's fire, the task laid upon his regiment was beyond achievement. But Antill, who was the main influence in the command of the brigade, had already received the news that one of the red and yellow flags had been seen in the enemy's trench. . . . He replied, therefore, that the 10th regiment must push on at once.

Bean, *Official History*, vol. 2, p. 617. The only modification from Bean's history is that in the film, this exchange occurs before the third wave of assault, which was the penultimate wave, not the last one, as the film makes it appear.

45. Gammage, p. 75. Even if this remark were accurate (I believe that it bears repeating that no one else refers to it), as used in Weir's film it does a great disservice to the British forces.

46. Gammage, pp. 74–75, n.65.

47. Gammage, p. 74. Bean also mentions White. Bean, *Official History*, vol. 2, p. 614.

In the screenplay, Barton says, "I can't ask my men to do what I wouldn't do myself." Williamson screenplay, scene 151.

48. Weir is incorrect in this regard. The previously mentioned recruiting film *The Hero of the Dardanelles* ends with the Australians landing at Gallipoli. According to Scott Murray, this scene, now lost, "is suspected to have been re-used for the 1928 *Spirit of Gallipoli*," which was directed by Keith Greenwood and William Green. Murray, *Australian Cinema* p. 11.

49. Fonda-Bonardi, p. 42.

50. Fonda-Bonardi, p. 42.

51. Fonda-Bonardi, p. 42. Obviously, though, if only judging by the testimonials in Bean's books, this statement is erroneous.

52. Roddick, review of *The Year of Living Dangerously*, p. 149.

53. Lucien Ballard quoted in Paul Seydor, *Peckinpah: The Western Films* (Urbana: University of Illinois Press, 1970), pp. 125–26.

54. An underwater swimming scene with a comparable function occurs in *The Year of Living Dangerously*. See chapter 5.

55. In certain respects this scene anticipates Guy Hamilton's dream of swimming underwater in *The Year of Living Dangerously*, particularly with regard to the abrupt transition from the idyllic to the horrifyingly real.

6. Puppet Show

1. Lacour-Gayet, p. 384.

2. Lacour-Gayet, p. 384.

3. Lacour-Gayet, p. 309.

4. Lacour-Gayet, p. 309.

5. Lacour-Gayet, p. 309.

6. Lacour-Gayet, p. 309.

7. Lacour-Gayet, p. 310.

8. Lacour-Gayet, p. 310. Interestingly, Papua New Guinea (as it had come to be known) achieved independence on September 16, 1975, exactly two weeks before the coup in Indonesia that eventually led to Sukarno's ouster.

9. Lacour-Gayet, pp. 388–89.

10. Lacour-Gayet, p. 389.

11. Lacour-Gayet, p. 389.

12. Lacour-Gayet, p. 389.

13. Guy's conflicted status is mirrored in Billy Kwan, who is half Australian and half Chinese and who, like Guy, eventually experiences opposing allegiances, in Billy's case between his Asian affinities and his realization that his Asian hero, Sukarno, is not what he initially believes him to be. Both men, then, are in many respects aliens in lands that have both literal and figurative aspects. As Billy notes of himself and Guy, "[we are] divided men . . . not quite at home in the world."

14. Indeed, all of the film's principal characters are, to varying degrees, puppets in the power of political, social, and emotional forces greater than themselves.

15. This dream aspect is made explicit in Koch's novel. At one point, as Guy begins his walk through an Indonesian market, the book's narrator notes, "Hamilton had the sense of entering one of those byways in a dream, which would soon dissolve into nothing." Christopher J. Koch, *The Year of Living Dangerously* (New York: Penguin, 1995), p. 16.

16. G. A. Feuerstein characterizes Arjuna as "the impersonation of restless activity." G. A. Feuerstein, *Introduction to the Bhagavad Gītā: Its Philosophy and Cultural Setting* (London: Rider and Company, 1974), p. 55.

17. In adapting Koch's novel, Weir deleted a fact that Koch makes available to the reader: that the *wayang* is based not only on the *Gītā* but also on another Indian text, the *Ramayana*.

18. This quote could just as well be attributed to Weir given his desire to emphasize story over style.

19. As critic Nick Roddick observes, "Sigourney Weaver's Jill seems grafted on to the story merely as a way of focusing Guy's growth and his rather crudely presented journalistic dilemma. . . ." Roddick, review of *The Year of Living Dangerously*, p. 148.

20. In Carolyn Durham's opinion, Guy's vision—or at least that of Westerners—becomes the predominant point of view in the film, as evidenced by the many shots from within his car of Guy looking out at events, with his figure dominating the frame. "Can Vision Be a Model For Knowledge?" *Jump Cut* 30 (March 1985), p. 6.

21. Robert Eberwein cites Jean-Louis Baudry and Frank D. McConnell's comparison of filmgoers to the inhabitants of Plato's cave. Although the analogy is somewhat faulty, in that filmgoers are not strapped into their seats, the fixation on shadow images, and the placement of a light source behind the "audience," does suggest an affinity between a cinema and the cave that adds resonance to the significance of Guy's dream (and, by extension, his swathed eyes) within the dream-like, Platonically influenced realm of *Year*. Eberwein, p. 24.

22. Billy misquotes from the *Gītā*, which states, "As fire is covered by smoke, as a mirror by dust, and as an embryo is enveloped by the womb, so this (knowledge) is covered by that (passion) . . . with these it bewilders the embodied soul, covering its knowledge." Deutsch, 3:38, and 3:40, p. 52.

23. Deutsch, 3:9, p. 48.

24. Deutsch, introduction, pp. 12–13.

25. Deutsch, 4:25, p. 57.

26. From Deutsch's commentary, p. 147, n.8.

27. From Deutsch's commentary, p. 163. Feuerstein seems to interpret the concept of sacrifice more materially than Deutsch; he feels that it refers to "forms of a lower order of organisation and complexity sustain[ing] the life of the more complex forms of existence by 'sacrificing' their individual lives" (Feuerstein, p. 65). If we read sacrifice metaphorically, though, we can view Guy's sacrificial act as an abjuring of the lower order of

material action in favor of an embracing of the spiritual dimension, a view that would bring Feuerstein in line with Deutsch's and my interpretation.

28. During the time that Guy lies on Billy's bed with his eyes bandaged, he hears in internal revery some of Billy's statements about the shadow play, prominent among which is the reference to everything being "clouded by desire."

29. McFarlane, p. 110. This reticence also applies to depictions of sexual behavior. Weir's films (with the exception of *Witness,* which, perhaps partially for marketing reasons, features a small amount of nudity) seem quite typical with regard to those of most other Australian filmmakers (some exceptions are the films about Barry McKenzie and some soft-core pornography films, many of which feature foreign actors), especially in their failing to graphically depict sexuality. There are exceptions to this rule, however, notable among which are Tim Burstall's *Two Thousand Weeks* (1969) and John D. Lamond's *Felicity* (1979).

30. Among those dissatisfied with the love affair part of *Year's* story, or the manner in which it is integrated into the film, are Glen Lewis (*Australian Movies and the American Dream* [New York: Praeger, 1987], p. 139); John Powers ("Saints and Savages, *American Film* 9:4 [January/February 1984], p. 40); Lindsy Van Gelder, "Gender Bending For Its Own Sake,"(*Ms.* 11:10 [April 1983], p. 73); and reviewers such as David Ansen (*Newsweek,* January 24, 1983, p. 66) and Vincent Canby (*New York Times,* January 21, 1983, p. C4).

31. Peter Weir quoted in Sue Mathews, *35mm Dreams: Conversations with Five Directors about the Australian Film Revival* (Melbourne: Penguin, 1984), p. 107.

32. Powers, p. 43.

33. Powers, p. 43.

34. See, for example, Koch, pp. 116–23.

35. Koch, p. 123.

36. Nonetheless, Koch received screen credit as one of the screenplay writers.

37. David Williamson wrote the last five drafts of the screenplay for *Year* after Koch, who had worked on the first draft with Williamson and Weir, left the project. Williamson says that Koch was very upset with the final screenplay and, apparently, the final version of the film. "[Koch] thought it should be a film of the book and Peter thought it should be a film *based* on the book and this sort of brought them to an impasse. That's when I came in. It was a tricky adaptation." David Williamson in Willibanks, p. 178.

Weir makes no secret of how demanding and difficult a collaborator he is. As he told the interviewer for *American Film,*

I think originals are preferable anytime because you have the freedom to include anything and it's your own. . . . I warned [Paul Theroux] when we first met to watch out, that I had a trail of writers behind me that won't speak to me and I won't speak to them. . . . I need somebody who will accept me on my own terms and be prepared to play second fiddle in a sense. Because even if my ideas are not

as well written, I can still do it, because I can film it. I can see the scene. Let's not worry about this piece of paper. Scripts often irritate me, frankly.
Peter Weir quoted in "Dialogue on Film," pp. 14–15.

38. Perhaps the only benefit of Hunt's casting (aside, of course, from her brilliant performance) is the potential androgynous effect that it brings to the role (I say potential because I'm not sure that on first viewing many audiences will realize that Billy's part is being played by a woman). Such confusion of sexual roles could be seen as contributing to Billy's inability to consummate his physical desire for the heterosexual Jill.

39. John Orr, "Peter Weir's version: *The Year of Living Dangerously*" in *Cinema and Fiction: New Modes of Adapting, 1950–1990,* ed. John Orr and Colin Nicholson (London: Edinburgh University Press, 1992), pp. 57–58. Interestingly, Orr is not overly troubled by Weir's jettisoning much of the novel's political information. See Orr, p. 57.

40. Orr, p. 60.

41. Orr, p. 60. Orr also refers us to Stanley Palombo's observation that Billy essentially scripts Guy's infatuation with Jill as does Gavin Elster for Scotty in *Vertigo*. See Palombo, p. 55.

42. Deutsch, introduction, p. 13.

43. Guy insists that he will not publish an article on the shipment until he gets outside verification of it, thereby supposedly protecting Jill's anonymity as a source. But as Billy points out, everyone will know that the story came from Jill.

44. Carolyn Durhham's excellent article concludes that the film's message is, "We reflect only ourselves; we should reflect on ourselves; only then can we learn to see beyond and behind our cultural assumptions." Durham, p. 7.

45. This theme is also present in *The Mosquito Coast*, in which, as in *Year,* native characters refer to one of the film's principals in terms that highlight a power imbalance. In *Coast*, Allie is repeatedly called "Father"; in *Year,* Kumar often calls Guy "boss."

46. This aspect may link Guy with the sexually exploitative Curtis and O'Sullivan.

7. The Eyes of a Child

1. *The Plumber* contains some brief shots of Jill undressing for a shower, but she is photographed from an oblique angle.

2. According to Russell Boyd, who was the cinematographer on *The Last Wave*, Seale "contributed [to *Wave*] greatly with imaginative ideas and angles. . . ." Nevertheless, neither *Picnic* nor *Wave* draw as much attention to the framing as does *Witness*. Boyd, p. 352.

3. As Weir stated in an interview, "John [Seale] approaches things from a different angle, but he has a far better eye than I do for framing . . . we look for the angle that is the most expressive of the idea. . . ." "Dialogue on Film," p. 15.

4. I am here borrowing terms from Richard Combs's review of *The Mosquito Coast* in *Monthly Film Bulletin* 54 (February 1987), p. 53

5. Richard Combs, review of *Witness* in *Monthly Film Bulletin* 52 (May 1985), p. 167.

6. Weir has stated that much of the film's visual style comes "from Flemish and German paintings." Weir, "Dialogue on Film," p. 14.

7. The statement can also serve as a comment on Book's dance with Rachel, during which, having taken her hand, he takes her into his heart.

8. This fact derives from Everett Corum, *Tantalizing Ambiguity: The Cinema of Peter Weir* (unpublished Ph.D. dissertation, University of Kansas, 1990), p. 22. Corum's source, Jack Searles's article "Colleagues Bear Witness to Weir's Ability" (*Los Angeles Herald Examiner*, March 17, 1986), p. B4, mentions that the film's original ending was bloody, involving "pitchforks and somebody being kicked to death by an animal"; however, Searles never makes reference to any final action involving Book's gun and Samuel. Since Corum is in all other respects a scrupulous writer, with a fine regard for details, I conclude that his information is correct but that he has apparently confused Searles's article with another piece that discussed a different ending to the film. Nonetheless, it is clear that the film's shaming of Schaeffer seems a far more satisfactory and appropriate resolution than any of the alternatives mentioned.

9. Robert Hostetter, "A Controversial 'Witness'," *Christian Century* 102:12 (April 10, 1985), p. 342.

10. Winer, p. 101.

11. Winer, p. 88.

12. Samuel is "hidden" during other scenes as well: not only is he not seen by Schaeffer after he returns to the farm at the film's end, but when he is at the police line-up, a one-way glass that promises anonymity shields him from the view of the men whom he watches. This anonymity provides protection from identification, yet Samuel would most likely have to testify in open court to his identification of the murder's perpetrators. Witnessing is thus quite often a reciprocal act, since it involves not only seeing but being seen.

13. Father figures loom large in the film. One can easily see Book's disappointment with Schaeffer's fall from grace as a blow against the father figure, an aspect that looks forward to Charlie's disappointment with his father in Weir's next film, *The Mosquito Coast*.

14. This shot virtually duplicates a shot from *The Cars That Ate Paris*, which shows the cars of some of the town's youth creeping over the edge of a hill before the destruction of the town.

15. According to Weir, during the shooting of *Witness* he became so caught up in the Amish point of view that he began to veer away from the cops and criminals aspect of the story. "When I started to become too Amish, [producer Ed Feldman] would remind me that this was a Western we were making, and to get some more shots in there." Weir, "Dialogue on Film," p. 14.

16. Weir views *Witness* as being part of "the American tradition" in which the hero "start[s] off with a flaw that is healed or cleansed. At the end, he walks off into the sunset, and he's a better man for the experience." Peter Weir quoted in McGilligan, p. 31.

8. Myopic Visionary

1. Turner, p. 3. Although there has been a great deal of debate about the validity of Turner's thesis and the analytical methods that he used, it is nonetheless true that his views have shaped American attitudes toward uncharted lands. For information on the controversies surrounding the Turner essay, see Ray Allen Billington's books *America's Frontier Heritage* (New York: Holt, Rinehart and Winston, 1966), and *The Frontier Thesis: Valid Interpretation of American History?* (New York: Holt, Rinehart and Winston, 1966).

2. Turner, p. 3.

3. Turner, p. 3.

4. For a discussion of the concept of the frontier as it relates to Australians, see Fred Alexander, *Moving Frontiers: An American Theme and Its Application to Australian History* (Port Washington, NY: Kennikat Press, 1969). Alexander feels that the Turner thesis does not really apply to Australia, whose "history has been in the main the story of a people inhabiting relatively narrow coastal belts in the eastern and south eastern sections of the continent and a less thickly populated strip in the remote south west." Alexander, p. 26. Nevertheless, it is doubtless true that the idea of rugged individualism attendant with the frontier concept is endemic to the psychology of many Australians.

5. Turner, p. 3.

6. Turner, pp. 2–3.

7. Turner, p. 30.

8. Marx, p. 65. There have been some obvious retoolings of this attitude in *The Mosquito Coast*. For one thing, when we meet him, Allie isn't living in the city but in the country; he only ventures into the city when he has to buy something that he can't find at the local dump. Despite the fine differences, though, Allie's attitude is quite similar to the one described by Marx.

9. Turner, p. 32.

10. Paul Theroux, *The Mosquito Coast* (Boston: Houghton Mifflin, 1982).

11. "I've attempted to eliminate my own style as much as possible, like some sort of personal cultural revolution. . . . I have consciously eliminated it from this picture and made it plainer, more straightforward. For other reasons, too—the material and essential ideas of this film are so contradictory to mainstream American filmmaking, are so deeply unconventional, that I felt the form and shape of it should be very conventional, in order not to repel the viewer. In fact, the opening sequence has some of the plainest opening images I've ever had, even bland. I shot another opening at the same time because I was aware of this problem. Originally, I shot a very mysterious, Peter Weir-style opening with dark figures on the horizon and all sorts of weird things going on, then I very cleverly realized what it was. I thought it might be too close to *Witness,* but I decided it was just my style. . . . I thought about it and thought about it and dropped it all. It was a symbolic gesture, but it did echo on throughout the film." Peter Weir quoted in McGilligan, p. 30.

12. Marx, p. 7.

13. Marx, p. 6.

14. Marx, p. 7. See also Henry Nash Smith, *Virgin Land: The American West as Symbol and Myth* (Cambridge: Harvard University Press, 1950).

15. Freud, *Civilization and Its Discontents,* p. 42.

16. See, for example, the promotional literature extant when atomic energy as a source of electricity was first being promoted in this country, notable among which was the government-induced propaganda in the book and film versions of the Walt Disney production *Our Friend the Atom* (1958).

17. Don Shiach points out a possible comparison between Weir's film and Graham Greene's *The Quiet American,* whose protagonist is "insensitive and shallow, creating havoc through his blundering initiatives while maintaining the pious air of someone carrying out good works." Don Shiach, *The Films of Peter Weir* (London: Charles Letts, 1993), p. 146.

A proselytizer for Western cultural values (in this case, pragmatic materialism and science), Allie is also like *The Last Wave*'s incognizant David, who penetrates into the mysteries of a black culture but is eventually revealed as an ignorant white man. Given Weir's nationality and strong sense of history, *Mosquito Coast*'s story must have had a special significance for him. Like Americans in general and Allie in particular, Australians robbed territory from a resident native population and then either displaced or destroyed the native population or attempted to "civilize" them with white culture, never taking cognizance of the integrity and intelligence of the culture that they were destroying. Indeed, just compare the pictures of urban Aborigines viewed by David's wife in *The Last Wave* with the sight of *The Mosquito Coast*'s distraught Mr. Haddy after his launch has been destroyed to see how similar their reactions to the negative consequences of white civilization are. In each case, the culture that has shocked these people is white culture, of which Allie is a prime example.

18. Joseph Conrad, *Heart of Darkness,* ed. Robert Kimbrough (New York: Norton, 1971), p. 16.

19. Conrad, p. 69.

20. Morrison, p. 67.

21. Ironically, Marlow's first name is also Charlie.

22. Conrad, p. 7.

23. Conrad, p. 7. Apparently, Marlow is here slyly referring to Kurtz's "unspeakable rites."

24. Conrad, p. 86.

25. Conrad, p. 86.

26. Stanner, p. 10.

27. It's also tempting to read the film as an autobiographical gloss on Weir's fascination with alternative cultures, which, with the best intentions, he "enters" via his filmic fictions. Like Allie and Kurtz, Weir inadvertently brings along with him the racial biases

of his civilization, which in this case reveal themselves in the unbalanced portrayal of *Mosquito Coast*'s people of color.

28. Peter Weir quoted in McGilligan, p. 30.

29. Combs, review of *The Mosquito Coast*, p. 53.

30. Combs, review of *The Mosquito Coast*, p. 53.

31. That the film is quite faithful to the book is attested to by Weir. Paul Schrader's screenplay adapts much of the book's tone and action. Although Weir says that he added material to Schrader's screenplay, he subsequently eliminated much of it at the editing stage. As a result, Weir says, "the cut that you see ends up being fairly close to Paul [Schrader], which is pretty faithful to Theroux." McGilligan, p. 30.

32. Weir, in Tulich, p. 9.

33. Tulich, p. 9.

34. Tulich, p. 9.

35. Peter Weir quoted in McGilligan, p. 30.

36. In Theroux's book, Charlie notes that Allie refers to the migrant workers as "savages," an appellation that Weir reserves for later in the film. Theroux, p. 30.

37. In this respect, *Mosquito Coast*'s final effect is unlike that of *Heart of Darkness*, whose end is referred to by its unnamed narrator as "inconclusive." Conrad, p. 7.

38. Critic Albert Guerard refers to this movement as "the night journey into the unconscious, and confrontation of an entity within the self." Albert J. Guerard, "The Journey Within," in Conrad, p. 170.

39. Conrad, p. 27.

40. Lillian Feder, "Marlow's Descent into Hell," in Conrad, p. 187.

41. Feder, p. 187.

42. Conrad, p. 50.

43. Conrad, p. 51.

44. Conrad, p. 27.

45. Conrad, p. 79.

46. Conrad, p. 79.

47. Peter Weir quoted in McGilligan, p. 32.

48. Some commentators on the film believe that Allie is intentionally lying about America's destruction (this is critic Don Shiach's view, yet he contradicts himself on this point 8 pages after making it), although I feel that such a view—which Charlie also shares—overlooks the most compelling reason for Allie's misrepresentation: the intensity of his self-delusion at this point in the film. See Shiach, pp. 146, 154.

49. Other characters who also disregard the distinction between two very different realms include *Witness*'s Schaeffer, *Fearless*'s Max, *The Year of Living Dangerously*'s Guy, and *Dead Poets Society*'s Keating, the latter of whom passes on advice about unconscious urgings without considering that the boys to whom he communicates this wisdom haven't the ability to apply these insights in a repressive setting without incurring disastrous consequences.

50. Later, though, when he refers to Mr. Haddy as a savage, Allie feels no remorse over his statement.

9. School Days

1. Campbell, p. 30.

2. Peter Weir quoted in McGilligan, pp. 25–26.

3. Peter Weir in the 1983 video interview for the Australian Film, Television, and Radio School.

4. Murray, "Australian Directors Overseas: 1970–1992," in *Australian Cinema,* pp. 153–55.

5. Murray, "Australian Director Overseas," p. 153.

6. The theme that composer Maurice Jarre uses at this point resembles the "Ode To Joy" from Beethoven's Ninth Symphony, which played during another essentially triumphant moment: when Keating's students lifted him up onto their shoulders. Viewers may also notice that Beethoven's Fifth Piano Concerto, used prominently in *Picnic at Hanging Rock,* is playing in the background when Todd visits Keating's room.

7. Tanya Modleski, "Dead White Male Heterosexual Poets Society," in *Feminism Without Women* (New York: Routledge, 1992), pp. 137–40.

8. Hentzi, pp. 2–12.

9. Hentzi, p. 3.

10. Hentzi, p. 3.

11. Hentzi, p. 3.

12. Hentzi, pp. 3–4.

13. Modleski, p. 138.

14. Hentzi, p. 3.

15. In a comparable misreading, Hentzi overlooks the rebelliousness of the town's youth in *The Cars That Ate Paris* in order to support his assertion that the town exemplifies "ritualized integration."

16. Modleski, p. 139.

17. Modleski also states that after Todd stands up on his desk at the film's end, "the other class members . . . follow suit," overlooking the fact that many of them, Cameron most prominently, remain seated. Modleski, p. 139.

18. Hentzi, p. 3.

19. Hentzi, p. 4.

20. Toni Morrison would probably refer to Conrad's book as an example of "European Africanism with a counterpart in colonial literature" (Morrison, p. 38).

21. Denby, "Jungle Fever," p. 128. Interestingly, Hentzi uses Denby's review of *Dead Poets* as support for his own assertion that there is a strong "suggestion in [the film's] final scenes of a teenager coming out of the closet" (Hentzi, p. 3). Hentzi states that "at least one reviewer [Denby] was led to remark that the film would have been more intelligible had this in fact been its subject" (p. 4). Unfortunately, Hentzi's implication that

Denby views *Dead Poets* as a film with a buried homosexual "text" is not necessarily supported by Denby's ambiguous prose. Denby's actual statement about Neil's father's response to his son's acting in *A Midsummer Night's Dream* is, "The amount of emotion generated by these impacted father-son scenes would make sense if Neil were announcing to his father that he was gay, but the filmmakers stay miles away from any such idea. This call for freedom seems rather conformist and repressed itself." David Denby, "The Boom-Boom Room," *New York* 22:24 (June 12, 1989), p. 78.

22. Morrison, pp. 46–47.

23. It would not be correct to assert that *Picnic at Hanging Rock* fits into this pattern of unwitting denial. As I pointed out in chapter 4, within the context of Australian culture, the film's references to Hanging Rock, which is situated on sacred Aboriginal ground, and its dialogue about Miss McCraw being "raped," clearly refer to fears of miscegenation.

24. Modleski, p. 137. Despite Modleski's quotation, nowhere in his article does Nowell-Smith use the term "hysterical text." Geoffrey Nowell-Smith, "Minnelli and Melodrama," in *Home Is Where the Heart Is: Studies in Melodrama and the Woman's Film,* ed. Christine Gledhill (London: BFI, 1987), pp. 70–74.

25. Nowell-Smith, p. 74.

26. Modleski, p. 138.

27. Modleski, p. 138.

28. Modleski, p. 138.

29. Modleski, p. 138.

30. Modleski, p. 139. On the previous page, Modleski characterized the "male boarding school" environment as being "possibl[y]" depraved. Modleski, p. 138.

31. Modleski, p. 140.

32. Hentzi, p. 4; Modleski, pp. 138–39.

33. Modleski, p. 138.

10. Jungle under Glass

1. Weir has remarked, "I admire [Depardieu], and it seems an awful loss that he is largely unknown to English-speaking audiences apart from real filmgoers. . . . I wanted to bring him something he could do in English. So, I tailored [the film for him]." Peter Weir interviewed by Tulich, p. 8.

2. Frye, pp. 182–84.

3. Scott Murray does not feel that *Green Card*'s ending is in any sense ambiguous: Instead of the usual kiss and fade-out, Weir has the couple declare love for each other at the very moment Georges in being arrested and deported. There is no indication that he will be back or that Brontë is off for Paris (other than for an end-credits song about everything being all right, but whose perspective does it represent?). The important thing is that Weir doesn't *show* everything being all right: while they may have found each other on some emotional/spiritual plane, Weir

closes with an image of an unbedded couple's being physically pulled apart. "Australian cinema in the 1970s and 1980s," in Murray, *Australian Cinema*, p. 122.

11. A Posthumous Life

The title of this chapter is a variation of a statement made by philosopher Abraham Maslow, who referred to the period after his near-fatal heart attack as his *"postmortem life"* (italics in original). Edward Hoffman, *The Right to Be Human* (Los Angeles: Jeremy D. Tarcher, 1988), p. 325.

1. There's a brief glimpse of the wrecked plane's fuselage in this shot, but the shot isn't held long enough to make this aspect of the image fully appreciable.

2. In this regard, although its text is religiously oriented, the teachings of the *Bhagavad Gītā* are instructive. Regarding the necessity of transcending oneself and concentrating attention on that which is greater, the *Gītā* (as commented on by translator Eliot Deutsch) asserts that "in order to act without attachment, without those egoistic motives for the fruits of action that bind one to the world, one must concentrate one's attention upon the Divine: one must fill one's consciousness with the power of loving devotion. Implicit in the whole teaching system of the *Gītā* is the belief that there is no other way to establish non-attachment than through a new attachment to that which is greater, in quantity and power, than that to which one was previously attached. One overcomes the narrow clinging to results, the passionate involvement with the consequences of one's action, only when that passion is replaced by one directed to the Divine." The correspondence between what the *Gītā* recommends as a prerequisite to enlightenment and Max's acceptance of the redemptive power of love seems quite evident. Deutsch, p. 163.

3. In Yglesias's book, Max actually does have a love affair with Carla. Rafael Yglesias, *Fearless* (New York: Warner, 1993).

4. I say "apparent" here because the second circumstance is a bit more complex than the first. When he drives his car into a brick wall, with Carla placed in the back seat, Max may be under the unconscious impression that he is hazarding his life in order to redeem Carla's, in which case his behavior looks forward to the act of salvation that he prompts in his wife at the film's end.

5. The scene involving Max, Carla, and the baby at the shopping mall to which I earlier referred may have been shot in a mirror as well, that is if we are to judge by the reversed lettering in a sign behind Carla.

6. The former is the title attributed to this work by Lynda Harris in her critical study *The Secret Heresy of Hieronymus Bosch* (Edinburgh: Floris, 1995), p. 198. The latter title is the one used by Walter S. Gibson in his *Hieronymus Bosch* (London: Thames and Hudson, 1973), p. 62.

7. The grouping of the panels that I have adopted is the one proposed by Gibson (pp. 62–63). Two caveats are in order, though. Harris points out that "we do not know how these paintings were originally organized" (Harris, p. 197). Gibson observes that "crit-

ics are not unanimous in attributing [these panels] to Bosch; nevertheless, it would be difficult to ascribe their compositions [sic] to anyone else" (pp. 62–63).

8. Gibson, p. 63.

9. Gibson, pp. 64–65.

10. Harris, p. 200.

11. The situation that Max describes bears comparison with that of Job although, unlike Job, Max repudiates God when his "family" is inexplicably taken away from him.

12. As Carl Jung has stated of psychoanalysis in an assertion quoted in this book's introduction, "human wholeness [is] the goal to which the psychotherapeutic process ultimately leads." Jung, *Psychology and Alchemy,* p. 27.

13. Jung, *Psychology and Alchemy,* p. 27.

14. Max's predicament obviously involves an essential crisis of identity that is being expressed in visual terms. As Carl Jung notes, "the mandala plays a great role in Eastern cults [in which it is] used as a psychological aid to individuation." Carl Jung, *Seminar on Dream Analysis,* ed. William McGuire (Princeton: Princeton University Press, 1984), p. 303.

15. Jung, *Psychology and Alchemy,* p. 29.

16. The text appended to the reproduction of the Bosch painting that Max's wife views reads, "The soul comes to the end of its long journey and, naked and alone, draws near to the divine." These words suggest that when Max (who is now no longer involved with Carla, and is thus without external support and alone) meets his wife after he is discharged from the hospital, he is, after the long spiritual journey that *Fearless* dramatizes, moving toward the woman he has finally recognized as a legitimate source of divine love: his wife. The fact that the meeting between Max and his wife takes place immediately after the one in which she views the Bosch painting seems to confirm this reading.

12. A Nightmare

1. See, for example, Richard Corliss, "Smile! Your Life's on TV," *Time,* June 1, 1998, p. 78.

2. Michael Sragow, "The Free Willies" (review of *The Truman Show*), *San Francisco Weekly,* June 3–9, 1998.

3. Alain Robbe-Grillet, *For a New Novel,* trans. Richard Howard (New York: Books for Libraries Press, 1970), p. 45.

4. The film commits a serious error with regard to this scene, since its "documentary" concerning "The Truman Show" states that "the world stood still for that stolen kiss," yet Truman and Sylvia were out of camera range at that time. The most that the audience of "the show" could know about this very private moment is whatever ex post facto information the man pretending to be the father of Lauren (the name of Sylvia's character) could have conveyed.

5. This beautiful piece of music is reminiscent of the Beethoven Fifth Piano Concerto, which Weir uses in both *Picnic at Hanging Rock* and *Dead Poets Society.*

6. Freud, *Civilization and Its Discontents,* pp. 51–52.

7. Freud, *Civilization and Its Discontents,* p. 52.

8. And just what is the difference between "counterfeit" and "somewhat counterfeit?" It's as specious a statement as the comparison that the actor playing Marlon (that is, the actor in "the show" playing Marlon) draws between fakery and a world in which things are only "controlled."

9. Karen Horney, *Feminine Psychology* (New York: Norton, 1967), p. 115.

10. It's unlikely that Truman doesn't care if he lives or dies, so the second "he" probably refers to Christof.

11. Freud, *Civilization and Its Discontents,* p. 26.

12. Freud, *Civilization and Its Discontents,* pp. 34, 51–52.

13. Freud, *Civilization and Its Discontents,* p. 32.

14. Freud, *Civilization and Its Discontents,* p. 32.

15. Freud, *Civilization and Its Discontents,* p. 32.

16. Freud, *Civilization and Its Discontents,* p. 32.

17. See Jesse Weston, *From Ritual to Romance* (New York: Doubleday/Anchor, 1957), especially pp. 12–13.

BIBLIOGRAPHY

A. G. Review of *The Last Wave*. *Positif* 204 (March 1978), p. 54.

Alexander, Fred. *Moving Frontiers: An American Theme and Its Application to Australian History.* Port Washington, NY: Kennikat, 1969.

Bean, C. E. W. *Anzac to Amiens.* Canberra: Australian War Memorial, 1983.

―――. *The Official History of Australia in the War of 1914–1918, Volumes I and II.* Sydney: Angus and Robertson, 1921, 1924.

Bertrand, Ina, ed. *Cinema in Australia: A Documentary History.* Kensington: New South Wales University Press, 1989.

Billington, Ray Allen. *America's Frontier Heritage.* New York: Holt, Rinehart and Winston, 1966.

―――, ed. *The Frontier Thesis: Valid Interpretation of American History?* New York: Holt, Rinehart and Winston, 1966.

Birchard, Robert S. "Witness/John Seale, ACS." *American Cinematographer* 67:4 (April 1986), pp. 74–78.

Booth, Wayne. *The Rhetoric of Fiction.* Chicago: University of Chicago Press, 1961.

Bordwell, David, Kristin Thompson, and Janet Staiger. *The Classical Hollywood Cinema.* New York: Columbia University Press, 1985.

Boyd, Russell. "Photographing *The Last Wave*." *American Cinematographer* 59:4 (April 1978), pp. 352–55.

―――. Video interview for the Australian Film, Television, and Radio School, 1984.

Brownlow, Kevin. *The Parade's Gone By.* New York: Bonanza, 1968.

Cage, John. *Silence.* Middletown, CT: Wesleyan University Press, 1961.

Campbell, Joseph. *The Hero with a Thousand Faces.* Princeton: Princeton University Press, 1949.

Castell, David. "Weir, weird, and weirder still." *Films Illustrated* 6 (November 1976), pp. 93–94.

Combs, Richard. Review of *The Mosquito Coast*. *Monthly Film Bulletin* 54 (February 1987), pp. 52–53.

233

———. Review of *Witness*. *Monthly Film Bulletin* 52 (May 1985), pp. 166–67.

Conrad, Joseph. *Heart of Darkness*. Edited by Robert Kimbrough. New York: Norton, 1963.

Corum, Everett. *Tantalizing Ambiguity: The Cinema of Peter Weir*. Unpublished Ph.D. dissertation. University of Kansas, 1990.

Dawson, Jan. "Picnic under Capricorn." *Sight and Sound* 45:2 (1976), p. 83.

Dempsey, Michael. "Inexplicable Feelings: An Interview with Peter Weir." *Film Quarterly* 33:4 (Summer 1980), pp. 2–11.

Denby, David. "The Boom-Boom Room." Review of *Dead Poets Society*. *New Yorker* 22:24 (June 12, 1989), pp. 77–78.

———. "Jungle Fever." *New Yorker*, November 6, 1995, pp. 118–29.

Deutsch, Eliot, trans. *The Bhagavad Gītā*. New York: Holt, Rinehart, and Winston, 1968.

Durham, Carolyn. "Can Vision Be a Model for Knowledge?" *Jump Cut* 30 (March 1985), pp. 6–8.

Eberwein, Robert. *Film and the Dream Screen*. Princeton: Princeton University Press, 1984.

Encel, S. "The Nature of Race Prejudice in Australia." In *Racism: The Australian Experience,* vol. 1, edited by F. S. Stevens, pp. 30–40. New York: Taplinger, 1971.

Feuerstein, G. A. *Introduction to the Bhagavad Gītā: Its Philosophy and Cultural Setting*. London: Rider and Company, 1974.

Fiedler, Leslie. *Love and Death in the American Novel*. New York: Anchor, 1992.

Fonda-Bonardi, Claudia, and Peter Fonda-Bonardi. "The Birth of a Nation: An Interview with Peter Weir." *Cineaste* 11:4 (1982), pp. 41–42.

Frazer, J. G. *The Golden Bough*. Abridged edition. New York: Macmillan, 1963.

Freud, Sigmund. *Civilization and Its Discontents*. Translated and edited by James Strachey. New York: Norton, 1961.

———. *The Complete Psychological Works of Sigmund Freud*. Volume 17. Edited by James Strachey. Translated by James Strachey, Anna Freud, Alix Strachey, and Alan Tyson. London: Hogarth Press, 1955.

———. *The Interpretation of Dreams*. Translated and edited by James Strachey. New York: Basic, 1955.

———. *On Dreams*. Translated and edited by James Strachey. New York: Norton, 1952.

Freud, Sigmund, and C. G. Jung. *The Freud/Jung Letters*. Translated by R. F. C. Hull. Edited by William McGuire. Princeton: Princeton University Press, 1974.

Frye, Northrop. *Anatomy of Criticism*. Princeton: Princeton University Press, 1957.

Gammage, Bill. *The Broken Years: Australian Soldiers in the Great War*. Canberra: Australian National University Press, 1974.

Gibson, Ross. "Formative landscapes." In *Australian Cinema,* edited by Scott Murray, pp. 45–59. Australia: Allen and Unwin, 1994.

Gibson, Walter S. *Hieronymus Bosch*. London: Thames and Hudson, 1973.

Glaessner, Verina. Review of *Green Card*. *Monthly Film Bulletin* 58 (March 1991), pp. 79–80.

Harris, Lynda. *The Secret Heresy of Hieronymus Bosch.* Edinburgh: Floris, 1995.

Hartigan, Karelisa V. "Artemis in South Australia: Classical Allusions in *Picnic at Hanging Rock.*" *Classical and Modern Literature* 11:1 (Fall 1990), pp. 93–98.

Hentzi, Gary. "Peter Weir and the Cinema of New Age Humanism." *Film Quarterly* 44:2 (Winter 1990–1991), pp. 2–12.

Hoffman, Edward. *The Right to Be Human.* Los Angeles: Jeremy D. Tarcher, 1988.

Horney, Karen. *Feminine Psychology.* New York: Norton, 1967.

Hostetter, Robert. "A Controversial 'Witness.'" *Christian Century* 102:12 (April 10, 1985), pp. 341–42.

Jackson, Kenneth T. "Gallipoli." In *Past Imperfect: History According to the Movies,* edited by Ted Mico, John Miller-Monzon, and David Rubel, pp. 192–95. New York: Henry Holt, 1995.

Jameson, Fredric. *The Geopolitical Aesthetic.* Bloomington: Indiana University Press, 1992.

Jung, C. G. *The Basic Writings of C. G. Jung.* Edited by Violet Straub de Laszlo. New York: Modern Library, 1959.

———. *Psychology and Alchemy.* 2nd edition. Translated by R. F. C. Hull. London: Routledge and Kegan Paul, 1953.

———. *Psychology and Religion: West and East.* Translated by R. F. C. Hull. New York: Pantheon, 1963.

———. *Seminar on Dream Analysis.* Edited by William McGuire. Princeton: Princeton University Press, 1984.

Kael, Pauline. "Doused." Review of *The Last Wave. New Yorker* 54:49 (January 22, 1979), pp. 102–4.

———. "Plain and Simple." Review of *Witness. New Yorker* 61:1 (February 25, 1985), pp. 78–81.

———. "Stonework." Review of *Dead Poets Society. New Yorker* 65:19 (June 26, 1989), pp. 70–71.

———. "Torrid Zone." Review of *The Year of Living Dangerously. New Yorker* 59:1 (February 21, 1983), pp. 120–25.

Kass, Judith. "It Doesn't Take Any Imagination At All to Feel Awed." *Movietone News* 62/63 (December 1979), pp. 2–8.

Kierkegaard, Søren. *Fear and Trembling* and *The Sickness unto Death.* Translated by Walter Lowrie. New York: Doubleday, 1954.

Kinder, M. Review of *The Plumber. Film Quarterly* 33:4 (Summer 1980), pp. 17–21.

Kobal, John. Review of *Witness. Films and Filming* 368 (May 1985), pp. 45–47.

Koch, Christopher J. *The Year of Living Dangerously.* New York: Penguin, 1995.

Kuhn, Thomas. *The Structure of Scientific Revolutions.* 2nd edition. Chicago: University of Chicago Press, 1970.

Lacour-Gayet, Robert. *A Concise History of Australia.* Translated by James Grieve. Australia: Penguin, 1976.

Landon, Brooks. *The Aesthetics of Ambivalence: Rethinking Science Fiction Film in the Age of Electronic (Re)Production.* Westport, CT: Greenwood, 1992.

Lévi-Strauss, Claude. *Structural Anthropology.* Translated by Claire Jacobson and Brooke Grundfest Schoepf. New York: Basic, 1963.

Lewis, Glen. *Australian Movies and the American Dream.* New York: Praeger, 1987.

Liddle, Peter. *Men of Gallipoli.* London: Pan, 1974.

Lindsay, Joan. *Picnic at Hanging Rock.* Melbourne: Penguin, 1970.

Magill, Marcia. Interview with Peter Weir. *Films in Review* 32 (1981), pp. 474–75, 478–79.

Marx, Leo. *The Machine in the Garden: Technology and the Pastoral Ideal in America.* London: Oxford University Press, 1964.

Mathews, Sue. *35mm Dreams.* Melbourne: Penguin, 1984.

McFarlane, Brian. *Australian Cinema 1970–1985.* London: Secker and Warburg, 1987.

McFarlane, Brian, and Geoff Mayer. *New Australian Cinema: Sources and Parallels in American and British Film.* Cambridge: Cambridge University Press, 1992.

McGilligan, Pat. "Under Weir . . . and Theroux." *Film Comment* 22 (November/December 1986), pp. 24–32.

McQueen, H. O. "Racism in Australian Literature." In *Racism: The Australian Experience,* vol. 1, edited by F. S. Stevens, pp. 115–22. New York: Taplinger, 1971.

Mico, Ted, John Miller-Monzon, and David Rubel, eds. *Past Imperfect: History According to the Movies.* New York: Henry Holt, 1995.

Modleski, Tanya. *Feminism Without Women.* New York: Routledge, 1992.

Moorehead, Alan. *Gallipoli.* New York: Harper and Brothers, 1956.

Moorehouse, Geoffrey. *Hell's Foundations: A Social History of the Town of Bury in the Aftermath of the Gallipoli Campaign.* New York: Henry Holt, 1992.

Morrison, Toni. *Playing in the Dark: Whiteness and the Literary Imagination.* New York: Vintage, 1993.

Murray, Scott, ed. *Australian Cinema.* Australia: Allen and Unwin, 1994.

———, ed. *Australian Film 1978–1992: A Survey of Theatrical Features.* Melbourne: Oxford University Press, 1993.

Murray, Scott, and Peter Beilby, eds. *The New Australian Cinema.* London: Elm Tree Books, 1980.

Nadeau, Maurice. *The History of Surrealism.* New York: Macmillan, 1966.

"The 'New Vintage' Cinematographers of Australia Speak Out." *American Cinematographer* 57 (September 1976), pp. 1038–39.

North, John. *Gallipoli: The Fading Vision.* London: Faber and Faber, n.d.

Nowell-Smith, Geoffrey. "Minnelli and Melodrama." In *Home Is Where the Heart Is: Studies in Melodrama and the Woman's Film,* edited by Christine Gledhill, pp. 70–74. London: BFI, 1987.

Orr, John. "Peter Weir's Version: *The Year of Living Dangerously.*" In *Cinema and Fiction: New Modes of Adapting, 1950–1990,* edited by John Orr and Colin Nicholson, pp. 54–65. Edinburgh: Edinburgh University Press, 1992.

Palfreeman, A. C. "The White Australia Policy." In *Racism: The Australian Experience,* vol. 1, edited by F. S. Stevens, pp. 136–44. New York: Taplinger, 1971.

Palombo, Stanley. "Hitchcock's *Vertigo:* The Dream Function in Film." In *Images in Our*

Souls: Cavell, Psychoanalysis, and Cinema, edited by Joseph Smith and William Kerrigan. Baltimore: Johns Hopkins University Press, 1987.

Pike, Andrew, and Ross Cooper. *Australian Film: A Guide to Feature Film Production.* Melbourne: Oxford University Press, 1980.

Poe, Edgar Allan. *The Complete Tales and Poems of Edgar Allan Poe.* New York: Vintage, 1975.

Powers, John. "Saints and Savages." *American Film* 9:4 (January/February 1984), pp. 38–43.

Price, A. Grenfell. *Island Continent: Aspects of the Historical Geography of Australia and Its Territories.* Australia: Angus and Robertson, 1972.

Pugsley, Christopher. *Gallipoli: The New Zealand Story.* Auckland: Hodder and Staughton, 1984.

Pulleine, Tim. Review of *The Last Wave. Monthly Film Bulletin* 45 (April 1978), pp. 66–67.

Pym, John. Review of *Gallipoli. Monthly Film Bulletin* 48 (December 1981), pp. 244–45.

Rank, Otto. *The Double: A Psychoanalytic Study.* Translated and edited by Harry Tucker Jr. Chapel Hill: University of North Carolina Press, 1971.

Rattigan, Neil. *Images of Australia: 100 Films of the New Australian Cinema.* Dallas: Southern Methodist University Press, 1991.

Reade, Eric. *History and Heartburn: The Saga of Australian Film 1896–1978.* Rutherford, NJ: Fairleigh Dickinson University Press, 1979.

Review of *Picnic at Hanging Rock. Positif* 183/184 (July/August 1976), pp. 97–98.

Robbe-Grillet, Alain. *For a New Novel.* Translated by Richard Howard. New York: Books for Libraries Press, 1970.

Roddick, Nick. "The Day of Living Dangerously: Indonesia, September 30, 1965." *Monthly Film Bulletin* 50 (June 1983), pp. 148–49.

———. Review of *The Year of Living Dangerously. Monthly Film Bulletin* 50 (June 1983), pp. 147–48.

Rousseau, Yvonne. *The Murders of Hanging Rock.* Melbourne: Scribe, 1980.

Seydor, Paul. *Peckinpah: The Western Films.* Urbana: University of Illinois Press, 1980.

Shattuck, Roger. *The Banquet Years: The Origins of the Avant Garde in France, 1885 to World War I.* New York: Vintage, 1968.

Shiach, Don. *The Films of Peter Weir.* London: Charles Letts, 1993.

Shirley, Graham. "Australian cinema: 1896 to the renaissance." In *Australian Cinema,* edited by Scott Murray, pp. 7–14. Australia: Allen and Unwin, 1994.

Smith, Henry Nash. *Virgin Land: The American West as Symbol and Myth.* Cambridge: Harvard University Press, 1950.

Stanner, W. E. H. "Australia and Racialism." In *Racism: The Australian Experience,* vol. 1, edited by F. S. Stevens, pp. 7–14. New York: Taplinger, 1971.

Stevens, F. S., ed. *Racism: The Australian Experience.* Vol. 1. New York: Taplinger, 1971.

Stratton, David. *The Last New Wave: The Australian Film Revival.* London: Angus and Robertson, 1980.

Strick, Philip. Review of *The Cars That Ate Paris. Monthly Film Bulletin* 42 (May 1975), pp. 100–101.

Terrill, Ross. *The Australians: In Search of an Identity.* London: Bantam Press, 1987.

Theroux, Paul. *The Mosquito Coast.* Boston: Houghton Mifflin, 1982.

Thomson, Alistair. *Anzac Memories: Living with the Legend.* Melbourne: Oxford University Press, 1994.

Travers, T. H. E. "Gallipoli: Film and the Traditions of Austrailian [sic] History." *Film and History* 14:1 (February 1984), pp. 14–20.

Tulich, Kathleen. Interview with Peter Weir. *Cinema Papers* 80 (August 1980), pp. 6–10.

Tulloch, John. *Australian Cinema: Industry, Narrative, Meaning.* Sydney: Allen and Unwin, 1982.

Turner, Frederick Jackson. *The Frontier in American History.* New York: Holt, Rinehart, and Winston, 1962.

Van Gelder, Lindsy. "Gender Bending for Its Own Sake." *Ms.* 11:10 (April 1983), p. 73.

Wallace-Crabbe, Chris. *Melbourne or the Bush.* Melbourne: Angus and Robertson, 1974.

Weil, Jonathan. "The Role of Ambiguity in the Arts." *etc* 43:1 (Spring 1986) pp. 83–89.

Weir, Peter. "Dialogue on Film." *American Film* 11 (March 1986), pp. 13–15.

———. Video interview for the Australian Film, Television, and Radio School, 1983.

Wernick, Andrew. "The Shifting Image of the Modern Car." In *Cultural Politics in Contemporary America,* edited by Ian Angus and Sut Jhally, pp. 198–216. New York: Routledge, 1989.

Weston, Jesse. *From Ritual to Romance.* New York: Doubleday/Anchor, 1957.

Wilkins, Nigel, ed. *Two Miracles.* Edinburgh: Scottish Academic Press, 1972.

Williamson, David. Screenplay for *Gallipoli.* No publisher or date listed.

Willibanks, Ray, ed. *Australian Voices: Writers and Their Work.* Austin: University of Texas Press, 1991.

Winer, Robert. "Witnessing and Bearing Witness: The Ontogeny of Encounter in the Films of Peter Weir." In *Images in Our Souls: Cavell, Psychoanalysis, and Cinema,* edited by Joseph Smith and William Kerrigan. Baltimore: Johns Hopkins University Press, 1987.

Wood, Robin. "An Introduction to the American Horror Film." In *The American Nightmare,* pp. 7–28. Toronto: Festival of Festivals, 1979.

Yglesias, Rafael. *Fearless.* New York: Warner, 1993.

INDEX

239

Michael Bliss teaches English and film criticism at Virginia Polytechnic Institute and State University. Among his previous books are *Justified Lives: Morality and Narrative in the Films of Sam Peckinpah; Doing It Right: The Best Criticism on Sam Peckinpah's "The Wild Bunch";* and, with Christina Banks, *What Goes Around Comes Around: The Films of Jonathan Demme.* Bliss's critical article "Back Off to What? Violence, Capitalism, and Enclosure in *The Wild Bunch*" was recently published in a collection of essays. Having just completed *Between the Bullets: The Spiritual Cinema of John Woo,* Bliss is now working on a study of Paul Schrader's films.